Womanhood in the Making

Womanhood in the Making

Domestic Ritual and Public Culture in Urban South India

Mary Elizabeth Hancock

Westview Press
A Member of the Perseus Books Group

Published in 1999 in the United States of America by Westview Press, 5500 Central Avenue, Boulder, Colorado 80301-2877, and in the United Kingdom by Westview Press, 12 Hid's Copse Road, Cumnor Hill, Oxford OX2 9JJ

Library of Congress Cataloging-in-Publication Data
Hancock, Mary Elizabeth.
Womanhood in the making : domestic ritual and public culture in urban South India / Mary Elizabeth Hancock.
p. cm.
Includes bibliographical references and index.
ISBN 0-8133-3583-3 (hc)—ISBN 0-8133-3889-1 pb
1. Women, Tamil—Rites and ceremonies. 2. Women, Tamil—Religion. 3. Women, Tamil—social conditions. 4. Urban women—India—Madras. 5. Women in Hinduism—India—Madras 6. Sex role—India—Madras. 7. Spatial behavior—India—Madras. 8. Madras (India)—Social life and customs. 9. Madras (India)—Religious life and customs.
I. Title.
DS432.T3H33 1999
305.48'8948110548—dc21 98-47288
CIP

The paper used in this publication meets the requirements of the American National Standard for Permanence of Paper for Printed Library Materials Z39.48-1984.

PERSEUS POD ON DEMAND

10 9 8 7 6 5 4 3 2

Contents

Figures

Acknowledgments

This book has been long in the making, and I have accumulated debts to many individuals and institutions. Paramount among those on whom I have depended are my friends and colleagues in India. Without the hospitality, help, and interest of Mr. and Mrs. S. V. Raman, Mr. and Mrs. Rodney Easdon, Mr. and Mrs. A. Balasubramanian, Mr. and Mrs. S. Mahalingam, Mr. and Mrs. R. Arjunan, as well as their respective families, my research would not have been possible. I am grateful to Vijayalakshmi Gourishankar, who shared her insights and questions with me. For reasons of privacy, I cannot mention by name the many other people with whom I worked; I remain, however, deeply in their debt and grateful for their friendship. My first two periods of fieldwork were funded by the Department of Anthropology of the University of Pennsylvania (October–November 1985) and by the American Institute of Indian Studies (February 1987–February 1988). My fieldwork in 1996 (August–December) was funded by the University of California through a Faculty Career Development Award, an Interdisciplinary Humanities Center Faculty Research Award, and a UCSB Faculty Research Award. Dr. P. Venugopala Rao, of the AIIS, Dr. G. Prakash Reddy of Sri Venkateswara University, and Dr. D. Sundaram of the University of Madras facilitated my work and were gracious guides.

The book began as a doctoral dissertation submitted to the Department of Anthropology at the University of Pennsylvania in December 1990. The influence of my teachers and colleagues there, including Arjun Appadurai, Carol Breckenridge, David Ludden, and V. S. Rajam, was and remains an important anchor for my work. My studies at Penn were supported by a university fellowship (1982–1983), a FLAS fellowship (1984–1986) for the study of Tamil, and a university dissertation fellowship (1988–1989).

The teaching demands of a three-year Mellon fellowship at the University of Chicago (1990–1993) slowed my writing but were the catalysts that helped me rethink the dissertation and craft this book. I was fortunate to have many fine colleagues willing to listen, argue, and make constructive suggestions; among them are Eytan Bercovitch, Barney Cohn, Malathi De Alwis, John MacAloon, McKim Marriott, Diane

Mines, and Catherine Peyroux. I especially appreciate the suggestions and assistance provided by Jim Nye, Southern Asia bibliographer at the University of Chicago's Regenstein Library, over the past several years as I completed this project and embarked on new ones. I wrote the first draft of the book during the year (1993–1994) I spent at the School of American Research as a National Endowment for the Humanities Fellow, and I thank Doug Schwartz and his staff, as well as my colleagues there (Michael Brown, John Forrest, Jenny Joe, Jon Ingimundarson, Kirin Narayan, James Snead, and Henry Wright), for that wonderfully creative and peaceful year.

Since 1994, I have taught in the Department of Anthropology at the University of California, Santa Barbara. Besides funding my fieldwork in 1996, UCSB has supported several research visits to archives at the University of Chicago and the Library of Congress. My colleagues at UCSB have read, commented on, and helped me refine portions of the book. In particular, I wish to thank Roger Friedland, Barbara Harthorn, Elvin Hatch, Mark Liechty, Shirley Lim, Mat Mines, and Mayfair Yang. I have also benefited from sensitive and knowledgeable comments about my work offered by persons who have read or heard portions of it—Val Daniel, Sara Dickey, Dick Fox, Sandria Freitag, Chris Fuller, Ann Gold, Lindsey Harlan, Gene Irschick, David Rudner, Lee Schlesinger, Sylvia Vatuk, Kamala Visweswaran, and Joanne Waghorne. The preparation of this manuscript was made much easier by the assistance of Dorothy McLaren of the UCSB's Instructional Resources Department, who prepared the illustrations. Stephanie Brommer assisted me in editing the manuscript, and I appreciate her patient and thorough work. It has been a pleasure to work with Karl Yambert of Westview Press. He and Jennifer Chen have been helpful, interested, and marvelously efficient. A special thanks is owed, as well, to an anonymous reader for detailed and constructive comments that I valued greatly.

Throughout the text, many lengthy quotations are attributed to particular informants. The statements are based on detailed notes that I took during interviews and excerpted from my field notes. Interviews were conducted in both English and Tamil, depending on the speakers' abilities and preferences. Unless otherwise noted, translations were prepared by me with the assistance of Mrs. Mythili Raman and my Tamil language tutor, Mr. S. Maruthavanan.

Throughout the entire period of research and writing, my family has remained steadfastly (if quizzically, at times) supportive of and interested in my endeavors. My partner, Toby Lazarowitz, has been uprooted too many times to count and (when not being uprooted) has borne my long absences; all the while he has helped me bring this work to completion by reading and rereading it. My mother, Cecilia, died in 1985, while I was visiting India for the first time. Had she not insisted that I take that trip, I probably would not have gone (or, for that matter, have completed graduate school). Here, at last, is its outcome. I hope that she would have been pleased.

Although I am grateful to all of the above mentioned persons and institutions, the final responsibility for this book rests with me. Any errors of fact or interpretation are mine.

Mary Elizabeth Hancock

Guide to Pronunciation

Tamil words are transliterated according to accepted conventions; I have used the *Tamil Lexicon* (1982) and *Kriyāvin̲ Tar̲kālattamil̲ Akarāti* (Dictionary of Contemporary Tamil) (1992) as guides for the spelling of most words. When standard, Anglicized forms for words exist, those usages (without diacritics) have been adopted (though Tamil versions are included in the glossary). The Sanskritized Tamil terms that are frequently found in Brahman religious discourse are not transliterated according to Sanskritic convention. Names of deities, characters in literature or folklore, famous historical personages, and castes are printed with diacritics unless an Anglicized form is in common use (e.g., "Brahman"). Geographical names appear without diacritical marks, as they would in signs or maps. Names of contemporary individuals appear without diacritics. Tamil words that recur in the book are defined in the glossary.

Credits

Portions of Chapter 1 originally appeared in "Unmaking the 'Great Tradition': Ethnography, National Culture and Area Studies in Postcolonial India," *Identities: Global Studies in Culture and Power* 4, no. 3–4 (1998): 343–388, and have been reprinted with permission of Gordon and Breach Publishers. A revised version of Chapter 5 originally appeared as "The Uncertain Subject(s) of Womanhood" *Nivedini* 5, no. 2 (1997): 5–27, and has been included here with permission from the journal's editor, Selvy Thiruchandran. A revised version of Chapter 8 originally appeared as "Hindu Culture for an Indian Nation: Gender, Politics, and Elite Identity in Urban India," *American Ethnologist* 22, no. 4 (1995): 907–926, and is included here with permission from the American Anthropological Association.

PART ONE

Introduction

Prologue: Making and Unmaking the "Great Tradition"

My first visit to the city of Chennai,[1] in southern India (Figure I.1), was in the autumn of 1985, just in time for Navarāttiri, a nine-night festival honoring the goddess.[2] Known also as Mahānavami or Dasara, it was described in the Devipurana. It became renowned in southern India during the Vijayanagar period (thirteenth through sixteenth centuries C.E.) as a ritual of kingship and was performed annually as a renewal of sovereignty (Stein 1980, 384–392; Dirks 1993, 39–44). Presently, the stage for Navarāttiri has shifted. Though observed in some goddess temples, it is largely a domestic affair celebrated by upper-caste families who perform nightly rituals and display collections of miniatures, as seen in Figure I.2.[3] In one home, small painted figures of the god Rama and his wife Sita stood next to a set of porcelain cats purchased in Singapore. Another family's display included an elaborate village scene, complete with a tiny train station and Hindu temple. The collections, whatever they included, were the centers of attention. People proudly showed off new pieces and experimented with arrangements, and they compared displays. Some families boasted collections that had been assembled over several generations. Nowadays, the objects are mostly mass-produced. When I arrived in October, the open-air markets near the temples overflowed with hundreds of items destined for these displays.

Each evening of the festival, the women of the household worshiped[4] the goddess, whose icon was normally included in the collection, and families opened their homes to their friends and neighbors. Visitors were served snacks, sang devotional songs with their hosts, gossiped and joked, and received small gifts. Indeed, women were expected to distribute gifts to their female visitors. Combs, mirrors, cups, and bowls were given; all were considered emblems of feminine beauty and domesticity. I was told that Navarāttiri was done for the pleasure of women and children, and, for the most part, it was women and children who acted as hosts and guests. The responsibility for accumulating and caring for the collections also fell to women.

FIGURE I.1 Map of India

This festival thus had strong associations with women and with normative representations of femininity. The moral value of feminine beauty and adornments, domesticity, hospitality, and fecundity were underscored through association with the goddess. Not surprisingly, it, like other festivals associated with goddesses, was a time when women's devotional groups, some of long standing, met at temples for prayer and song.

I decided then that I wanted to know more about women's devotionalism and the domestic focus of women's ritual. When I returned to Chen-

FIGURE I.2 An Assemblage *(Kolu)* of Figures Displayed During the Festival of Navarāttiri, 1996. Photograph By Author.

nai a little more than a year later, I intended to make women's devotional groups the subject of my fieldwork. I was intrigued by the role of ritual in urban women's day-to-day interactions, and I was curious about the different kinds of social spaces that ritual practice created. Homes were periodically transformed into meeting halls while street corners and small shrines were claimed by devotional groups—suggesting that conventional Euro-Western distinctions between "public" and "private" domains needed to be rethought in these settings. Finally, I wished to better understand the place of consumption in ritual contexts and thus map the ways that gender ideologies informed and were informed by both caste- and class-based forms of distinction and status production.

I sought to understand these issues in light of previous work. In the 1950s and 1960s, Milton Singer had found in Chennai a generalizable case of the modernization of tradition, and he considered public ritual practices of the sort I had encountered to be important vehicles for these changes (Singer 1972, 62–64, 70–80). He used the phrase "cultural performances" to designate expressive activities, like music, dance, theater, and ritual, that represented the concerns and identities of performers. He argued that they could be treated as the primary units of analysis in the study of civilizations undergoing modernization.

Singer's work on predominantly male and upper-caste[5] devotional groups had established that such groups and the cultural performances they authored were constituent features in south India's urban landscape. They typified the networks thought to characterize modern social worlds, and they illustrated a pan-Indic model of modernization: one that drew on an indigenous Great Tradition rooted in Sanskritic Hinduism.[6] By Great Tradition, he meant the body of historically sedimented, textually inscribed ideas and practices. He stressed that the Great Tradition was synthesizing rather than orthogenetic, and he considered Smārta Brahmans important exponents of it. Smārtas, also known as Aiyars, are a community with roots in Tamil-, Telugu-, and Kannada-speaking areas of peninsular South Asia. He argued that they were among the culture brokers who had disseminated Sanskritic Hinduism regionally and transregionally and thereby incorporated localized, orally transmitted, Little Traditions into a composite Great Tradition. This process helped Smārtas broker alliances among different castes and classes in urban south India. Simultaneously, caste and class distinctions and inequalities (and presumably those of gender, though Singer did not explicitly state this) were also actuated.

I initially viewed women's devotional groups through the lens of Singer's work, seeing them as sites for cultural brokerage and for the modernization of tradition. I wanted to know, first, how upper-caste women's groups differed from those that Singer had studied and what the consequences of those differences were. Second, I wanted to understand how their emergence and ongoing practice derived from Singer called "compartmentalization": the adaptive process whereby upper-caste, professional men bifurcated their lives into a modernized sphere of the workplace and a traditional domestic domain.

I did explore these questions in my fieldwork and subsequent dissertation. In the course of my work, however, I came to understand the significance of these questions differently. Instead of presuming the objective existence of tradition and modernity (and the contrast between private and public they implied), I began to ask what those categories signified, how and why they had been objectified, and how and by whom they were created, deployed, and debated.[7] These are the questions that I explore in this book.

When discussing my interests with Indian academics, many of them Smārtas, I discovered that Singer's text—a gatekeeping work on urban India—continued to be invoked by some Indians in the course of framing their identities for Indian and non-Indian audiences. Some of my acquaintances, conscious of being both subjects and readers of his text, re-presented Singer's ethnography to me. On one occasion, when I was outlining my project to some anthropology graduate students from Madras University, one woman offered, "So, it's the relationship between the Great and Little Traditions that you want to learn about?" A more portentous "meeting" of text and context took place a couple of months after my arrival as I spoke with a senior scholar—a Sanskritist and Smārta Brahman affiliated with a college in Andhra Pradesh, the state immediately north of Tamil Nadu. "L.G." listened thoughtfully as I explained my research interests and then suggested that I work under her direction. She indicated that she would assign appropriate readings (translations of Sanskrit works), introduce me to priests and other "reliable" informants, and arrange for me to view examples of "correctly" performed domestic rituals. She then lent me a book, *Festivals, Sports and Pastimes of India* (1979), as my first assignment, adding that its author, V. Raghavan, the Smārta intellectual with whom Singer had collaborated while doing fieldwork in Chennai, had been one of her teachers.

I was grateful for her guidance but found myself caught in an uncomfortable bind. I did not agree with her methodological prescription, although I respected her intellect, her independence, and her professional accomplishments. And I was acutely aware of the limits of my own knowledge and abilities. In not welcoming her guidance, I risked insulting a senior colleague. If I became her student, I would gain rapid access to domestic ritual arenas, but I would in effect be transcribing her sophisticated notions of orthopraxy as generalized principles of religious belief and practice. Although I knew that ethnography was always a matter of situated knowledge, I resisted the scenario she described, mainly because I wanted to work out methodologies as my personal relationships with people in Chennai developed.

Finally, instead of apprenticing myself to her, I continued in the open-ended fashion in which I had started, soon settling into several overlapping networks of religious practice. Minakshi, a married Smārta woman who became my assistant and close friend, initiated me into these networks. She was a devout Hindu, though her tastes and practices were more eclectic than L.G.'s. My concerns in this book have been shaped to a large extent by Minakshi's enthusiasms, desires, and interests. It was in the course of my work with her that I perceived the contradictions embedded in Brahman women's devotional experience and the complexity of its relation to caste, class, and nationhood. This was the wedge that shifted my work away from an account based implicitly on the assumptions of modernization theory. I became skeptical of narratives about the "displacement" and "fragmentation" of "indigenous traditions" by the external (Western) forces of modernization, curious about how the paradigm that framed the tradition-modernity dichotomy had become authoritative. Throughout my stay in Chennai, L.G. remained cordial, though she rebuked me more than once about my "haphazard" approach to research, which she feared would publicize "inauthentic" versions of Hindu practice including, no doubt, some of the activities to which Minakshi introduced me. L.G. will certainly find this book flawed, and I concede that it *is* flawed from her stance. However, the nature of the contestation implied in her judgment is what interests me.

In many respects, L.G. exemplified the sort of person anthropologists consider an ideal informant. As interlocutors in the space-time of the "field," such persons are recognized as fountains of information and exegesis, issuing the oral narratives (and in some cases, writing the books and articles) that anthropologists absorb. When textualized, these women and men are remade as spokespersons for holistic and wholly Other cultures (Appadurai 1988b).

Interrupting this image, however, was L.G.'s objectification of Indian culture and her concerns about authenticity. She was vexed with me because I remained unwilling to transcribe her vision of Hindu India, despite the fact that she had offered her accomplishments and professional status as guarantees of the authority of that vision. Another interruption was L.G.'s refusal of the form of womanhood idealized in Brahman orthodoxy. She undermined the image of the docile, husband-worshiping wife, the *cumaṅkali*, by being unmarried and by pursuing a successful career in a setting that was dominated by men. She did not, however, exhibit any of the trappings of the career woman depicted in India's mass media: a person who appears alternately in saris and jeans and who has two children, a husband who helps with housework, and a fiercely traditional mother-in-law. L.G. was conservative in matters of dress, grooming, and everyday etiquette, and she regarded herself as deeply orthodox. These aspects of self-presentation, coupled with her program for directing my work, amounted to a refusal to be a token in cultural feminist baggage that I carried, unwittingly, into the field. She did not wish to make common cause with me as a woman; she neither sought approval for what might be seen as a westernized challenge to local gender roles, nor was she caught in a discourse of essentialized feminine virtues. Instead, she spoke as an elite gatekeeper of Indian tradition, defined in terms of a textualized and self-consciously modern Hindu orthodoxy.

Both her claims and her refusals invite a postmodern interpretation of society and cultural forms. This approach recognizes that historical and cultural truths are always partial and that ethnographic work is enmeshed and implicated in a world of enduring but always changing power relations. It advocates a dialogical understanding of culture as an "inscription of communicative processes that exist, historically, between subjects in relations of power" (Clifford 1986, 9). L.G. had slipped out of (and in fact rejected) the unidimensionality of the "informant" role. Her stance was strategic and harbored contradictions stemming from her negotiation of both gender and caste identity, as well as her experience of class privilege.

For her, the provision of ethnographic information was an act of self-representation. It actuated her identity (and status) as an intellectual and as a Smārta Brahman even as it placed her outside the orthodox images of womanhood. In fact, though she refused to conform to canonical representations of womanhood, she endorsed the ideology that buttressed them. Finally, and on a purely practical level, she depended on other women's consenting to these norms, for she lived in a joint household in which her brother's wife was responsible for most of the domestic labor—cooking, cleaning, marketing, child care, and domestic ritual.

These contradictions emerged at the moment of our interaction, and they introduce the matters that I probe in this book. I take seriously Lila Abu-Lughod's challenge to anthropologists to write "against culture" (1991; see also Abu-Lughod 1992; Fox 1989, 1990, 1991), that is, to write against the vision of culture as the anchor of authenticity, homogeneity, and synchronicity among bounded social groups.[8] With this in mind, I concentrate on the specific, immediate circumstances of people's action: their life history and personal experience narratives, ritual practices, and aesthetic sensibilities. In this way, I intend to draw forth the disjunctions and improvisations that are parts of the everyday invention of culture.

In the chapters that follow, I look at the stake that Smārta elites have in the official nationalism of the Indian state and at the practices of self-representation with which they transmit their vision of India's "national" culture. I find normative images of womanhood, domesticity, and tradition at the heart of these domains. In an effort to understand how these hegemonic discourses are reproduced and ruptured, I ask how Smārta Brahman women in urban Chennai created, used, manipulated, and contested womanhood and tradition through ritual practices and in the personal narratives that framed and were framed by their ritual activities. Moreover, the location of these practices in domestic space, as well as their functions as social and spatial signifiers of domesticity, reveal the ways that domesticity itself comes to be defined through cultural debates on tradition and womanhood. This book thus considers women's ritual and the domestic realm as interpenetrating zones of cultural production and contestation, and it explores the contexts and consequences of these practices.

Notes

1. Chennai is the capital of Tamil Nadu state in southern India. With a population of over 5 million, it is the fourth largest city in India. During the colonial period, it was known as Madras. In 1996, its name was changed to Chennai by the state government. This, along with contemporaneous changes in other place-names, was undertaken to make place-names consistent with Tamil vernacular usage.

2. Navarāttiri is a Sanskritic term that literally means "nine nights." It refers here to a festival period of nine nights during which rituals honoring the goddess in the forms of Lakshmi, Durga, and Saraswati are performed. There are two Navarāttiri periods during the Tamil year, one during the lunar month of *Paṅkuṉi* (mid-March to mid-April) and the other during the lunar month of *Puraṭṭāci* (mid-September to mid-October).

3. Among lower castes, it is observed as a solemn ceremony honoring deceased ancestors.

4. *Pūja* (Tamil, *pūcai* or *pūjai*) is a paradigmatic form of Hindu worship, in which the deity is praised, anointed, and honored with offerings that include food, incense, camphor, flowers, money, and jewelry. The ritual is concluded with the redistribution of the food offerings among worshipers. *Pūja* is performed in temples as well as in homes, and it can be done with varying degrees of elaboration.

5. Caste, glossed as *jāti* in Tamil and other Indic languages, is used in scholarly literature to refer to the system of ritually ranked, occupational groups that has been described throughout South Asia. The principles of ranking have been identified as relative purity or pollution (Dumont 1970), styles of transaction and exchange (Marriott 1976), and/or differential access to valued resources (Bailey 1957; Mencher 1974). Caste can also refer to the individual, named groups that are in principle, and at times in practice, endogamous. It should be noted, though, that the term *jāti* has a broader set of usages than caste, for *jāti* is used colloquially to mean kind, category, or type.

6. See Hannerz (1980) and Sanjek (1990) for reviews of social anthropological literature on urban sociology, networks and voluntary associations. Studies of urban networks and social organization in India include, besides Singer (1972), L. Caplan (1987), P. Caplan (1985), Cohn and Marriott (1958), Khare (1970), Lewandowski (1980), Sharma (1986), and Singh (1976).

7. I have found Talal Asad's criticisms of anthropological treatments of religion and ritual, especially Chapters 1–2 of *Genealogies of Religion* (1993), to be extremely valuable guides for the argument that I pursue in this book. In his complex and wide-ranging presentation, Asad urges anthropologists to be more attentive to the culturally and historically specific genealogies of the analytic categories that they employ. "My argument . . . is not just that religious symbols are intimately linked to social life (and so change with it), or that they usually support dominant political power (and occasionally oppose it). It is that different kinds of practice and discourse are intrinsic to the field in which religious representations . . . acquire their identity and their truthfulness. . . . The anthropological student of particular religions should therefore begin from this point, in a sense unpacking the comprehensive concept which he or she translates as 'religion' into heterogeneous elements according to its historical character"(Asad 1993, 53–54).

8. Abu-Lughod (1991) reviewed three modes currently in use. The first is to focus on discourse and practice, and thereby analyze social life without presuming coherence or boundedness. The second entails seeking connections, historical and contemporary, between the groups with whom anthropologists work and the anthropologists themselves. Such connections might include the historical circumstances that bring them together, institutional arrangements that foster such work, and the past and ongoing dependencies between societies. Finally, she describes the efforts to write narrative ethnographies of the particular lives/communities in which Others are made less Other, the constructed qualities of what appears to be typicality (in sentiments, social practices) are highlighted, and the crucial roles of particularities in the constitution of experience are revealed.

1

Tradition, Modernity, and Their Gendered Places

"Tradition" and "modernity" are ubiquitous terms in the lexicon of contemporary nationhood. As Benedict Anderson (1991) has shown, the nation is imagined, through language mediated by print capitalism, as a community that shares both a past and a destiny. The nation is the historically fated, modern surface of tradition. Comparisons among nationalisms reveal modernity and tradition to be gendered, implicitly and explicitly, with tradition carrying female associations and modernity, male connotations. Tradition and modernity, especially as deployed in nationalist discourse, are entangled in what Teresa De Lauretis (1987, 2–3) has called technologies of gender. By this she means popular and mass-mediated representations of gender identity and difference as well as individuals' ways of understanding and responding to those representations.

Domestic space and practice are implicated in nationalist formulations of tradition and modernity in India (Chakrabarty 1994; Chakravarti 1990; Chatterjee 1993; Grewal 1996; Patel 1988; Sangari 1993; Visweswaran 1990). Homes are places in which struggles to define these categories take place, and the boundaries and meanings of the home itself are worked out in these debates. Though he may not have intended it, Singer's notion of compartmentalization illustrates this. Singer wrote that modern Indian industrialists (1972, 272–366) took care to separate their personal and professional lives spatially, temporally, and socially. He considered this a response to modernity understood as secularization, industrialization, and democratization. The industrialists' personal lives were governed by orthopraxy that was enacted vicariously by the ritual practices of their wives and mothers at home. Their professional lives, by contrast, were thoroughly secular and organized around the regimes of the modern workplace. Singer used compartmentalization to denote a functional adaptation that permitted people to manage the contradictions of modernity. It was a means of modernizing without abandoning tradition. Indeed, inasmuch as compartmentalization denoted the ongoing, everyday process of modernization, it encapsulated Singer's larger intellectual project of "indigenizing" modernization theory.

A different take on compartmentalization comes from reading Singer against the grain. Instead of being framed as adaptation, compartmentalization might be interpreted as an effort to displace the contradictions fostered by alienation—of producer from product, among producers, and in the realm of subjectivity—that Marx would associate with industrial capitalism (Tucker 1978, 70–81). In this light, compartmentalization would be explicable as a strategy for claiming that a realm of unalienated, natural labor (understood in the broadest sense as practice that transforms the social and natural world) existed within the confines of domestic life. As such, it masked the relations of patriarchal power that underpin domestic labor and consumption. It also concealed the domestic reproduction of systems of class and caste domination by allowing aestheticized distinctions and exclusions, such as those associated with notions of pollution, to be recuperated and labeled as "traditions," *pāramparīyam*. Without explicitly stating it, Singer's own account showed that compartmentalization reproduced gendered spaces and patriarchal relations by embedding particular styles of ritual practice in the domestic realm. He observed that the ritual neutrality of modern, male-dominated workplaces was accompanied by the gender and ritual marking of domestic space:[1]

> Even within the more modern types of homes, however, the older customs continue. The wives, who may not speak English, and other females of the household tend to remain in the background; they usually do not eat until the males and guests have been served, and they participate more faithfully in ritual observances and cultural performances than do the industrial leaders and other males of the household. (Singer 1972, 322)

Put simply, a compartmentalizing (male) subject required an at-home, compartmentalized (female) subject: a wife, mother, sister, daughter and/or daughter-in-law. The process of compartmentalization thus reiterated metonymic connections among women, religion, and the home in a way that incorporated them as cultural capital for the production of bourgeois status and power. It created a spatial and psychological interior wherein tradition was crafted, contained, and feminized. Yet what is less obvious in Singer's account is the fact that this process was always precarious and its outcome uncertain, for it rested on continual renegotiations of labor and consumption among kinswomen, between female employers and servants, and between men and women. Contrary to appearances, "traditional" ritual practices were not merely holdovers from the past but had been revised, and in some cases reinvented, in response to the elements of modernity that colonialism introduced (Lakshmi 1984, 2–30).

Thus I agree with Singer about the existence of compartmentalization. I depart from him in that I do not see it as a straightforward adaptation to modernity, but as a strategic claim by elites that is at once *about* modernity and *prompted by* modernity. In an influential argument, Partha Chatterjee (1989; 1993, 116–157) has claimed that nationalist elites in late nineteenth-century Bengal bifurcated their lives in ways similar to those described by Singer. They conceded the realms of work and governance to the modernity that was part of the apparatus of colonial rule, but they preserved in their domestic lives a space of local identity and incipient nationalism, constituted as tradition. This bifurcation, in turn, entailed men's efforts to control women's actions and appearances (Chakrabarty 1994; Chakravarti 1990; Sangari 1993). Although this hardly constituted an invention of patriarchy, it reshaped patriarchal relations in the service of an emerging bourgeois ideology of nationhood. Chatterjee did not refer to Singer's work in his analysis, yet the parallels are suggestive. Here I would draw on Chatterjee's argument to interrogate Singer's and suggest that compartmentalization be understood as a style of social practice and a normative discourse about social practice. It describes and prescribes, while remaining subject to contestation and revision.

Chatterjee (1989) offered linguistic evidence from Bengali to demonstrate that the origins of the home-world dichotomy, and its rhetorical potency, predated the colonial era. There are parallels in Tamil, which also has a well-developed vocabulary for making relational distinctions between interiority and exteriority. The term *akam* refers to the house, the self, and womanhood. These relational interiors stand in opposition to exteriors, *puṟam*—which can include spaces, like the street or the yard outside a house, and activities, like war and governance. A. K. Ramanujan (1985, 229–297) has found this distinction within Tamil poetry of the Caṅkam era (ca. 100 B.C.E.–250 C.E.). He characterized *akam* poems as a genre of love and longing, whereas *puṟam* poems celebrated heroism, community, and conquest. However, in vernacular as well as literary usages, the distinctions made are complex and subtle; *akam* and *puṟam* are treated as aspects of a single, often cosmological whole.

Under colonial rule, the languages of interiority and exteriority were employed by subaltern elites[2] as they developed a nationalist lexicon (often with some loss of their nuanced and complementary vernacular meanings). In late nineteenth-century usage, the interior constituted the impenetrable (and feminized) essence of the nation, which harbored resistance to colonial rule. The exterior was the world of wage labor, governance, and material production; it was the zone into which Western mores and power penetrated. Elite nationalists acceded to the exterior conditions of colonial rule, but they claimed the interior—women, home, family—as the principal site in which nationalist subjects were to be formed in opposition to colonialism.

Chatterjee found that nationalist resistance to colonialism in the twentieth century made further use of this emotionally charged set of distinctions. Gandhian projects inverted the hierarchical relations between exteriority and interiority by claiming a moral superiority for nonviolence *(ahimsa)* in achieving self-rule. Gandhi viewed nonviolence—and the humility, patience, chastity, and self-sacrifice it entailed—as essentially feminine and women (mothers and widows especially) as its exponents. The domestic interior was thus the center of a new way of imagining the nation.

Chatterjee's criticism of the modernization paradigm offers a useful contrast to Singer's position. Nevertheless, Chatterjee, like Singer, stopped short of critically analyzing either domesticity or female agency. Instead, Chatterjee considered domesticity as a redemptive, albeit fragmentary signifier of the national community. Feminist scholars (Chakravarti 1990; Mani 1990; Patel 1988; Visweswaran 1990, 1996) have taken issue with Chatterjee, emphasizing that women were treated as icons of tradition in the patriarchal ideologies of elite nationalism (see also Chakrabarty 1994). It is telling that the upper-caste Tamil women who had supported Gandhian projects from the 1920s through the 1940s interpreted *kaṟpu* (the culturally valued quality of wifely devotion to a husband, sometimes translated "chastity") as an expression of *ahimsa* (Lakshmi 1984, 24–25). At the same time, however, characterizations such as this created new spaces for female action. Such actions are exemplified in women's own efforts to support anticolonial nationalism and social reform by opposing child marriage, agitating for women's education, and participating in Gandhian civil disobedience. Such challenges revealed (even as they intervened in) the patriarchal underpinnings of bourgeois nationalism.

In their own "compartmentalizing" practices, contemporary Smārta elites such as L.G. (see Prologue) appeared to subscribe to the gendered language of tradition and modernity that crystallized under colonialism. But taking a cue from feminist arguments, I argue that everyday practice requires attention. In everyday practice, the meanings and boundaries of the home and the world are always negotiated and contested, even among those women whose elite status might suggest that they complied with a moral etiquette consistent with compartmentalization. L.G.'s own life, as I have suggested, was not ordered in deference to these dualities. She was an unmarried woman who worked outside the home and traveled abroad occasionally. The Sanskrit texts that she studied contained assertions that a woman's first lord was her husband. Yet L.G.'s own enactment of Hindu orthopraxy was through disciplined intellectual activity coupled with formal ritual rather than the embodied practices of wifehood. Other women I knew were not as well versed in the Hindu canon, but they also made—and unmade—the boundaries between the home and the world. Some women performed domestic rituals for audiences of friends and neighbors who admired these women's skills and intense religiosity. A few were goddess mediums; like other ritual specialists, they often performed within (and thus resculpted) domestic space. Unlike other Brahman ritual specialists, however, these mediums were sometimes initiated by low-caste and Harijan practitioners and maintained close (though contradiction-laden) relationships with them. In these contexts, domestic space was reconstituted with practices that both deconstructed and reconstructed caste and class inequalities. Finally, there were still other women who transplanted household ritual into public venues, such as temples or meeting halls, thereby domesticating (if only provisionally) those public spaces. All whom I discuss challenged the home-world distinction implied by compartmentalization but did so from within the domestic realm, using its own logic to transform its boundaries.

Domestic Ritual and Its Practice

My argument in this book begins with domesticity as practice. Tamil glosses for domesticity, *illaṟam* and *ilvāḻkkai,* denote the way of life of a householder, a man with a wife and worldly duties (in contrast to the man who has renounced such things). This way of life has a place, spatially and behaviorally, for ritual actions. As is discussed in Chapter 3, shrines and kitchens are the key areas that define the domestic realm. Household ritual repertoires include the generic forms known as *samskāra*s (ceremonies marking life cycle transitions) and *paṇṭikai* (calendric festivals), as well as various fasts and vows to which individuals commit themselves. Tamil Brahmans consider these events part of domestic life (even when they perform them indifferently or not at all). When they are performed, it is usually women who see to them, interweaving their performance with other activities such as cooking and cleaning. Women's own rituals, such as weekly worship of the goddess in the form of an oil lamp *(tiruviḷakku pūja)* or cycles of fasting and prayer *(nōṉpu and viratam),* are also aspects of domestic life. All domestic rituals involve ways of doing things—of cleaning objects and serving foods, for example—that are not unlike the performance of comparable actions in nonritual contexts.

Because of the observable continuities between rituals and other domestic actions, I find Catherine Bell's (1992, 88–93) use of "ritualization" to be applicable. Bell noted that efforts to create a generalizable definition of ritual (and the corresponding effort to distinguish rituals from non-rituals) have floundered because of the cultural and historical specificities of the category and its resistance to translation. She did not go so far as to jettison the term from the scholarly lexicon but suggested instead that attention to "ritualization" might be more productive. By ritualization she intended the linguistic and behavioral pragmatics that actors employ in defining ritual in particular sociocultural and historical contexts, writing that "formality, fixity, and repetition are not intrinsic qualities of ritual so much as they are a frequent . . . strategy for producing ritualized acts" (Bell 1992, 92). This, she argued, would allow scholars to focus on the situational and strategic aspects of ritual rather than engage in the fruitless and intellectually suspect exercise of trying to categorize some actions as "ritual" as opposed to, say, "utilitarian."

Bell's intervention was informed by the theorization of practice found in the work of Bourdieu (1977, 1990), Foucault (1979, 1980), and De Certeau (1984), and it is compatible with existing scholarship on South Asian Hinduism. Much scholarship on conceptions of self and personhood among Hindu South Asians has identified underlying ethnosociological principles. These writers argue that the person is conceived as dynamic and relational: The biomoral boundaries of the person are considered porous, subject to the influences of place, food, cloth, and others' (including deities') bodies and their voiced and unvoiced intentions (Daniel 1984; Marriott 1976; Marriott and Inden 1977; Trawick 1990).[3] As such, persons are never finished products but are always in the making, intersubjectively, throughout individual life cycles and across broader cycles of rebirth.

In tension with the fluidity of the person stressed in ethnosociological approaches, others have emphasized the fixity of caste as a category of identity. Dumont's (1970) attributional model described the caste system as a hierarchy of bounded categories that is based on relative degrees of purity and pollution. He pointed to the role that Sanskritic texts on law and morality—known as *shastras*—played in actors' conceptions of social order. These texts described an ideological grid of caste, gender, life stage, and occupational difference *(varṇāśramadharma)* into which all humans could be slotted; this, he maintained, was consistent with the ways in which people viewed themselves and others.

There have been efforts to combine these different models. Parry (1994), recognizing the salience among Hindus of both fluid and hierarchical models for personhood, has suggested that some sets of Hindu ritual practices acknowledge and resolve, at least situationally, the tensions between them. Following his argument, it could be suggested that for Brahmans, an ideological resolution of the tension between ethnosociological and attributional models of personhood was contained in the textualized life cycle rituals, *samskāras*, that include rituals of marriage, pregnancy and childbirth, tying and renewal of the sacred thread, and funerary ritual (Pandey 1969; Ramanujan 1978, 139–147). Pandits (textual scholars) and priests credited those rituals with the capacity to "refine" humans, ushering them through a series of different types of personhood over the course of the individual life cycle and, ultimately, across the broader cycles of rebirth. Because they served both as linchpins in the reproduction of *varṇāśramadharma* and as transactional modes of person making, *samskāras* can be treated as the mediating point for the two models.

It is not my aim to rehearse the debates about the relative merits of attributional and ethnosociological models of caste ranking here. My review is offered merely to point out the extent to which Hindu rituals have been treated as embodied practices. Taking this as my point of departure, I wish to make two kinds of claims. First, borrowing Foucault's (1980, 98) terminology, I argue that ritual is a "local center" for the exercise of hegemonic power and that an analysis of ritual can point to ways in which gender, class, and caste hierarchies might be reproduced. One way of framing this process is with Althusser's notion of ideology, which, he asserts, works by shaping subjects who are imbued with its terms and consciously subscribe to them. Thus ritual "hails," or interpellates, subjects as occupants of certain kinds of class and status positions. In so doing, it reproduces relations of differential power (Althusser 1971). Second, although I would argue that ritual has ideological functions in the sense of representing and enforcing sectional interests, I would not claim that it does this simply by duping subjects, that is, by creating false consciousness. Here I depart from Althusser's position. As a local center of power, ritual is a site of force and resistance; in terms of subject formation, it creates complex subjects who are both compliant and resistant, subjects who can and do intervene in the streams of action that constitute ritual. Thus the struggles comprising hegemony are not only between subjects but are intrinsic to the very constitution of those subjects (Grosz 1990).[4]

My understanding of ritual has been strongly influenced by post-Marxist and poststructuralist theory, but I maintain that this can speak to and be enriched by the classic work on ritual and symbolic practice associated with Victor Turner (1967, 1969). Turner's interpretation of ritual form, specifically his notion of liminality (antistructure) as transformative core of ritual action, remains a major paradigm for ritual analysis. His understandings of ritual as a site for the negotiation and resolution of societal contradiction and as embodied symbolic practice are helpful in framing questions about the emergence of critical subjectivity. If, as an Althusserian reading would predict, orthodox Hindu ritual "hails" persons as occupants of categories of gender and caste, then as people experience these rituals they are imbued, over and over again, with these categories—they become what orthodoxy declares them to be. And, following Turner, if there is a process of "hailing" or assimilation in the context of ritual practice, it must be enacted at the point of ritual transformation, which is the liminal. But, as Turner writes, the liminal, while being the core of transformative experience, is also the point at which people objectify those representations and stand outside them as "uncommitted" beings (1967, 106–108). I argue that this standing outside is one condition (not the only one, certainly) that makes critical consciousness possible. Is not critique predicated on the possibility of imagining that things might be different from their appearance and from their authoritative representation?

The notion that ritual is a practice that produces and reproduces meaning follows arguments made by Bourdieu (1977, 1990) and De Certeau (1984), and it illuminates the functions and persistence of some forms of Hindu orthopraxy. The persistence of structured systems of thought, action, and social life was explained by Bourdieu with his notion of habitus, defined as

> systems of durable, transposable dispositions, structured structures predisposed to function as structuring structures, that is as principles of the generation and structuring of practices and representations which can be . . . "regular" without . . . being the product of obedience to rules . . . [and] without presupposing a conscious aiming at ends of an express mastery of the operations necessary to attain them. (Bourdieu 1977, 72)

In accounting for how habitus and its encoded systems of domination were reproduced without appealing solely to actors' rational calculations of interests or to all-powerful institutions of social constraint, Bourdieu stressed its tacit and aesthetic mediation. To illustrate, he pointed to the sense of honor among the Kabyle, writing that it was "embedded in the agents' very bodies in the form of mental dispositions, schemes of perception and thought . . . and also, at a deeper level, in the form of bodily postures and stances, ways of standing, sitting, looking, speaking or walking" (Bourdieu 1977, 15; see also Bourdieu 1990, 66–79). Similarly, Foucault's analysis of modern state power focused on its diffused and localized operation through practices of bodily discipline, surveillance, and classification (1979). He claimed that the individual as conceived in post-Enlightenment discourse was an effect of this decentered and capillary power. Both Foucault and Bourdieu emphasized that these practices operated as modes of domination; in Bourdieu's terms, as euphemized or symbolic violence.

Drawing on these arguments, I argue that the styles of everyday actions in which women's rituals were embedded—actions that include cleaning oneself, eating, and touching others—should be understood as making and marking caste, gender, and class, and the relations of power that those identities encode. These processes could be apprehended cognitively by actors and thus disputed or resisted. They were also aesthetic, that is, they were modes of sensory experience whose apprehension was only partially a matter of conscious cognition, or "discursive consciousness" (Giddens 1984, 5–7). They were technologies of identity written on and in the body, in the sensations, desires, and fears that sometimes eluded linguistic expression.

Their embodied qualities might make gender, class, and caste appear to be intricate and hyperdetermined identities—pieces of a perfectly self-reproducing and hegemonic system. However, in suggesting that caste and gender are made and remade through the body in everyday practices, I have also introduced the possibility of "unmaking," whether by accident or intent. Here I rely on De Certeau's readings of Bourdieu and Foucault. De Certeau acknowledged, following Foucault, that the "grid of 'discipline' [that was] everywhere becoming clearer and more extensive" made it imperative that the analysis of everyday practice "bring to light the clandestine forms taken by the dispersed, tactical, and makeshift creativity of groups or individuals already caught in the nets of 'discipline'" (De Certeau 1984, xiv–xv). He described the object of his own study as the "network of 'anti-discipline'" (De Certeau 1984, xv).

The image of human action as cutting paths into, remaking, and appropriating pieces of preexisting worlds of meaning runs through De Certeau's work. The performers of and participants in ritual were engaged in what he called consumption: the selective use, ingestion, and absorption of the representations delivered in ritual. Their practices of consumption could take the form of consent, resistance, and the myriad possibilities lying between those two poles. To get at the ambiguities of consumption, De Certeau distinguished between strategic and tactical practices. Tactics are the arts of the weak—"poaching" on terrain controlled by dominant powers and making use of "cracks that particular conjunctions open in the surveillance of the proprietary powers" (De Certeau 1984, 34). Strategies, on the other hand, are the privileges of power: "calculation[s] . . . that become possible as soon as a subject with will and power . . . can be isolated" (De Certeau 1984, 36). Strategies are visible exercises of power that reproduce relations of domination, whereas tactics work invisibly. Neither form of action is the exclusive property of a single actor or social group; rather, they are situational practices that can be combined in varying ways and to different ends. Informed by De Certeau's insights about the reproductive and resistant dimensions of practice, I treat ritual as an aesthetic practice that can both reproduce and resist domination and as a transformative "technology" that produces complex subjectivities (see also Boddy 1989; Comaroff 1985).

I claim that rituals only superficially enact textual recipes. More fundamentally, they are performances attributed with the power to transform participants. As such, they are acts of appropriation and reinvention, driven by what actors know, intend, or desire, that can also change the contours of knowledge, intention, and desire. They also have experimental qualities. People use ritual instrumentally, testing and modifying their techniques in light of their perceived effects. This is not a simple matter of rational calculation, however, because their understanding of the nature and signs of a ritual's efficacy also shift over the course of a performance cycle. Practice theory accommodates these changing applications and helps explain Brahman women's positioning by and in Hindu ritual, as they are compelled to negotiate between forms of female subjectivity that include both figures of desire (e.g., the auspicious wife) and figures of abjection (e.g., the inauspicious widow). Such an analysis contributes to the efforts of feminist theorists who want to understand how women are "caught" in systems of gendered inequality and want to demonstrate that alternatives to these systems are not only thinkable but have concrete, historical existence.

Feminisms

Feminist theorists and activists concerned with India have contributed to scholarship on the practical constitution of gender and the ways in which different systems of structural inequality become enmeshed with it. Rajeswari Sunder Rajan has put it this way:

> If we acknowledge (a) that femaleness is constructed, (b) that the terms of such construction are to be sought in the dominant modes of ideology . . . and (c) that therefore what is at stake is the investments of desire and the politics of control that representation both signifies and serves, then . . . what is required . . . is an alertness to the political process by which such representation becomes naturalized and ultimately coercive in structuring women's self-representation. (Sunder Rajan 1993, 129)

This passage asserts the inextricability of feminist theory and feminist politics. Sunder Rajan found in the specificities of women's experiences the means for decoding the practices by which womanhood is negotiated by women within the shifting fields of power associated with class, race, caste, and gender.[5] With Sunder Rajan, I argue that feminist analysis is characterized by the effort to understand the contextually variable representations of femininity, female sexuality and gender as sociocultural systems of difference. This understanding attends to the everyday politics of gender through which representations become meaningful, that is, how they come to operate as lenses by which people make sense of and question their lives, their relationships, their desires, fears, and habits. Moreover, the capacity to penetrate the intimate politics of representation may also enable people to create alternative repertoires of gendered practice—new ways of being male or female.

Sunder Rajan's concerns are shared by feminist ethnographers, folklorists, and historians who document the material and social conditions of particular women's lives in order to recover silenced subjects and locate emancipatory possibilities in those conditions. For example, there is a growing body of anthropological and ethnohistorical work committed to making visible and analyzing South Asian women's interrogations of and improvisations around canonical representations of femininity (Forbes 1996; Harlan 1992; Karlekar 1991; O'Hanlon 1992, 1994; Raheja and Gold 1994; Stree Shakti Sanghatana 1989; Thiruchendran 1997; Visweswaran 1990, 1996; Wadley 1982). These works foreground women's "voices"—their understandings of themselves and their worlds, and their oral and gestural forms of expression. The authors also show the limits of canonical representations of womanhood. In their work on North Indian women's speech and song, Gloria Raheja and Ann Gold reviewed these approaches. They suggested, citing Margaret Trawick (1990, 5), that representations of Indian women as repressed and submissive are "half-truths" (1994, 9) that not only misrepresent women but also orientalize South Asian culture and society, concluding that

> far from speaking only in a language dominated by males, the women we have come to know imaginatively scrutinize and critique the social world they experience and give voice to that vision in a poetic language of song and story. . . . Those songs and stories may enter their lives and shift, however slightly or however consequentially, the terms in which their lives are led. (Raheja and Gold 1994, 26)

A related approach that links the recovery of women's voices with critical political practice is illustrated in the work of the Stree Shakti Sanghatana in India, a Maoist feminist collective who gathered the oral histories of women who had participated in the Communist-led Telangana movement in southern India in the 1940s and 1950s (Stree Shakti Sanghatana 1989). They intended to bring to light previously unknown aspects of the movement by documenting women's experiences, but they also sought to interrogate the methods and descriptive categories that other historians had taken for granted, notably the tacit assumption that political action is undertaken in a "public" realm that excludes the "private" spaces and relationships of domestic life. The testimonies collected from women revealed the extent to which images of family life pervaded the Communist party's rhetoric and organization. This was a source of security for some women who had left their families to join the insurgency; others recognized and lamented the patriarchal relations that persisted among party members. The accounts also revealed the shrewd usage of social conventions by women. To help men elude police officials, women hid them in the female quarters of affluent households or provided disguises of female clothing, including the face and head covers worn by women in purdah.

A third direction taken by those seeking to recover silenced subjects has inquired about the intentional and expressive aspects of silence and nonverbal actions. Silence—the absence of documentation or speech—has been explored as an expression of subaltern resistance and as a refusal to collude with a discourse in which one is constituted as Other (Visweswaran 1990, 184–215; Spivak 1987). De Lauretis (1987) and Sunder Rajan (1993, 83–102) have taken this further by inquiring into forms of resistance and representation that exist outside the speech/silence problematic, specifically in nonverbal practices. Their work contains a critique of the idea of autonomous subjectivity (i.e., the Euro-Western "individual"), with its locus in the act of speech, but also suggests ways of thinking about subjectivity as positional and *inter*subjective.

These arguments about the retrieval of women's voices and subjectivities, about the meanings of silence, and about the critical interventions enabled by such understandings are deeply relevant to the issues I address in this book. Hinduism sanctions women's silence in a variety of contexts and further defines womanhood through such silences. The Brahman woman is "muted" in orthodox ritual settings, and on an everyday basis she is enjoined to be modest and self-effacing, for example, she is expected to avoid uttering her husband's name on the grounds that it will hasten his death. This latter practice is not reciprocal—a man can refer to his wife by name—and it reproduces patterns of deference and status distinction. From a woman's perspective, however, these silences are more complicated, and it is with this complexity that I am concerned.

Such silences, interpreted against that which is spoken and that which is performed, are traces of complex and shifting subjectivities located in the actions of real, historical women. For example, a woman's nonverbal actions could stem from desires for valued kinds of female personhood, though they may have subversive qualities as well. Her silence, which might appear deferential, could be experienced differently and more ambiguously—as a moment in which wifely identity is both asserted and relinquished. The more complex silences of women who act as goddess mediums offer another case in point. On the one hand, these women explain their bodies, voices, and desires as having been overtaken by the intentionality and agency of a divine being. They describe themselves as vehicles for a divine Other who expresses her wishes and her creative energies by displacing those of her host. On the other hand, these women also see themselves as partners with the goddess who "comes to" them. That is, the goddess only partially and provisionally displaces her devotee's intentions and desires. The result is that during a medium's performances there are always ambiguities about whose voice speaks and whose intentions are relayed. The medium's own social identity is unstable as well. Though she may be a wife, mother, daughter, or daughter-in-law, as a medium she often renegotiates the relations of obligation, emotion, and entitlement that define those statuses—authoring new, and different, relationships and identities that extend to contexts outside those of ritual action.

Attending to the interplay of speech and silence, then, may reveal disjunctions and emancipatory possibilities that exist within ideological systems of gender representation. This is the point of departure from which, in the chapters that follow, I reflect on the ways in which religious imagery mediates subjectivity and opens up spaces for improvisation. Inspired by my women friends in Chennai, I ask how women attempt to alter the horizons of the thinkable and the doable through the very discourses and practices that define womanhood as the anchor of Hindu tradition.

The Public Culture of Domestic Ritual

By framing ritual as an ensemble of strategies and tactics, I recognize that as much as ritual can be said to create contexts, it is located in sociopolitical and historical contexts that are not of its own making.[6] Chennai, the site of my ethnography, is a city shaped by the political economy of colonial power, industrialization, and the administrative structures of the Indian state, not by pilgrimage or royal patronage (Basu 1998; Lewandowski 1977; 1980, 41–64; 1984). The recent designation of Tambaram (a town within the greater municipality of Chennai) as an export processing zone reflects the growing presence of multinational capitalism in the city. Domestic rituals, like other cultural practices, have been transformed by contestatory nationalisms, transnational processes, commodification, and class formation—the same forces that have shaped other areas of life. Among Smārtas, domestic rituals are actions by which self-defined "middle-class"[7] persons characterize the ways in which they differ from the poor and from non-Brahmans (whom upper castes often labeled "Sudras"[8]) and represent their Indianness. The questions of class and nation that are part of domestic ritual, moreover, are themselves embedded in a set of larger issues concerning modernity. Domestic ritual, therefore, should be analyzed among the cultural practices that appropriate, resist, and reshape modernity—as public culture.

Most of the families I knew were supported by men who held white-collar jobs as entrepreneurs, teachers, accountants, managers, doctors, and architects. Many, moreover, were civil servants who depended directly on the central government for livelihoods and, as state functionaries, represented the state apparatus to the populace. Brahman recruitment to the civil service began under colonial rule, and most of the people with whom I was acquainted in Chennai were second- or third-generation urban migrants. Some had relocated in Chennai from villages elsewhere in southern India to pursue education and employment opportunities. For others, Chennai was a temporary residence—one of a succession of temporary postings that took them to cities throughout India.

Patterns of middle-class domesticity among urban Smārtas correspond easily to what Singer called compartmentalization. Reflecting the general pattern of low labor force participation found among middle- and upper-class Indian women, the majority of women with whom I worked were not formally employed (Caplan 1985). All, however, had received at least a secondary education, and some had attended college. Those who worked for wages were teachers, accountants, administrative assistants, and doctors. Even those not formally employed often contributed to the household's income or maintained personal funds by providing services that ranged from private tutoring to casting astrological charts. The women who acted as goddess mediums frequently received donations from clients, which could amount to a considerable income.

All women, employed or not, performed a variety of household tasks (such as marketing, housecleaning, home decorating, coaching children with schoolwork, and entertaining guests) that were densely interwoven with ritual practices. Indeed, they often defined their feminine identities in terms of these tasks. Food preparation and household cleaning, for example, included the preparation of ritual food offerings and the ritualized purification of domestic shrines. Following Hannah Papanek (1979), I characterize women's domestic labor as status production work in order to signal its role in constituting elite class status for the household as a whole. Family status production work often extended outside the household as well. The relation between elite status and membership in international clubs, for example, the Lions and the Rotary, and in local voluntary associations has been well documented (Caplan 1985), and most of my informants were "joiners." Besides fostering class alliances among elites, the associations, which usually had philanthropic functions, were vehicles that perpetuated class inequality and ideology by cementing relations of dependency between elite women and poor women.

Women's production of family status accompanied intrahousehold negotiation of power and status among kinswomen and between servants and their female employers. The more onerous, time-consuming, and least ritualized tasks were assigned to lower-status women (often daughters-in-law) and servants, whom all families employed. The assignment and supervision of tasks, as well as the regulation of consumption, marked differential status—often in terms of women's relative purity, cleanliness, and propriety. The negotiation of housework among women thus reconstituted caste and class difference and inequality within the household, framing these differences in the substantive, often aestheticized terms of women's bodily qualities.

Status production within and among households also entails particular styles and levels of economic consumption. With colonial urbanization and subsequent industrialization, urban households have become units of consumption rather than production, and women have taken on roles as consumers. Household manuals and women's periodicals dating from the late nineteenth century register this shift, linking feminine virtue to thrift, rationalized expenditure and budgeting, and the exercise of taste. The introduction of postsecondary Home Science education (by and for middle-class women) further rationalized domestic labor as it promoted normative styles of consumption. It was not until the beginnings of economic liberalization in the early 1980s that consumer goods such as household appliances, televisions, and videocassette players became readily available to middle-class Indians, making consumption a more prominent feature in household status production. These developments cast women in a dual role as agents of class-specific styles of aesthetic judgment (taste) and as quasi-commodities themselves, accentuated by the increasing use of dowry as a channel for the acquisition of consumer goods.

With respect to domestic ritual, the impacts of changes in elite women's domestic labor and consumption have been significant. More commodified styles of domestic ritual have become arenas for displaying class status among urban elites. Families at times invited outsiders' scrutiny and evaluation of domestic ritual spaces and practices; in some houses shrines were moved out of kitchens and adjacent alcoves and into the front room. Ritual performances were occasions for inviting work associates and neighbors into one's home. The assemblages of objects that shrines comprised—deity figurines and pictures, incense burners, trays, lamps, metallic vessels—were by and large mass-marketed, sometimes produced by government-funded artisans and sold in the craft emporia that cater to the tourist market. The knowledge of ritual techniques had moved out of the control of domestic priests and were mass mediated with the result that there were more opportunities for individual innovations and adaptations. Several specific styles were popularized through devotional films, and nearly all domestic ritual formats were disseminated in instructional pamphlets and magazines as well as by audiocassette and videocassette.

The commodified reinventions of Hindu practice that I witnessed among Chennai Smārtas were contextualized by transregional and transnational processes. Transregionalism among Smārtas is long-standing, for as literati they enjoyed royal patronage under the succession of precolonial dynasties that ruled the southern peninsula. With colonial rule, their regional mobility expanded, and it was accompanied by transnational mobility. During the colonial era, it was not unusual for Brahman men to seek education abroad because the training and qualifying examinations for civil service postings were only administered in England. Similarly, some of my acquaintances had traveled abroad for schooling or jobs, and most had relatives living abroad. Indeed, current research indicates that South Asians are among the most dispersed populations in the world. Substantial South Asian communities can be found in Australia, Fiji, New Zealand, Southeast Asia, East and South Africa, England, Germany, France, the United States, and Canada (Clarke, Peach, and Vertovec 1990; Van der Veer 1995).

In short, because of their mobility and the class privilege that underwrote it, many Chennai Brahmans (along with other communities that the urban elite comprises) have acquired distinctly cosmopolitan outlooks and tastes. As "foreign-returned" (a colloquial usage in Indian English), they were like colonial elites elsewhere, whose sojourns abroad provided them with an advanced education that they could use to claim privileged positions in an expanding social structure. They possessed a general sophistication derived from exposure to metropolitan lifeways (Hannerz 1992, 228–229). The mobile cosmopolitan stands in sharp contrast to "rustics" (another colloquial usage), who are taken to represent tradition in its rough cut.

These contrasting terms are indicative of the ambivalence with which tradition was objectified and understood by Smārta elites in Chennai. As foreign-returned, they saw themselves as bridgeheads of transnational cultural processes. This enabled them to objectify the local, which they described using the English word "authentic"—distancing them from it while making it available for their consumption. Tradition as "authenticity" could be found in the "village," and my informants were unanimous in recommending that I go to the "village" to find "authentic" religious practice. They rarely specified any particular village by name; rather, they were referring to the "village" as an ideal type. The only qualifier was that it be south of Chennai. In fact, the farther south the village, the more authentic the practice.

Many Smārtas identified the state as a corrosive force on religious authenticity, and the presence of the state on the cityscape touched everyday religious practice in different ways. There is in Tamil Nadu a government agency that administers Hindu religious institutions such as temples, schools, and charitable organizations. This agency, the Hindu Religious and Charitable Endowments Department, was founded under the colonial state but has grown in size and bureaucratic intricacy since independence. Because the funds, personnel, and ritual calendars of large temples were monitored by this agency, the state's presence at many religious sites was tangible. All Hindus who patronized temples were keenly aware of this, and they often resented it. Their awareness of the state's interventions in temple operations affects their use of temples, sometimes leading them to use temples in ways not authorized by the state and at other times to negotiate with bureaucrats for degrees of autonomy. It is also common to create "private" temples—shrines built by families or voluntary associations in homes or on the grounds of domestic compounds and used only by audiences designated by their owners, founders, or regular users.

Another large-scale political project that affected (and continues to affect) everyday religious practice has been the burgeoning right-wing Hindu nationalist movement. Since the early 1980s such groups have tried to mobilize Hindus through a critique of the secular Indian state by claiming that the state has catered to religious minorities, especially Muslims and Christians. They appeal to the Hindus' general dissatisfaction with what they understand as state interventions in social and religious life, as well as to their particular resentment of the restrictions that many "foreign-returned" have experienced while working abroad, especially in Islamic countries. Beginning in 1989, Hindu nationalists sponsored public rituals in cities, towns, and villages throughout India to consecrate bricks for use in what they claimed was the rebuilding of Hindu temples previously destroyed by Muslims. These gestures were accompanied by other deliberately provocative actions, such as the organization of Hindu religious processions in Muslim residential areas. In October of that year, nationalist groups gathered at Ayodhya (a town in northern India) and attempted to destroy the mosque that they claimed had been built by Mughal forces in the twelfth century after demolishing a temple marking the birth site of the god Rama. They followed this with a similarly orchestrated effort in 1992. During that assault they destroyed the mosque and precipitated riots throughout the country. Despite public condemnation of these tactics, the political power of the nationalist Bharatiya Janata

Party (BJP) has grown, and in the 1998 general elections the BJP gained the parliamentary majority that enabled them to form a national government.

The sympathy that urban elites have for Hindu nationalism is evident in southern India (Hancock 1995b; Pandian 1990). Since the early 1980s, nationalist organizations have attracted members and support from Hindu religious leaders in the south. This is particularly evident when the nationalist platform filters through familiar ritual forms. For some, these developments reinvigorated the "authenticity" that city life threatened. A case in point, which I discuss further in Chapter 8, was a social movement headed by a Smārta religious leader that fused elite philanthropy with Hindu nationalist proselytization. The movement's leaders publicized their cause and sought to mobilize an elite constituency using a modified style of women's domestic ritual.

Smārta disparagement of urban life was tempered by the conviction that something identifiable as tradition continued to exist in the midst of contempory urban life. I found that ritual activity was bracketed and consumed by urban cultural elites as tradition. These cosmopolitan and often transnational Hindus valued certain rituals, particularly women's rituals, as a contrapuntal space, time, and morality that is distinct from modernity. Their leisure activities, for example, included movies as well as classical music and dance, and most read English-language and vernacular newspapers and magazines. All these connoted and embodied what they considered modernity, and yet they were also the means for defining and consuming tradition, for example, by packaging it on audio-cassette, in print, and in performance. Indeed, the presence of places, activities, and styles deemed traditional distinguished India's urban life from that in the West and was a source of pride for many middle-class Smārtas.

They pointed to bearers of Hindu "authenticity" such as the pandit (as opposed to temple priests, whom they dismissed as corrupt emissaries of the state). Some averred that women were emotionally attached to traditional ideas and practices. For example, elite families were keen to have their daughters study Bharat Natyam. This dance form was based on the ninth-century sadir style but had been reconstructed and classicized in the early years of the twentieth century by urban elites and incorporated in the repertoire of Indian culture that elite nationalists celebrated (Srinivasan 1985). Tradition was objectified, as well, in the paraphernalia found in household shrines, the silver eating and serving utensils favored for special occasions, and the nine-yard saris worn for weddings by upper caste brides and for everyday wear by orthodox women.

The importance of these examples lies in the cultural production of modernity and the contest over it that Smārtas' conscious engagements with tradition suggest. These examples show that modernity no longer derives from Western sources; the means for local productions of modernity are distributed widely (though not evenly) across the globe. Appadurai and Breckenridge (1988; see also Appadurai 1996; Breckenridge 1995) introduced the expression "public culture" to refer to cultural forms and practices of these dispersed and differential modernities. Public culture supercedes the notion of mass culture conceptually in that it does not presume that mass-mediated and commodified cultural forms signal the degeneration of political institutions. Instead, public culture furnishes the rubric for dealing with cultural consumption as political practice, following, for example, Hebdige's (1979) concept of resistance through style, or Mosse's (1975) argument of domination through aestheticization. Consistent with De Certeau, consumption is understood as underdetermined practice that can involve different ways of reading and responding to modernity.

Public culture, then, can be located in the space between domestic life and projects of the nation-state as different social groups constitute and contest identities that are classed, gendered, and nationalized. Here mass-mediated forms articulate with the practices of everyday life, that is, the public realm is taken to be an arena of cultural contestation rather than a group or apparatus standing between state and society and derived from bourgeois, propertied interests seeking to limit state interference in and regulation of daily life (Habermas 1989a).

The conceptual frame of public culture is a rich and suggestive place to situate ritual practice. What it does, first, is connect ritual with consumption as activity and modality of social life. An analysis of ritual that focuses on consumption invites the consideration of modernity in the frame suggested by Appadurai and Breckenridge (1988)—as the work of imagination tied to the constitution of new identities, forms of class politics, and national narratives. At the same time, by taking ritual and specifically domestic ritual as the focus, the boundaries of public culture are themselves thrown up for scrutiny. In situating public culture *between* the domestic world and the nation-state, Appadurai and Breckenridge, in effect, retained the separate spheres dichotomy and thus retained the baggage of the "public sphere" and "mass culture" problematics that they intended to move beyond. My argument in this book employs the rubric of public culture to interrogate the gendered boundaries of these putatively separate spheres. The public-private dichotomy is in some sense the work of modernity; the domestic world is not at the edge of modernity but is reconstituted in its projects. It is precisely because the domestic world has often been represented as a residue of the past—modernity's Other—in discourses of religious nationalism and ritual practice that domestic spaces and practices have been critical contexts to both contest and appropriate the modern. Construed by urban Smārtas as fragments of other times and places, domestic rituals were practices with which they read and reified possible pasts.

About the Book

This book is divided into four parts. Part 1 consists of this introductory chapter, "Making and Unmaking the 'Great Tradition.'" It is followed by Part 2, "Elite Cultures and Hybrid Modernities," which comprises two chapters. Chapter 2 provides a conventional point of ethnographic departure as I locate, historically and socially, the Smārta Brahmans who are the focus of the discussion in this book. I demonstrate the complexity of their social and cultural positioning in urban south Indian society. There is a high degree of coincidence between *high* caste and class status in urban south India (Driver 1982; Driver and Driver 1987), which is ascribable to past and ongoing educational and social advantages derived from their colonial status as subaltern elites. Brahman status is complicated by the fact that Smārtas who are privileged materially are not necessarily empowered politically. Though south Indian Brahmans are well represented in the elite corps of national civil servants (Singh 1976), the Indian Administrative Service (IAS), they exercise little political power at the state level. In the late nineteenth century, Brahmans dominated sections of the state bureaucracy that were open to Indians. Due to the success of populist, anti-Brahman social movements and political parties during this century, however, their access to such positions was sharply curtailed. Thus, although neither hegemonic nor dominant as a caste, they contend for status as elite cultural brokers in a variety of domains, such as performing arts, religious and social service institutions. In Chapter 2, I outline these processes, paying special attention to the roles and representations of women. Chapter 3 describes elite domesticity, focusing on the practical and material dimensions of the domestic world in the late twentieth century, thereby contextualizing the ideologies of Hindu femininity and moral etiquette that are both represented and resisted in women's practice of domestic ritual.

The two chapters in Part 3, "The World in the Home," introduce ethnographic material on women's religious practice. Chapter 4 considers the normative representations of femininity included in the life cycle and calendric rituals of Sanskritic Hinduism. This chapter theorizes ritual as a site for reproduction of and resistance to hegemonic images of female subjectivity. It lays the groundwork for Chapter 5, in which I address the ways that women remake subjectivities, households, and communities through their enactments and reworkings of Sanskritic Hindu ritual. I explore the dynamics of a particular women's devotional group by analyzing the personal narratives and ritual practices of participants. The group I describe was dominated by Smārta Brahmans, and it was centered on the worship of Karumāriyamman, a non-Sanskritic goddess often though to be more popular among non-Brahmans. Women participated in the group by becoming mediums for this goddess or by participating in rituals conducted by other mediums. This material reveals how women negotiate broader spheres of domestic and ritual authority through mediumship (after Lewis 1989) but shows the unfolding and remaking of female subjectivity in the interpenetrating contexts of ritual and personal narrative. Their stories reveal and are themselves the vehicles with which women complied with, appropriated, resisted, and questioned the representations of womanhood encountered in formal rituals of Sanskritic Hinduism.

Part 4, "The Home in the World," includes three chapters, all of which deal with the ways in which urban religiosity has been shaped by the Indian state's administration of religious sites and organizations and responds to it. With this material, I put the making and remaking of female subjectivity in contexts of socially and politically interpolated discourses and practices of Hinduism, not just Brahmanic orthopraxy. Chapter 6 is a descriptive overview of the shifting interface between the state and Hindu religious institutions during the past century and the ways that this has shaped the public culture of Hinduism in Chennai. Many Hindus, for a variety of reasons, resist the increased bureaucratization and rationalization of temple administration, which they regard as a sign of state corruption. In Chennai, this dissatisfaction has fueled the privatization of Hindu religious practice, for example, by creating venues for worship beyond the legal reach of the state. It has also been accompanied by an increased receptivity to Hindu nationalism among some Hindus who see state monitoring of Hindu institutions as a threat. I consider both kinds of responses to state intervention in religious discourse and practice in Chapter 7 and Chapter 8.

Chapter 7 focuses on the different ways in which two women, both ritual adepts and goddess devotees, fashioned new forms of collective worship and public space. One, Rajalakshmi, transformed her family's home into an exclusive (albeit "public") worship space for an elite, mostly male devotional group that she led. The other woman, Parvati, informally took over a goddess shrine in a local temple. She felt that the state-appointed temple authorities had neglected to care for it properly and in so doing had dishonored the deity. Her efforts attracted the attention of other neighborhood women, and within a short time a group of women of different castes and mostly working-class backgrounds joined her in a regular cycle of worship there. Parvati's group was more inclusive than Rajalakshmi's, and I contrast the two styles of resistance to state management of religious sites.

In Chapter 8, I look at the receptivity to Hindu nationalism that urban elites have shown—another area in which resistance to state intervention in religious practice has crystallized. I examine a short-lived social movement authored and led by a Smārta religious leader, Sri Jayendra Saraswati (the head of an important monastery in Kanchipuram just outside Chennai). This movement, Ja<u>n</u> Kalyāṇ, sought the involvement of upper-caste elites as dispensers of philanthropy and of Saraswati's own (nationalistic) version of Hindu doctrine. Embedded in its promotion of voluntary social service was an ideology of class inequality and dependency. In addition to what this movement reveals about the elite mediation of Hindu nationalism, it also reveals the importance of gender in the naturalizing representations of power and in enacting and perpetuating relations of class and caste inequality.

Ja<u>n</u> Kalyāṇ's appeal to women and its reliance on them goes to the heart of the issues explored in this book. Its caste- and class-inflected deployment of female idioms of devotion, service, and nationhood shows that the equation of women-tradition-nation, so powerful in anticolonial nationalist discourses, continues to exert force in the postcolonial imagination. It reveals, however, that those hegemonic discourses can at times be ruptured from within.

Notes

1. The phenomena Singer observed in the 1950s and 1960s derived from the explicit association of women's piety with domestic labor found in the household manuals and reformist tracts produced initially by social reformers and later by elite nationalists in India during the nineteenth century. Enjoined in these tracts was a normative etiquette of domestic labor that included "observation of festivals alongside socialisation of children, service of menfolk, management of money and servants" (Sangari 1993, 22). Sangari finds that the citation of the Laws of Manu (an early Sanskrit legal/moral text) was common in these tracts, and as such they "sacralised domestic labour into dharma (a process to which waged labour could not be subjected) and the Laws of Manu into a primer for embourgeoisment and class management"(Sangari 1993, 22).

2. Elite "subalternity" describes the condition of being subordinate to British colonial rulers while exercising authority over other Indians (Chatterjee 1993, 36).

3. For a provocative counterargument that draws selectively on principles of ego psychology to stress the individuality of South Asian persons, see Mines (1994).

4. My argument is predicated on the notion that hegemony is a mode of domination that operates through socially situated forms of "common sense" and relies on the "education of consent," and by implication on the constitution of subjects who are, in varying degrees and contexts, compliant (Gramsci 1971, 273, 323–343); see also Althusser 1971; De Lauretis 1987, 6–11; Laclau and Mouffe 1985; Williams 1977). This understanding of hegemony also entails recognition of

its dynamic qualities: that its educative function comprises struggles of a quotidian nature that involve various deployments of force and resistance. Last, hegemony as used here implies a complex subjectivity, one involving conscious and less-than-conscious processes (after Giddens 1984) and exhibiting fractured and conflictual qualities.

5. See also Brooks (1997), John (1996), Mohanty (1991), Riley (1988), Sandoval (1991), Joan Scott (1991), Tharu and Niranjana (1996), Visweswaran (1994).

6. Talal Asad (1983, 251) has made this argument.

7. See also Caplan 1987, 11–14; Dickey 1993.

8. The word "Sudra" refers to one of the four *varṇas*. In the mythic recounting of the origins of the world recorded in the Laws of Manu, humankind is classified into four discrete, ranked categories, or "colors" *(varṇa)*. These categories correspond to portions of the body of the primal man. The head is the source of Brahmans, the priestly classes; the arms are associated with Kshatriyas, the warrior and ruler classes; the torso and thighs are associated with Vaisyas, merchants and artisans; the feet are the Sudras, laborers. "Sudra" is sometimes used as a collective term that encompasses a variety of castes regarded, in the past, as agricultural laborers. It was also used by upper castes pejoratively, to describe the poor and other low-status persons—attributing uncleanness, crudity, and vulgarity to such persons.

PART TWO

Elite Cultures and Hybrid Modernities

2

Brokering Culture for the Nation

Caste, Culture, and Modernity

No one would deny that castes in general, and Smārtas in particular, exist and that the boundaries between castes are real, if contextual. Other issues, however, remain unsettled. How do people constitute caste as a sociocultural institution in practice? How do they affiliate as members? And to what degree do they share caste consciousness? In short, what does Smārta identity mean in the late twentieth century? The activities of a contemporary caste association, TAMBRAS (the Tamil Brahman Association, a statewide organization founded in 1980), can illustrate some strategies by which Brahman identity is constituted through social practices.

To commemorate the ninety-fourth birthday of the retired Shankaracharya[1] of Kanchipuram, Sri Chandrasekharenda Saraswati, local units of TAMBRAS sponsored public events in June 1987, several of which I attended. The memory of one remains vivid. Purnima, joint secretary of one unit, had invited ninety-four *cumaṅkali*s to perform *tiruviḷakku pūja* (worship of the holy flame) together at a small local temple to mark this special day. Flyers announcing the event were distributed and an announcement appeared in local editions of English and Tamil newspapers. The *pūja* took place on June 11 in the assembly hall connected to a temple, with thirty-four women attending as performers. Purnima welcomed everyone on behalf of TAMBRAS and conveyed the Shankaracharya's blessing of the occasion. Led by Purnima's guru (an elderly man who had adopted an ascetic lifestyle after retiring from the civil service), the women went through the steps of the ritual, their gestures and prayers synchronized. Most of the performers knew the steps of this *pūja* well, for it was done by many of them at home every Friday, a day dedicated to the goddess Lakshmi. An audience of over a hundred family members, friends, neighbors, and passersby looked on, joining in the prayers and songs and, at the end, coming forward for *prasadam.*[2] At the conclusion of the *pūja,* Purnima handed out pamphlets detailing the procedures for the ritual as souvenirs to the women who had participated. Later I spoke with the president of TAMBRAS, Gopalakrishnan, who emphasized the importance of such events for the organization in terms of recruitment and publicity, adding that TAMBRAS had been founded to combat the harassment and violence to which Brahman women were subjected by "anti-Brahman rowdies and gangsters" (see also Jagadheesan 1991).

A few months later, TAMBRAS was in the news again. Members had staged another public event—a demonstration in New Delhi in front of the parliament building.[3] Representatives had delivered a petition to Prime Minister Rajiv Gandhi officially protesting Tamil Nadu's policies of "reserving" a proportion of government jobs and school admissions for members of non-Brahman castes. They identified these policies, which had been inaugurated by the colonial government, as threats to the Brahman community, who, they claimed, were being systematically denied opportunities for employment and education despite their being otherwise qualified. They requested that economic disability be used as the sole determinant of eligibility for reservations, arguing that the caste criterion was unfair. Such positions have been espoused by TAMBRAS since its founding in 1980, and this particular petition was almost identical to others presented by TAMBRAS.

Since 1980, TAMBRAS has sought to consolidate Brahman identity and advance Brahman interests through direct political agitation, as well as through the transformative practices of ritual wherein women are visible as icons and actors. Ritual has been used hegemonically as well as in a way that mitigates class inequalities among Brahmans. TAMBRAS assumes the wedding expenses for poor Brahmans, and its officers often perform the ceremonies. The organization also sponsors charitable events, such as distributions of food and clothing that provide relief for poor Brahman families. TAMBRAS has been generally supportive of efforts by Brahman religious leaders to "Hinduize" India's public culture. Its activities in this area have been increasingly visible since 1981, when low-caste Hindus in the southern village of Meenakshipuram converted en masse to Islam. Groups allied with the Rashtriya Swayamsevak Sangh, a militant Hindu nationalist organization founded in 1926, called for government inquiries into the phenomenon and began a program of active proselytization in southern India. Sri Jayendra Saraswati, head of the Kanchipuram *maṭam,* endorsed their moves publicly (*Data India* 1981, 407) and in 1983 convened the three-day Hindu Arts Festival in Chennai, which was intended to "revive [the] nationalist spirit" (*The Hindu,* August 11, 1981).

TAMBRAS claimed to speak for Brahmans, but not all Brahmans supported it. I spoke to many who considered TAMBRAS to be little more than a vehicle for office bearers to gain social recognition and status. "It's no different from the Lions or the Rotary," one Brahman woman complained, scoffing at the association's supposed concern for women's welfare. Her son added that it was "an A–1 fraud." Although TAMBRAS officials claimed that the organization is supported by most Brahmans in the state, the demonstration in New Delhi was a small affair and probably had little significance nationally—indeed, more people attended the *pūja*.

Regardless of their affiliation with TAMBRAS, however, I knew no Brahmans who did not voice concerns similar to those raised by TAMBRAS. TAMBRAS, like other caste associations, was the product of an important and abiding contradiction—the simultaneous recognition and denial of caste by the Indian government. The Indian constitution abolished discrimination on the basis of caste in favor of equal rights for individuals but authorized an ever expanding system of positive discrimination that is based on caste. Caste quotas exist for civil service positions and for college and university admissions, giving a caste basis to important institutionalized forms of socioeconomic opportunity and constraint. The result is that the state elicits from and confirms caste identity for the populace in a variety of contexts, despite its official erasure of caste.[4]

Caste quotas for political representation, employment, and education have existed since the early twentieth century, when they were initiated by the British colonial government. Brahmans have been reckoned officially as a "forward" community, that is, one in which socioeconomic progress was not impeded by caste. Class privilege was thereby amalgamated with caste identity in the popular perception of Brahmanhood. Yet many Brahmans claimed that their welfare as individuals and as a community was threatened by the systems (state and national) of positive discrimination that have existed in India throughout much of this century. They argued that they could not claim the same types or levels of entitlements (e.g., jobs, seats in educational institutions) available to members of some non-Brahman castes and to former Untouchables, now known as Harijans or Dalits. They complained that merit is discounted as a qualification for such positions, implying that they themselves were the more intelligent, capable candidates. Brahmans also claimed that they were the recipients of day-to-day, informal discrimination—insults (including the degrading term *pārppaṉ*, which was sometimes used to refer to Brahmans), street harassment, and petty crime. They spoke of the "politicized" and "commercialized" atmosphere of Hindu temples and were critical of the ways in which the government administered temples, interpreting its actions as a form of discrimination. They attributed these situations to the influence of the regionalist, anti-Brahman parties that have controlled Tamil Nadu's state government since 1967. Many were convinced that caste-based collective action was a legitimate way to undo the system of caste-based reservations.

Caste, Class, and Status

In the context of such debate, the ritualized spectacles of the *pūja* and the demonstration might be considered artifacts of the politicization of caste and of the complex intersections of caste and class status. Embedded in the claims of reverse discrimination that fueled TAMBRAS activities were signs of the ways in which caste and class operate together as systems of domination. The Brahmans' charge of reverse discrimination was a strategy that sought to preserve or reclaim privileges ordinarily associated with middle- and upper-class status, such as access to elite educational institutions and opportunities to pursue professional employment. Although Brahmans were neither uniformly wealthy nor a ruling class (in the Marxian sense), urban Smārta Brahmans identified themselves, and were identified by others, as middle or upper class. Like other investigators (see Caplan 1987; Dickey 1993), I found that Smārtas used the term *naṭuttara makkaḷ,* which can be translated as "middle-quality people," interchangeably with "middle class" to describe themselves and to contrast their lifestyles with those of the very poor and the very wealthy.

The Smārtas with whom I worked in 1985, 1987–1988, and 1996 fell within the broad boundaries of India's urban middle classes. My informant population (1987–1988) comprised fifty-five households spread over several mostly contiguous areas in the city, including the administrative divisions of Mylapore, Raja Annamalai Puram, Teynampet, Alwarpet, and Adyar.

Some of the older men and women had migrated to Chennai from rural areas earlier in the century. The more recent urban migrants included individuals whose jobs required frequent transfers and who had, as a result, resided not only in Chennai but also in other metropolitan areas of India. Most adult males (heads of households and others) held professional jobs as lawyers, doctors, engineers, accountants, civil servants, or educators; a number of them were self-employed businessmen. Middle-aged and elderly women were rarely employed formally but did contribute monetarily to their households' incomes through other avenues, such as private tutoring. Most had brought dowries, property, or money to their husbands' households. Younger women were more often employed, their jobs being as various as men's jobs. Taking the contributions of all members into account, monthly household incomes in

1987–1988 ranged from Rs. 800 to Rs. 3,000.[5] These figures should be taken as minimums, however, because most households derived some of their income from sources other than standard wages and sought to keep such information concealed. Also contributing to the net worth of a household were individual members' property holdings. Few families lacked members who owned parcels of residential property in the city and/or rural, agricultural, or undeveloped land.

Material privilege was not simply a matter of income, property, and education. At issue is their transmutation into status, the culturally recognized forms of value that inform the ways in which people evaluate and rank themselves and others. Hannah Papanek observed that for urban middle classes in India, the production and evaluation of relative status is often a domestic matter and thus is tied to gendered labor (1979). That is, the reproduction of class ideology and material privilege for middle classes was as much a matter of unremunerated domestic labor as it was of the occupations, incomes, and educations of those who participated in waged (or salaried) labor. The latter was more often undertaken by men, whereas the former was done by women and was termed "status production work" (Di Leonardo 1986; Papanek 1979). It typically included coaching children, entertaining guests, making decisions about the purchase and display of consumer goods, and club involvement. Nearly all informants, male and female, were members of voluntary associations, ranging from international clubs such as the Lions or Rotary to local groups such as neighborhood ladies' clubs, temple organizations, and *bhajana*s (devotional music groups). Women were more active than men and often used their homes as meeting areas. The women's organizations had agendas that included informal education (e.g., needlework classes) and "social service"—a term that English-speaking informants applied to charitable activities. Patricia Caplan found that since independence India's central and state governments have relied heavily on middle-class women's voluntarism for the implementation of state-mandated social welfare (1985, 124–133). Finally, I would extend the notion of status production work to domestic ritual. For Smārtas, it is an important component in the maintenance of family status, functioning not as a mystification of class inequality but as a key means of status maintenance and improvement.

Household composition was variable. Most households consisted of nuclear family groups, though complex households (comprising extended, joint, and supplemented nuclear family groups) were also prominent. Increased occupational mobility has led in many cases to an overall increase in nuclear households in urban areas, but I found that families opted for some sort of complex household for varying lengths of time in order to mitigate socioeconomic uncertainties and pool resources needed for purchasing residences. Flats have become more common as middle-class residences. Multistoried complexes contained anywhere from six to twenty identically laid out, autonomous residences. The oldest were built in the 1960s to house government employees; by the mid-1990s flat complexes had multiplied in all areas of the city due to the efforts of private developers. Prior to the 1960s, apartments had been carved out of bungalows or "garden houses." Unlike the flats, the apartments created from houses were not always fully autonomous. Clusters of two or three rooms might be allotted to a family, but these areas often communicated with other parts of the house via shared hallways and courtyards. Wells, lavatory facilities, and occasionally kitchens might also be shared. It was not unusual for related families to live contiguously, thus approximating joint households in some respects.

All of my informants were literate in at least one language (Tamil), and both men and women were often literate in two or three languages, including English. Levels of education tended to be higher among men of all ages and among women born in the 1950s and after due to the improved facilities for women's education. Brahmans have also recognized the prestige that female education confers on women and their families, as well as opportunities for employment.

A distinctive mark of middle-class status and aspirations was the visibility of consumer goods in people's homes. These goods included sofas and lounge chairs, appliances (refrigerators, fans, televisions, audiocassette players, electric food processors), family photo displays, decorative plaques and figurines. These things were intentionally displayed to selected audiences of kin, neighbors, coworkers, and other visitors in the context of social gatherings and informal visits. In some households, ritual spaces and practices have become part of this cultural economy. For example, in 1986 a married businessman in my neighborhood had joined a devotional group comprising several male coworkers and relatives. To inaugurate the group's annual pilgrimage to Sabarimalai[6] in 1987, he invited neighbors, relatives, and business associates to participate in a special *pūja* at his home. The pilgrims and their leader conducted the *pūja* in the family's elaborately decorated *pūja* room while an audience of about thirty guests looked on. The opulent ritual accoutrements attested to the existence of disposable income and to styles of consumption (including but not limited to that associated with ritual) that provided cultural markers of class privilege.

The material advantages and stylistic distinctions of Smārta lifestyles that I observed were consistent with the findings of an earlier study by Driver (1982). Relatively high levels of status summation (the covariation of caste and class status) were observed among Brahmans in urban south India, despite low rates of status summation within the population as a whole. The higher status summation among Smārtas was due, in part, to mechanisms that mitigated material inequalities. These include kinship obligations, strategic deployments of social service, and the informal use of hiring preferences.

Defining Class

Although the negotiation of caste and class identity are obviously interlocked, it would be a mistake to view Brahman identity politics as merely a gloss for class domination, narrowly understood as control of labor and resources. Rather, the work of an upper-caste association like TAMBRAS points to the need for a contextually sensitive understanding of class formation and ideology in urban India. Here I intend "class" broadly as a system of domination associated with capitalism that (1) derives from and reproduces material inequalities and (2) glosses intergroup relations of inequality involving both dependency and antagonism. It is important for analyses of class to recognize that the formation, maintenance, and contestation of such systems are historically specific processes and—just as important—not limited to strictly "economic" spheres but encompass cultural practice. This underscores the necessity of attending to people's own notions of inequality—its sources, its manifestations, and its mitigation (cf. Thompson 1963). People's own understandings of class are not just outcomes of material inequality but are elements of the way in which class identities and inequalities are reproduced (see Bourdieu 1984; L. Caplan 1987; P. Caplan 1985; Dickey 1993) .

Lionel Caplan (1987) has made a persuasive argument to this effect. He maintains that it is necessary to foreground class analytically, for Indian metropolitan centers were initially created and developed by and for benefit of British capitalism and became loci of multinational and indigenously generated industrial growth (1987, 6). However, the class divisions produced and the modes of domination enacted (the means whereby some persons gained capacity to nominate others as equal or unequal) are not mirror images of Western industrial capitalism. This is the case in part because ownership of means of production rests with state or multinationals, so that the indigenous capitalist class (owners of means of production) is small, highly compact, and barely visible (Caplan 1987, 14). The relatively larger, more extensive elite of which they are a part is fragmented—possessing different lifestyles, work, and values. The lower classes are similarly fractionated and the differences among and within classes are matters of continuous negotiation and struggle, not merely over control over resources and labor but also about the cultural institutions, practices, and meanings that mediate these struggles. Consequently, class-based collective action has been limited. In these contexts, differences associated with class (broadly defined) are "consciously recognized, cognitively salient, experientially real and behaviorally motivating" (Dickey 1993, 9). If class is to be dealt with, it should be treated as a cultural as well as an economic formation that encompasses competing meaning systems, modes of self-attribution, discourses of distinction (such as taste), and forms of consumption. Caste, insofar as it derives from and is reproduced through these cultural practices, has to be seen in dynamic interaction with class.

Both the *pūja* and the demonstration sponsored by TAMBRAS can be regarded as performances that constitute identities that fuse elements of caste and class. Those who sponsored them sought to persuade other participants of the value of certain styles of political action and to valorize the identity claims that such actions preserved or were predicated on. In these ways, they were vehicles for what Steven Barnett (1977), influenced by Dumont (1970) and Marriott (1976), has called substantialization. By this Barnett meant the reckoning of social identity in terms that foreground substantive elements such as blood, though he departed from both Dumont and Marriott in his effort to link discourses of substance to processes of class formation. Barnett argued that claims about substance are now the dominant features in ideological and increasingly racialized representations of caste and class identity, and they have supplanted local notions of caste as a hierarchy maintained by strict behavioral codes (see also Dirks 1996).

Though I could not corroborate the historical shift that Barnett suggested, I noted the prevalence and ideological importance of substantialization among urban Smārtas. The founding of TAMBRAS, as well as its charter and functions, were symptomatic of these concerns. Brahmans (Smārta and others) whom I knew talked about Brahmanness in substantive terms as embodied qualities; they favored styles of consumption that sustained those qualities. Brahman friends, for example, described "cooling" vegetarian foods as being suitable for their tastes and bodily qualities; they contrasted their preferences with the tastes for chili-laden *acaivam* (nonvegetarian) foods that they attributed to non-Brahmans.

For Brahmans, the most important context for caste substantialization was the domestic realm; sexuality, commensality, and ritual were its principal arenas. It was in domestic realms that caste was made, through transactions of substance and through the moral etiquette and aesthetic sensibilities with which those transactions were laden. Although this amounted to forming zones of Brahman exclusivity, these are context-specific, which means that resulting relations of inequality were situational rather than fixed. In these contexts, women were positioned both as dependents who derived class and caste status from men, and as agents who "conjointly lived out class relations and participated in their reproduction" (Sangari 1993, 869). They accomplished this through their own remunerative labor, through the social service work that is requisite for middle-class women, through domestic practices centered on ritual and commensality, and through their interactions with servants.

Seen in this light, TAMBRAS's usage of the rubric of domesticity makes sense. The public performance of domestic ritual, weddings, and the food and clothing distributions presented Brahmanness as a "privately" achieved and substantive phenomenon that is dependent on women's action. In turn, TAMBRAS claimed that zone—the zone of naturalized identity—as a basis for political mobilization and justified its own existence with the rhetoric of its defense of female modesty. Class interests were served by this, though not by caste serving as the proxy for class. Instead, class ideology and relations were mediated by the cultural practices and styles that for Brahmans were encompassed by caste, understood not as a hierarchy rooted in behavior but as one rooted in the naturalness of bodily substance. Smārta Brahmans' self-designation as "middle-quality people" conflated notions of material privilege as well as tastes, desires, and qualities that confirmed and re-created that privilege. How has this fusion of caste and class practice come about? And how have these processes implicated and transformed Smārta womanhood?

Smārta Brahmans in Chennai: Historical Roots of Contemporary "Middleness"

Though culturally and linguistically identified with the populations of peninsular South Asia, Smārtas are (and have long been) a mobile community. In the past, royal patronage enabled Smārtas, like other Brahman literati, to develop networks anchored by monasteries, schools, and temples throughout southern India and across the subcontinent. This gave the community an identity that was at once locally rooted and decentralized. Ties of common language and cultural practice bound them to Telugu-, Tamil-, and Kannada-speaking populations of the south. Their command of Sanskritic learning tied them to royal centers such as Tanjavur and to the transregional network of temples and monasteries founded by or associated with the eighth century (C.E.) preceptor Adishankara, whose teachings Smārtas follow.

This bifurcated pattern continues to the present day. Smārtas in Chennai constitute no more than 3 percent of the city's population but maintain wide sociocultural and economic networks.[7] Currently, Smārtas live and work in urban areas throughout India and abroad, where most are employed in a business or professional capacity. Following a pattern that has become common among India's urban elites, all of the Smārta families I knew in Chennai had members residing outside India—in the Middle East, Southeast Asia, Japan, England, and the United States. Most had left in order to pursue higher education and/or employment. Such endeavors were facilitated in the 1970s and 1980s by the relaxation of immigration laws in the United States and by the expansion of petroleum and electronics industries in the Persian Gulf region and Southeast Asia, respectively. Brahmans' willingness to resettle abroad was also due to their sense of relative deprivation in Tamil Nadu, which they attributed to the "anti-Brahman" policies of the state government.

Despite the relocations that were permanent for many, Brahman emigrants were always present on Chennai's social and spatial horizons. They contracted marriages in India, relying on the brokerage of local friends and family members. They donated to local temples. The Indian government's liberalization of regulations pertaining to investments by foreigners has fostered further connections. Many Indians living abroad have invested in the high-rise apartment complexes (such as that shown in Figure 2.1) that have proliferated throughout India during the past two decades and own fully furnished flats that they use as pieds-à-terre during visits to India and rent out for the remainder of the time. Smārtas living abroad also owned other commercial properties jointly with locals, as well as shares in local business and industrial enterprises.

Local (and contested) reinscriptions of Indian culture and history have accompanied the patterns of geographic dispersal already described. Although Chennai Smārtas live and work throughout the city, certain areas, notably Mylapore and its environs, have had higher populations of Brahmans historically and are popularly regarded as Brahman enclaves.[8] Recently, Mylapore has been identified in elite discourses on "heritage" as a site warranting cultural conservation. Its Brahman-inflected public culture, represented in its religious and domestic architectures, has been marked as a cultural resource endangered by economic development and with that universalized as "Indian culture" (D'Souza 1992). A 1993 INTACH[9] report observed that Mylapore's history

> dates back in legend to the third century and in existing physical structures to the eighteenth century with sculptural remains dating to the ninth century. In this one area the co-existence of Christianity, Hinduism, Jainism, and . . . Islam . . . can be experienced. . . . Associated with . . . these areas are the special residential patterns of the primarily traditional Hindu streets surrounding the temple areas and the more spacious colonial prototype settlement patterns and bungalows in a large section of the Santhome [a section of Mylapore] area. (INTACH 1993, 1)

Structures such as the residences on the street pictured in Figure 2.2 and activities such as the temple procession shown in Figure 2.3 were

FIGURE 2.1 A New High-Rise Flat Building in Mylapore, 1996. Photograph By Author.

FIGURE 2.2 An Older Residential Street in Mylapore, 1996. Photograph By Author.

FIGURE 2.3 A Festival Procession Near the Śrī Kapalēswarar Karpakampal Temple in Mylapore, 1987. Photograph By Author.

deemed under threat by real estate speculation. An elaborate plan for conservation was advanced involving the removal and/or relocation of an open vegetable market, the rerouting of city buses, and the creation of a pedestrian mall on the streets that flanked the large Shiva temple that the report identified as Mylapore's center. Though contested and not successful to date, the project was significant. By identifying the spaces of Smārta daily life as sites of Indian tradition, it underwrote a claim that echoed Smārtas' own contentions at various times in the past.

The Past in the Spaces of the Present

Mylapore has long been a site of cultural production and contestation; indeed, it is a social space produced in some measure by and through Smārta negotiation of culture and identity. The relative density of Brahmans and their current visibility are products of Mylapore's early role as a temple center and its subsequent importance as a residential area for those elite Indians employed in the colonial civil service. Smārta Brahmans initially settled in Mylapore several centuries ago. Formerly a separate village and pilgrimage center, Mylapore is home to hundreds of temples, mosques, and churches. One of its most famous religious sites is a ninth-century temple complex, Śrī Kapalēswarar Karpakampal, dedicated to the god Shiva and his consort.

Mylapore's Smārta Brahman population had long claimed high ritual status as priests and scholars, though that did not automatically imply political or economic dominance. Evidence indicates that Brahmans achieved such power only in contexts in which they controlled land (as in the Tanjavur region to the south) or people (Beteille 1965). As recipients of royal patronage, Smārta Brahmans held hereditary rights of occupancy and temple service. Veḷḷāḷas, the local landholding group, as well as other banking, merchant, and trading castes, exercised political and economic dominance (Neild-Basu 1977, 244; Rudner 1994, 42–49).

From the mid-seventeenth through the mid-nineteenth centuries, as the area developed from a mercantile entrepôt into an urban center of colonial administration and commerce, Mylapore was brought into closer articulation with the European settlements to the north such as Fort St. George and Black Town, with their government institutions, warehouses, and businesses (Lewandowski 1977, 206; Neild-Basu 1977, 309). Europeans built garden houses in and around Mylapore, some of which still stand. Because of its temples and associated cultural institutions, Mylapore tended to attract wealthy Indians whose fortunes and influence had grown with the stimulus of European trade. The residential areas of Europeans and local elites were spatially and stylistically distinct. European garden houses contrasted with the central courtyard houses favored by the local elite, which opened directly onto narrow streets and radiated from the *agraharam* (Brahman neighborhood) surrounding the temple.

During the first half of the nineteenth century, the structure of the region's economy changed as European traders sought regional political dominance. The composition of the local elite shifted as well. The East India Company was reorganized between 1812 and 1832. Company operations and profits were brought under the administrative control of the British Crown, and the autonomy of individual European merchants and traders was constricted. Consequently, the volume and value of transactions changed, and with this the composition of the local elite. Landholders and rich merchants retained a power base and used their wealth to fund commercial ventures as well as to support art, religious institutions, and philanthropy. Brahmans (specifically Brahman men) whose education and background enabled them to serve in the expanding colonial administration emerged as a new local elite (Neild-Basu 1977, 339).

With the official declaration of the Crown's authority in 1858, Brahman presence and wealth in the city increased and Brahman voices in its public culture became more prominent. Brahmans' transregional networks, as well as their Sanskritic learning, positioned them as interlocutors with the colonial state, as translators and interpreters of local law and custom. With the expansion of the colonial bureaucracy, Brahmans served as administrators, clerks, jurists, legislators and publicists. In growing numbers, Smārta Brahmans migrated to Chennai, and to Mylapore especially, from rural areas. There men and (to a far lesser degree) women pursued secondary and postsecondary education and then took up administrative posts, often secured with the help of family members and caste mates. Mylapore's population grew dramatically during the latter half of the nineteenth century. The 1908 Imperial Gazetteer recorded that at 6 percent of the city's population, Brahmans were "more than usually numerous" (1907–1909, 372). By the late nineteenth century, Brahmans dominated the professions, including the civil service, and led other caste groups in the attainment of the B.A. degree (Barnett 1976, 18–21; Irschick 1986, 21). As late as 1931, the majority of gazetted officers in the province were Brahmans.

Historian David Washbrook related Brahman assumption of elite status in southern India to the centralization of the Madras presidency's administration during the latter part of the nineteenth century (1975, 159–162). This process created new kinds of administrative positions for educated Indians, as well as more possibilities for higher education among this emergent elite. Washbrook further argued that the forces associated with regional political centralization led to the formation of provincial-level interest groups—nascent caste associations—among these elites (Washbrook 1976, 261). This in turn fostered denser networks of marriage and ritual alliance as well as an elaboration of distinctive ritual styles and attachments to particular temples and *maṭams*—in effect, creating a public culture of Brahman Hindu practice, with stylistic details elaborated according to sectarian affiliation.

Exemplifying and contributing to this process was the Smārta Brahman family to which prominent nationalist lawyer and legislator C. P. Ramaswamy Aiyar belonged (Washbrook 1975, 160–161). By the 1910s, the family was established in Chennai, having already expanded outward from villages in North Arcot district to Tanjavur. Washbrook documented the combination of marital alliances and access to key government posts that enabled this expansion, and he argued that caste cohesion was intensified by the Smārtas' distinguishable ritual style and by their attachment to particular preceptors, temples, and monasteries, including the monastery-temple complex currently located in Kanchipuram.

Washbrook's data illustrated the process by which Chennai became a stopping point on what Anderson has called bureaucratic pilgrimages (1991, 114–116). By the end of the nineteenth century, these circuits, connected by new rail and shipping lines, telegraphic communications, and print media, extended across the subcontinent and beyond. Rural hinterlands fed into provincial capitals, cities linked to each other and to other colonial cities in South and Southeast Asia, and to European metropoles. Men with professional aspirations were compelled to enter this circuit because qualification for civil service and other professions required advanced education, often abroad, as well as successful completion of a sequence of examinations administered in various cities in British India and in Britain itself. These patterns, enacted over several generations, were the means by which Smārta Brahmans were fashioned as a subaltern elite for whom privilege was defined and delimited by their relations with the colonial state. Male professionals helped consolidate colonial rule through their labor as clerks, lawyers, and publicists even as they articulated nationalist opposition to the colonial state. Their wives, daughters, and sisters—status tokens by virtue of their nonparticipation in waged labor—became the embodiments of an emergent nation. These women represented an authenticating past that was both redemptive and stultifying. Diverse individuals were brought together by cosmopolitan experiences and collective sensibilities. What they shared was not a class consciousness (as that term is usually used) but a habitus intimately tied to their middleness as subaltern elites.

Colonialism and Nationalist Imaginaries

Unlike the earlier generations of dubashes,[10] the local elite that was reconfigured during the nineteenth century was not absorbed within European society. Susan Neild-Basu observed that they "took advantage of the period of political tranquility and relative prosperity to rediscover their own cultural heritage to enhance their prestige by supporting traditional South Indian arts and scholarship" (Neild-Basu 1977, 354).[11] Subsequent scholarship, particularly Eugene Irschick's (1994) thoughtful analysis, has suggested that this efflorescence is not as much a "rediscovery" of South Indian culture as it is a matter of dialogue and contestation with Europeans and other Indians. Out of this came new cultural forms and the reconstitution of existing ones. On this discursive substrate, new communities of imagination—some nationalistic, others linguistic and ethnic—took shape.

In the intensified translocal flows of people, information, and commodities of the latter nineteenth century, regional arts and scholarship were celebrated, often by refashioning forms and marking them as "authentic" as well as by creating new evaluative standards. These cultural expressions were mediated by print capitalism, by the activities of voluntary associations and clubs, and by the proliferation of schools and performance venues. These processes gave shape and substance to a range of distinct and often contentious cultural nationalisms and associated reform movements that came to the fore in the late nineteenth century. With this, Brahman and non-Brahman elites revisited, revised, and contested Brahmanness, Hinduism, and Tamilness.

One notable development in this regard was the pure Tamil movement, sometimes described as a Tamil renaissance (Barnett 1976, 16–18; Kailasapathy 1979). At its core was *ta<u>n</u>ittami<u>l</u>*, or "pure Tamil," often pictured as a goddess or mother (Ramaswamy 1997). Inspired by the poetry of the Tamil saint, Ramalingam (who in the mid-nineteenth century attempted to eliminate Sanskritic words from his work), and by Tamil Shaivite devotionalism, writers advocated the colloquial use of "pure Tamil." And because "pure Tamil" was closely linked to the regional religious doctrine of Shaiva Siddhanta and to regional styles of music, drama, and poetry, they were celebrated as emblems of the region's cultural and ethnic distinctiveness.

Ta<u>n</u>ittami<u>l</u> proponents maintained that it represented the language and worldview of the region's original Dravidian population. With the arrival and domination of northern Aryan populations, both people and language had been denigrated and corrupted. Sanskrit and its doctrinal counterpart, Vedic Hinduism, were thought to support a system of caste hierarchy with which the invaders—ancestors of Brahmans—oppressed the indigenous population. Though *ta<u>n</u>ittami<u>l</u>* had Brahmans among its advocates, its anti-Brahmanism was adopted later as the ideological core of the Non-Brahman movement (and its electoral wing, the Justice Party) and of the rationalist critiques of caste and Hinduism associated with the Self-Respect movement and subsequent Dravidianist parties.

Tanittamil was one of the identity movements that found expression in the late 1800s. Another community of imagination was constituted transregionally. Although it was not solely a Brahman endeavor, it became identified with Brahman interests by the early twentieth century. Drawing on their knowledge of Euro-Western political institutions and theories, the doctrines of Hindu universalism exemplified in the work of Swami Vivekananda, emerging theories of eugenics, and the discourse of social reform, urban elites crafted a self-consciously modern style of Indian nationalism during the late nineteenth century.

This discourse on national sovereignty served as a means of attacking colonial domination in its own terms. Elite nationalisms spread transregionally among the subaltern elite classes through voluntary organizations, philanthropic groups, cultural associations, and branches of larger bodies, such as the Arya Samaj. It was from these dense and proliferating networks that the Indian National Congress (INC) emerged in 1885. The leaders of the INC sought to mobilize public opinion among this stratum and to represent their interests to colonial rulers. Smārtas played prominent roles in these developments. In 1878, a weekly English-language newspaper, *The Hindu*, was founded by G. Subramania Iyer to convey nationalist interests. Mylapore Smārtas founded the Mahajana Sabha, often described as a precursor of the INC, in 1884 (Sadasivan 1974, 10). Its aims were to provide a forum for deliberation among members of the educated elite and to convey their interests and concerns to the government. During that same year, Mylapore was selected as the site for initial planning meetings for the Indian National Congress. P. Ananda Charlu (a member of the North Arcot Smārta family alluded to on page 54) and another prominent Smārta, S. Subramania Iyer, took the lead in this. Subsequently, the 1887, 1894, 1898, 1903, and 1908 meetings of the INC were convened in Chennai (Sadasivan 1974, 10).

In the decades around the turn of the century, elite nationalism in the south escalated. The year 1892 saw the founding of the Madras Hindu Social Reform Association. In the first decade of the twentieth century, paired nationalist organizations, the Sons of India and the Daughters of India, were founded to promote Gandhi's swaraj campaign by Annie Besant, a Fabian socialist, Theosophist, and feminist. The roles of the Theosophical Society, and Besant in particular, deserve mention. The society was headquartered in Chennai on a vast property bounded on the north by Mylapore and comprising the current administrative divisions of Adyar, Besant Nagar, Indira Nagar, and Tiruvanmiyur. Besant led the organization during the early twentieth century, and it served as the node around which a cross-caste but Smārta-dominated nationalist elite was constituted. The affinity between Theosophy and contemporary Hindu universalism provided ideological ballast for Besant's commitment (as well as that of other leaders) to elite philanthropy and reform and to anticolonial nationalism. The society's buildings and grounds were used by affiliated voluntary groups as headquarters and public meeting sites. Several nationalist publications, including *The Indian Social Reformer, Young India,* and *Stri Dharma,* were subsidized by the society.

Besant herself drew directly on these constituencies to contest the presidency of the INC and to organize a splinter group, the Mylapore-based (and Smārta-heavy) Home Rule League. At the time of its formation, the Home Rule League represented the interests of those within the INC who sought complete independence rather than a gradual program of constitutional reforms. It was also Brahman dominated—making it a target for both anti-Brahman agitation and colonial repression. Subsequently, the Home Rule League and the INC were sought as a core constituency in Gandhi's nationalist campaigns.

Embedded in these interventions in colonial governance were the efforts of Brahman elites to claim and circumscribe "authentic" regional culture, operations that were directed simultaneously against the colonial state and against cultural claims of non-Brahman proponents of Dravidianism. The appropriation of bhakti devotionalism by urban elites can illustrate.

By 1900, Chennai Smārtas had created a network of voluntary associations for the performance of devotional music, the Radha-Krishna *bhajana*s that continue to exist today in the city (Singer 1972, 200). These groups gathered in members' homes and community halls to sing devotional songs (*bhajan*s).

Accompanying these performances were Hindu rituals of worship and acts of philanthropy such as distributing food and clothing to the poor. The leaders were Smārtas who had moved from the southern district of Tanjavur to Chennai. They used a set of Sanskritic texts and commentaries codified in the seventeenth century by three musician-saints from Tanjavur (Singer 1972, 204–205, 218–222). The Smārta-dominated membership was recruited from professional and voluntary associations and from caste and kinship networks.

The *bhajana*s were forums for elite cultural expression, as well as intra-elite cultural debate. The individualized and voluntaristic devotion of *bhakti,* with its musical and poetic emphases and its universalistic ethos, augmented and, for some, supplanted the more formal styles of worship authorized by the Smārta religious leaders. The *bhakti*-influenced styles became hallmarks of new, nationalized, and self-consciously modern elite sensibilities that as such were points of contention among elites. The more orthodox sections, including the *maṭam* leadership, regarded the *bhajanas* (along with social reform measures) as threats to the integrity of Hindu doctrine and to the exclusivity implied by *varṇāśramadharma*. In contrast, *bhajanas* were employed by Gandhian workers in their campaigns to remove caste restrictions on temple entry, rehabilitate slums, and eliminate Untouchability.

Though the *bhajanas* were used in different sociopolitical contexts and for different ends, their presence, popularity, and persistence heralded new styles of class culture. Despite the discourse of universalism in which they were cast, *bhajanas* reproduced and naturalized class difference using aesthetic criteria. In giving ideological sanction for elite philanthropy, *bhakti* contributed to the reproduction of dependencies deriving from the conflations of class and caste inequalities (Subramaniam 1988; see also Fuller 1992, 161–162; Hancock 1995b).

Femininity and Elite Nationalism

The contentious discourses on nationalism—from the ethnic/linguistic nationalism celebrated by the Dravidian movement to the constitutional nationalism of the INC and allied groups—employed and modified popular conceptions of womanhood. A common rhetorical strategy used in early nationalist writing (by men) was to represent the incipient nation—be it Indian, Tamil, or Bengali—as a woman, usually a mother, and often defiled (Chakravarti 1990; Jayawardena 1986; Ramaswamy 1997). Bankimchandra Chattopadhyay's Bengali anthem "Bande Mataram" (Hail to the Mother) was an early expression of this. Later Bengali nationalists, notably Aurobindo Ghose, developed this metaphor further by identifying the incipient nation as *shakti,* a term used as a name for the female consort of the god Shiva and, more generally, for the feminized creative energy of the cosmos. In southern India, the *taṉittamiḻ* movement made similar use of feminine imagery (Ramaswamy 1997). Alongside these metaphoric deployments of femininity, there was a growing prescriptive literature in which the merits of specific educational and social reforms were debated and the boundaries of appropriate feminine action recast in nationalist terms (Chakrabarty 1994; Chatterjee 1993; Hancock forthcoming; Lakshmi 1984; Sadasivan 1974, 113–122).

Using women's welfare as an index of civilizational progress, these efforts extended the social reformism initiated earlier in the nineteenth century. Like the earlier work, they incorporated explicit resistance to Euro-Western models of reform and to the feminist interests thought to be associated with them. The new regimens of women's action were thought to have the capacity to improve women's lot and actualize the new national community by regenerating families, by inculcating values of citizenship, by selectively appropriating modern (often scientific) forms of knowledge and technologies, and (borrowing the popular ideas associated with eugenics) by improving its "racial stock" (Chakravarti 1990; Hancock forthcoming).

Nationalist recalibrations of normative femininity, however diverse in content, raised questions about female agency that affected the everyday lives of men and women. Should women be educated? If so, to what ends? What should be the content and aim of their education? When should women marry? What styles of life were appropriate for widows? These questions carried implications for the ongoing public debates on widowhood, prostitution, divorce, age of consent, and property rights. Chennai Smārtas participated in these debates but were divided in their positions. Those sympathetic to nationalist and reformist goals, who were affiliated with organizations such as the Madras Hindu Association, the Arya Samaj, or Theosophical Society, were receptive to arguments in support of girls' education, raising the minimum age of marriage, women's property and inheritance rights, and widows' remarriage. On the other hand, those who resisted such measures did so by appealing to Hindu orthodoxy as interpreted by the Shankaracharya and/or neotraditionalist leaders of the Sanatana Dharma movement. They asserted that child marriage was a Hindu tradition, and they opposed both divorce and the remarriage of widows. In his *Melliyalar Cutantiram* (1918; Women's Freedom),[12] K. Vasudeva Iyer, a Smārta moralist, warned women against "ruining the greatness of Bharat" by straying from their domestic duties of cleaning, cooking, and thrift (cited in Lakshmi 1984, 10).

Cultural debates on womanhood in turn-of-the-century Chennai were mediated by voluntary associations, educational institutions, and the rapidly expanding print culture (see Lakshmi 1984, 1–26; Visweswaran 1996). Women themselves encountered new behavioral possibilities and subject positions, as well as new conflicts and dilemmas. The work of one Smārta reformer, Sister Subbalakshmi, illustrates the shape and trajectory of these debates. In 1912, after obtaining a B.A. from Madras University, a Brahman widow, Subbalakshmi Ammal (later known as Sister Subbalakshmi), founded the Brahman Widow's Home in Chennai (Ramanathan 1989). It was a residence and school for young widows like herself. The home was established to further women's education while enabling widows to become economically self-sufficient by training them to be teachers.[13] In time, the caste exclusivity of the home was contested, as was Subbalakshmi's leadership. In 1932, she stepped down as headmistress. The home continued as the Government Widows' Home and was open to widows of any caste or sect. Subbalakshmi continued to advocate reforms in women's education and legal status; she was president of the Women's India Association, a nationalist women's organization, in

1945–1946, and she founded several schools and social service clubs for women in the Mylapore area.

Womanhood was implicated in nationalist debates on "high culture" during the early decades of the twentieth century. The classicization of regional dance forms offers a well-documented example of this.[14] The primary context for this type of dance was (mainly Shiva) temple worship. Performance techniques, instrumentation, and accoutrements had long been maintained and transmitted among hereditary communities of temple servants—instrumentalists, teachers, and performers. Performers were generally women, whereas instrumentalists tended to be men. The social organization of these communities was distinctive. Women dancers were "married" to the reigning deity of the temple with whom they were associated, although they took lovers from among temple patrons and donors. Property was transmitted through women. Male offspring who remained within the community served as instrumental accompanists and sometimes teachers. Children from other communities were adopted by the dancers. Under colonial rule, the dancers (known by the Sanskritic term *devadasi* "servant of the god") were categorized as prostitutes; after 1863 adoptions by *devadasi*s were outlawed, and their offspring were deemed illegitimate. While the state was instituting legal restrictions, local reformist organizations targeted *devadasi*s as victims in need of rehabilitation. By the 1920s, moreover, the demonization of *devadasi*s on grounds of "social hygiene" was accompanied by upper-caste appropriation of the style and technical details of *devadasi* dance. A scriptural basis for dance was adduced, and its original practitioners were characterized as chaste, nunlike "wives" of the god. In an effort to "restore" the original form and function of regional dance (which scholars dubbed "Bharat Natyam," the dance of Bharat), elites moved dance out of the temple and onto the performance stage. Dance training became part of the aesthetic repertoire of upper-caste women, who as young girls received lessons and later were expected to give fancy recital performances.

The classicization of dance and Sister Subbalakshmi's reformism were indicative of women's stakes and modes of participation in the cultural debates of elite nationalism. In the first two decades of the twentieth century, women's efforts were mediated through their own periodicals and associations. The Women's India Association (WIA), an early nationalist women's organization affiliated with the INC, exemplified this process. It was founded in 1917 by Annie Besant, Margaret Cousins, and Dorothy Jinarajadasa, and it was one of the earliest transregional organizations founded and controlled by women, primarily urban elites.

The WIA initiated programs on behalf of women and children, Through meetings and its monthly publication, *Stri Dharma,* it sought to be forum for women's public deliberation about matters of collective concern—education, governance, health, poverty, and caste inequality. One WIA leader, Dr. Muthulakshmi Reddy, authored measures for reforming *devadasi* life. As the first female legislator in the Madras presidency, she pressed for an official ban on temple dancing. Local WIA chapters offered basic education for women, including classes in literacy (English and vernacular), Indian history, domestic arts like sewing or embroidery, and health and hygiene. Some chapters adopted social service projects such as rescue homes, schools, and health centers. Most included *bhajans* and other ritual observances as regular features of their meetings.

Though the group's social reform measures were fused with a nationalist political program that included both constitutional reform and acts of collective resistance, the combination of political and social goals caused debate within the organization. In 1926, the All-India Women's Conference on Social and Educational Reform (AIWC) splintered from the WIA to pursue educational and social reforms that were avowedly apolitical. WIA leadership was left in the difficult position of having to negotiate both a critique of colonial rule and the "modernity" of the West and a critique of the oppressiveness of local institutions and ideologies. The organization and its journal, *Stri Dharma,* were venues for a range of contending positions that ranged from Dravidianist repudiations of the caste and gender hierarchy to the espousal of constitutional reforms to orthodox assertions of women's innate spirituality.

Domestic space was a root metaphor for these varied discourses and an important site for the work of reform and nation building. Both Gandhian nationalism and the Tamil linguistic/ethnic identity movements had conceived of the home as the site from which new kinds of collective identities might be forged. The nationalist organizations controlled by elite women emphasized the political importance and visibility of the home in order to argue for women's right to education, suffrage, and property. Orthodox resistance to the societal reforms proposed by nationalists existed among urban Smārtas, but this resistance shared key images of femininity and domesticity as the natural grounds of sociopolitical communities. Within diverse nationalisms and the orthodox resistance to nationalism, then, home was a place to suture the categories of tradition and modernity through styles of consumption, dress and grooming, and everyday domestic labor. Indicative of this convergence was the WIA's endorsement of Home Science (a field of study modeled on Home Economics) in 1921. That field introduced practical grammars of daily life governed by scientific notions about hygiene, nutrition, and child care. Nationalist women's espousal of Home Science recognized domesticity as a laboratory for "indigenizing" modernity by transforming the regimens of daily life.[15]

Both elite nationalist ideologies and elite "high culture" illustrated (in different ways) how women appropriated and were appropriated by nationalized images of femininity and how they drew on these images to create spaces of female agency. In so doing, they preserved the tensions embedded in earlier reformist projects that identified women as victims of tradition in need of benefits of social, educational, and political reforms and as regenerative sources of tradition. Elite women also contributed to the cultural formation of class identity and difference, for elites constructed images of idealized womanhood that subsumed class and caste privilege. The ideal woman was portrayed as a dedicated mother, pious ritual actor, and rational consumer. This contrasted with poor and low caste women (often laborers), who were defined as ignorant and haphazard mothers, victims of male greed, and generally in need of the reforms that elites administered. The uneasy conjunctions of feminism and nationalism in colonial India enabled bourgeois domesticity and femininity to be reframed as "natural" emblems of nationhood.

Elite Identity and Postcolonial Cultural Politics

The nationalist imaginaries described above germinated in opposition to colonial rule, though still within the structure of opportunities and constraints imposed by the colonial state. Such structures are particularly important in evaluating the situation of subaltern elites like Smārta Brahmans, for whom daily life was shaped, though not wholly permeated, by colonialism in significant ways because of their role in the colonial bureaucracy.

The contributions of upper-caste elites to anticolonial nationalism were noted by the British. In the early twentieth century, British administrators began to devise mechanisms to restrict Brahman access to influential administrative, legislative, and judicial positions (Washbrook 1976, 282–287). By 1910 the senior members of the secretariat had come to regard the nationalist threat as a Brahman threat. The efforts to oppose Brahman "nepotism" (as it was glossed by the British) included the initiation of a system of caste-based, or communal, reservations of legislative seats. Caste-based quotas were also introduced for civil service postings and in institutions of higher education.

It was in the wake of these administrative measures that the non-Brahman political movement gained ground. Though ideological bases had been laid with the earlier *taṉittamiḻ* movement, indigenous efforts to mobilize non-Brahmans politically came in the second decade of the twentieth century. The non-Brahman movement was formally inaugurated by the 1916 Non Brahman Manifesto, authored by P. Thyagaraja Chetti (a wealthy non-Brahman merchant-banker and philanthropist).

With the newly formed South Indian Liberal Federation, known subsequently as the Justice Party, the wealthy Veḷḷāḷa and Cēṭṭiyar leaders of the movement intended to broker a cross-caste movement that challenged Brahman political and socioeconomic power. Initially the movement was a failure, since participation by poor and low-caste groups, as well as by Muslims, Christians, and Anglo-Indians, was minimal. Their efforts succeeded in the retention and expansion of caste-based reservations—a program that primarily benefited wealthy non-Brahmans.

Non-Brahman populism was reconstituted and strengthened with the founding of the Self-Respect League in 1925. The league advocated atheism and radical social reform, an agenda molded by E. V. Ramasami, a former Congress nationalist who had come to oppose its Brahmanical character under Gandhi. The league cooperated with the Justice Party until 1936, when it disbanded after losing the elections. In 1944, the league's agenda was incorporated into the secessionist platform of a new regional non-Brahman party, the Dravida Kazhagam (DK). Since 1967, Tamil Nadu has been ruled by offshoots of the DK—the Dravida Munnetra Kazhagam (DMK) and the All-India Annadurai Dravida Munnetra Kazhagam (AIA-DMK). Under these parties, the reservations authored earlier in the century by the British government were expanded to current levels of up to 70 percent.

These developments have had important consequences for Brahman socioeconomic and political status. Brahman access to political power at the state level gradually diminished during the first half of this century, as did their access to state-controlled jobs and educational opportunities. They attempted to mitigate the effects of these changes through private enterprise and through claims of entitlement made on the central government rather than at the state level. Because India's central government maintains a more limited reservations system than does the Tamil Nadu state, Brahmans have sought education at private or centrally administered schools, and they have obtained employment through the central government.[16] In the early 1970s, Singh (1976) noted that 82 percent of all Tamil Brahman men residing in New Delhi (India's capital city) were employed by the central government in service and administration. These proportions have not shifted appreciably since then, despite efforts to create reservations for non-Brahman castes and to extend those already in existence for former Untouchables and tribal groups. Relying on their backgrounds in civil service and the professions, Brahmans have also sought employment through private industry, which has grown considerably since decolonization and particularly since the economic liberalization measures of the early 1990s. Singer's (1972, 284) study of Chennai industrialists suggests that Smārtas may have been especially advantaged in making the shift to industrial employment and management,[17] and Driver's (1982) findings on status summation among Brahmans, though not statistically significant, were consistent with this.

Smārtas As Cultural Brokers

The socioeconomic and political dependency of the Smārtas on India's central government dovetailed with their support for the Congress party and for the official nationalist agenda of unity, sovereignty, secularism, economic self-sufficiency, and socioeconomic welfare (Brass 1990, 10) that the Congress-led central government has promulgated since independence. The interest that Smārtas have in the cultural dimensions of official nationalism have influenced cultural politics in India and the knowledge produced about South Asia. Singer's book *When a Great Tradition Modernizes* described and actually was a product of Smārta cultural brokerage. Urban Smārtas' claims about their own collective identity as cultural interlocutors and their views on the Sanskritic content of Indian national culture were mediated by Singer. Threaded through Singer's description and analysis of South Asian modernity, is a regulatory description of social life—a Smārta-authored set of "shoulds" and "oughts." The book has been read as a description of urban elites' adaptation to modernity, but it might also be read as a vehicle of urban elites' cultural production of class and nation.[18]

During the first two decades after independence, increased agricultural production and rapid industrialization were sought under India's modified form of state socialism. The central government implemented large-scale projects such as building dams and hydroelectric plants and mechanizing agriculture to meet planning objectives. Accompanying the centralization of the political economy was the expansion of governmentality[19] through efforts to nationalize language and cultural forms such as music, drama, plastic arts, and literature. Professionals attached to the central ministries of education and of information and broadcasting sought to consolidate the central state's control over media infrastructure and in many instances to promulgate a Sanskritized "high culture" as official nationalism. The expansion of All-India Radio in the 1950s was marked by programming decisions calculated to create a distinction between classical and popular genres and to promote a national music derived from Sanskritic sources (Lelyveld 1995). In a similar vein, national "akademis" of letters, arts, and performance were established by the central government in 1953 and 1954 as part of the National Cultural Trust. Through their publications, awards and grants-in-aid, the akademis were meant to conserve a Sanskritized canon.

It was during these decades that Singer conducted fieldwork in Chennai. Singer sought from his cosmopolitan and mostly upper-caste informants an authoritative version of the Great Tradition of Sanskritic Hinduism. He considered Smārta Brahmans important exponents of the Great Tradition and attributed their modern "catholicity" to their past roles as textual scholars and literati (Singer 1972, 70, 227). He made less of the fact that, as civil servants and white-collar professionals, they were actively engaged in building the cultural and educational institutions through which they derived social and material privilege and from which they sought to exert influence.

Singer's privileging of Smārta voices corresponded with his dependence on Smārta informants. In the book, he describes several, including a prominent Indologist, V. Raghavan. Singer worked closely with Raghavan for five months in 1954–1955. In 1960–1961 and 1964, he completed two additional field studies during which he relied on Raghavan only indirectly. In 1960–1961, Singer studied Smārta-led devotional groups, which he described as embodying Smārtas' historical predisposition to cultural brokerage. In 1964, he studied industrialists (Smārtas were numerically preponderant in his sample) and the particularly Indian ethos that (contra Weber) he found to be an ideological prod to capitalist expansion. These field studies formed the basis for *When a Great Tradition Modernizes.* Singer's arguments reflected his abiding interest in the integrating work of cultural brokerage in a modern, which for him included national, context. And it was the work with Raghavan that refined this focus.

Raghavan's interest in cultural hegemony within India predisposed him to working with Singer even as it drove his work as scholar, educator, and administrator.[20] Singer's association with V. Raghavan began during his first visit to India in 1954.[21] Raghavan's position was epitomized by his argument in favor of Sanskrit as India's national language. Raghavan depicted India's incipient cultural integration as the work of elites. For audiences in India, he published newspaper articles (mostly in the English-language press) that were broadcast on All-India Radio and delivered speeches to fellow Sanskritists. He envisioned an integrated Indian culture centered around Hinduism and used Sanskrit sources to document its crucial features—performing arts, ritual practices, and basic values.[22] He also suggested that installing Sanskrit as the medium of both popular discourse and state ceremony (in anthems, oaths, mottos) would produce a citizenry shaped by the values of Indian culture. Sanskrit was conceived as the means for creating a new national subject: a modern, tradition-infused citizen.[23]

Raghavan identified *bhakti* as an important medium for these subjective transformations. In a series of nationally broadcast lectures presented on All-India Radio in 1964, Raghavan reframed popular Hinduism, placing Sanskritized *bhakti* at its center (1964, 16). In Raghavan's reading, *bhakti* was shorn of the oppositional qualities that other writers have since stressed (e.g., Ramanujan 1973; Turner 1969) and was identified on the basis of its "catholic acceptance of many paths" and its monistic orientation. Socioeconomic and political equality were deferred in favor of the "cultural" and "emotional" integration that *bhakti* was thought to effect. In singling out "emotional integration," Raghavan borrowed a key word from official nationalism.[24] What he meant by it was an interior transformation brought about through devotion. The subject constituted through the catharsis of "melting moods" *(bhava)* was one in which "sympathy, equanimity, humility, and tolerance have taken root" (Raghavan 1964, 56–58) and one that could be pressed into the service of the nation. Besides seeking union with the deity, the devotee also established connections with others—ideally philanthropic ties of dependency—which again obviated the question of socioeconomic and political equality. Evoking the bourgeois appropriation of *karmayoga* (devotion through service) as a definitive feature of Hinduism (Subramaniam 1988), Raghavan advised *bhakti* as a practical immersion in the human world, a "doing good for others" (1964, 44) that included scholarly endeavors (1964, 96). *Bhakti* was thereby Sanskritized and made available as a vehicle of bourgeois nationalism.

Mediated by Singer, this proved to be a powerful concept in South Asian area studies. As a style of religiosity that could serve as a vehicle of liberal humanism, *bhakti* represented a suturing of modernity and tradition (Singer 1959, 144–149; 1972, 200–241). Though Singer had not relied on Raghavan directly in his 1960–1961 field study of devotional groups in Chennai, he had drawn on Raghavan's work to place *bhakti* firmly within the Great Tradition of Sanskritic Hinduism. He thereby underwrote Smārta claims about their identity as mediators of an Indic culture aligned with liberal humanism, modernity, and progress, downplaying the roles played by urban *bhajana*s in the formation of distinctive class cultures.

In addition to having class dimensions, Sanskritization was deeply gendered in ways that derived from elite nationalist recalibrations of gender difference and were consistent with the ways that women were cast as status producers among urban elites. As used by Raghavan, the concept of Sanskritization sutured the rifts between tradition and modernity, between Great and Little Traditions, and between the public and private realms associated with modern urban life. He likened the noncanonical domestic rituals of Brahman women to the Little Tradition, the encompassed interior of the Great Tradition of Sanskritic Hinduism (Raghavan 1956, 502). He pointed to the orthodox ceremony for Hindu marriage as a metonym of the way that Vedic Hinduism "incorporated" local customs, suggesting that the relation between the Great and Little Traditions was like that of male, Brahmanical, and priestly ritual to the practices of women and "common folk" (Raghavan 1956, 502). Taking this reasoning to its logical conclusion, Raghavan admonished scholars to study Brahman families' domestic rituals as residues of the great tradition. Armed with that knowledge, they could then remake a national culture that had been derogated by a succession of foreign conquests (1956, 502). Their practices, he noted, should be recorded in order to retain these traditions in their authentic forms and thereby contribute to "national consolidation" (Raghavan 1956, 505). Here the work of official nationalism was to formulate models of how culture that was generated in the feminine space of the home could be made continuous with a nationalized public realm.

Raghavan's argument was reframed by Singer with his notion of compartmentalization—a "functional adaptation" in which bourgeois males divided their lives into separate but complementary spheres (Singer 1972, 296, 315–366) of a traditional (feminized) home, as well as a modern (masculinized) workplace. Singer's model of compartmentalization thus contained a regulatory description of bourgeois social reality, available to and deployed by both Indian elites and Western social scientists.

Conclusion

My discussion of Singer's work closes this chapter appropriately, since it contains a useful description of modes by which Smārtas fashioned collective identity as cultural brokers. By contextualizing the work—specifically linking it to his relation to Raghavan as informant and collaborator—it is possible to see strategies by which Smārtas developed a discourse on national culture that has been influential in Indian cultural politics and in the production of scholarly knowledge about South Asia. Raghavan's engagement with Singer's project was consistent with already established Smārta interventions in cultural debates on India. I argue that scholarly paradigms should be seen as by-products of Smārta cultural history rather than the products of Euro-Western paradigms. If these projects are dialogic, they are also power laden—they have been inscribed by colonial repression as well as by negotiation and deployment of material privilege and inequality among Indians.

This raises questions about class, but not class as usually treated in Marxist or Weberian terms. Instead, I have defined class broadly as deriving from a system of domination associated with capitalism that is based on and reproduces material inequalities and glosses relations that involve both dependency and antagonism among groups in society. This recognizes the salience of Marxian arguments about the exploitative and antagonistic features of the class system. However, by also incorporating Weber's attention to status and consumption, as well as his concern with issues of meaning, I recognize that class is always historically emergent and culturally grounded. Thus class cannot be treated simply as a matter of material privilege and inequality, but of the local and historically contingent meanings of those characteristics. What I have sought to demonstrate with this chapter's exploration of Smārta cultural history is the nationalist genealogy (and interconnectedness) of Smārta cultural production and class formation, and the centrality of female bodies and labor in those projects. The next chapter focuses on current domestic practice, including ritual, and the way that differences—of gender, caste, and class—are made.

Notes

1. Shankaracharya is a Sanskritic title used among monastic brotherhoods that designates its bearer as a preceptor of the tenets of Adishankara, the eighth-century (C.E.) religious teacher who formalized the Hindu school of thought known as *advaitavēdanta*. In 1987, the formal head of the Kanchipuram *maṭam* (monastery and teaching center) was Sri Jayendra Saraswati. He had succeeded Sri Chandrasekharenda Saraswati, who remained at the *maṭam* until his death in 1994. The elder man was revered by Hindus of various sects as well as by non-Hindus and was known as Paramacharya (Supreme Teacher). Also at the monastery was a younger monk, the Shankaracharya-designate, who will take office when the current leader steps down.

2. *Prasadam* glosses the food offerings made during *pūja* that are redistributed at the end to participants. The literal Tamil transliteration would be *piracātam*. *Prasadam* is the more common form of this Sanskritic word.

3. "Brahmins Team Meets PM," *The Hindu* [Madras edition], November 3, 1987. At its 1989 state meeting, TAMBRAS again passed similar resolutions. See "Ignoring Brahmans' Demands Undemocratic," *The Hindu*, December 26, 1989, and "Economy-Based Reservation for Secular Order," *The Hindu*, December 27, 1989.

4. See Beteille (1996).

5. At that time, US$1 equaled about Rs.13. In 1996, the exchange rate had shifted, with Rs.35 equaling US$1.

6. Sabarimalai is the site of a large temple in Kerala dedicated to the god Aiyappa. Aiyappa devotionalism is marked by rigorous purity rules and is for the most part restricted to men (premenstrual girls and postmenopausal women are the only females who normally participate). Devotion can include four separate pilgrimage cycles per year, though the major one takes place in January. Each pilgrimage is preceded by several weeks of fasting, celibacy, and ritual teachings.

7. In the 1931 census, the last to enumerate caste, Brahmans made up 3 percent (19,350) of the total population of Chennai (then Madras City), 645,000, and

Smārtas constituted no more than half of the Brahman population (Singer 1972, 61–64).

8. Weinstein (1974, 42–48) and others (Driver and Driver 1987, 8–9; Wiebe 1975, 17) found the city to be heterogeneous socially and economically but noted higher Brahman densities in Mylapore and adjacent areas of Tiruvalluvar Nagar and Vivekananda Puram (Weinstein 1974, 67–65). The way such places were perceived was suggested to me anecdotally when an acquaintance, a Smārta woman and longtime resident of Mylapore, commented that Mylapore and Mambalam (a local name for Thyagaraja Nagar, a division west of Mylapore) were the places where one could always see the "typical Brahman women, wearing nine yards [sari] and gold jewelry."

9. INTACH is an acronym for the Indian National Trust for Art and Cultural Heritage. It is a nationally based voluntary association formed in 1984 for the identification and preservation of cultural resources, including parks, wildlife refuges, archaeological sites, and historic buildings.

10. "Dubash" is the Anglicized term for translators and other brokers who facilitated interactions between European traders and local producers and merchants.

11. See also Haynes (1991) for an insightful discussion of comparable processes in colonial Surat.

12. The Tamil word *melliya* is an adjective literally meaning "soft-voiced."

13. Similar principles informed women's efforts to found rescue homes for prostitutes, and for female beggars and petty criminals—all of whom were identified as victims of inadequate education, poverty, corrupted home life, and male greed. For example, at the Avvai Home in Chennai, destitute women were rehabilitated by being relocated in a substitute home, a dormitory-like residence that combined time discipline, behavioral restrictions, medical attention, limited education, and productive labor (handicrafts, usually). They were subject to the disciplinary surveillance of matrons and expected to contribute their labor to the maintenance of the home—through practices of "homecraft"—thus making the home self-sufficient as well as rehabilitative (*Women's India Association Annual Report,* 1933–1934, appendix 2, pp. 24–26).

14. Sources consulted include Srinivasan (1985) and Nair (1996).

15. Consider a Tamil gloss for Home Science—*kuṭumpam cāstiram.* It refers literally to family or household *shastras* (*shastra* being the blanket term used for the corpus of Hindu moral-legal texts compiled between 500 B.C.E. and 500 C.E.). It thereby dislocated science from its Euro-Western contexts of production and dissemination. These processes echo Prakash's observation about the Hindu elite's appropriation of science education in colonial Bengal: "Formed in this hybridity, the Hindu elite relocated science's authority in its use in this world, not in its signification as a mark of western superiority" (Prakash 1996, 81).

16. A separate system for reservations is maintained by the central government; the national civil service (IAS, Indian Administrative Services), the centrally controlled universities, banking and industry, and both houses of parliament (Rajya Sabha and Lok Sabha) have a proportion of slots reserved for women, minorities, and members of those castes (mostly former Untouchables) and tribes listed on a "schedule," based on their having experienced systematic

discrimination that limited their social and economic mobility. In Tamil Nadu state, the Central Schedule is augmented by the state's own list of "backward" castes and classes.

17. Of the nineteen industrial leaders that Singer (1972, 283–286) studied in the 1950s and 1960s, seven were Smārtas. No other caste group was as well represented. Singer did not construct the sample to be statistically representative, but his findings can be taken as qualitative indicators of this stratum of the population. The industrial leaders studied had been identified by other industrialists, by the State Minister of Industries, and by Singer's own Smārta informants. All of the leaders surveyed had relied on kinship networks to gain power but had also used skills and contacts developed through employment in banking, government service, and private business. About 75 percent of his sample had attended college. My informants included only two households comparable to those of the industrial leaders studied by Singer, but most men and some women had experienced similar patterns of education and employment.

18. See Hancock (1998) for a more extended discussion of this.

19. Foucault described governmentality as a hegemonic exercise of state power that emphasized the use of tactics such as advertising that manipulated desire rather than rely solely on formal mechanisms of law to repress or punish (Foucault 1991, 95).

20. In 1954, when he met Singer, Raghavan was already well established as an academician. After receiving his Ph.D. in Sanskrit Language and Literature in 1935 from the University of Madras, Raghavan joined its Sanskrit Department, and by 1955 he was appointed professor and head of department. The Indian government recognized his work as a Sanskritist in 1953, with the award of the Kane Gold Medal; two years later he was honored with titles bestowed by an important religious leader, the Shankaracharya of Kanchipuram, in recognition of his creative writing in Sanskrit.

21. Singer explained his decision to focus on Chennai in light of its reputation as a center of traditional artistic, religious, and cultural expression (1972, 68–70). He later reiterated this but added that it was V. Raghavan, whom he met at a Ford Foundation–funded conference in Pune, who convinced him that Chennai was an exemplary locus for the Great Tradition (Singer. n.d. "Dr. V. Raghavan: A Personal Reminiscence," page 6, box 34, Milton Singer Papers, Department of Special Collections, Joseph Regenstein Library, University of Chicago). Singer described Raghavan as the ideal learned informant—a person who was a product of an "indigenous civilization" and its Great Tradition (1972, 81); it was Raghavan's vision of Indian civilization that Singer canonized as the paradigmatic form of the Great Tradition. Singer wrote, "Dr. Raghavan's version of the Great Tradition . . . represented only one of several interpretations, but it was nevertheless a broad and inclusive one that consolidated many elements from local and regional traditions. Although I stopped looking for *the* Great Tradition . . . I continued to find the comprehensiveness and catholicity of Dr. Raghavan's position highly productive of anthropological insight. Dr. Raghavan became more than a learned informant. . . . He also became a friend, a fellow inquirer, and a colleague with whom I could discuss and plan ongoing research" (Singer 1972, 82; emphasis original).

Raghavan influenced Singer's methods of study, as well. Singer wrote that to comprehend the Great Tradition, one had to study its sacred geography, its professional representatives and their social organization, and its cultural performances (1972, 62). Cultural performances were, he stressed, the methodological entry points. Brahmans were identified as learned representatives among whom Singer found cultural leaders with a comprehensiveness of outlook that was comparable to his own (1972, 63–64, 79–80).

Singer acknowledged his dependence on Raghavan in studying cultural performances (1972, 71). On Raghavan's advice and with his assistance, Singer identified those cultural performances worthy of analysis by consulting the daily engagements listings in the English-language newspaper *The Hindu*. Then, accompanied by Raghavan (or one of his sons, students, or associates), Singer attended. Raghavan provided introductions and often translated the proceedings for Singer. Singer depended on Raghavan for exegesis as well, and mentioned that he often went over his notes with Raghavan (1972, 81–82).

22. In 1958, Raghavan participated in the Sanskrit Commission. That group was convened by the Central Ministry of Education in October 1956, and members toured India during the early months of 1957. The final report, published in 1958, reviewed Sanskrit research and education, and made specific recommendations for the promotion of Sanskrit study by the central and state governments. A Sanskrit-saturated mass culture was envisioned as a means for lending security to Sanskrit education and for producing a culturally imbued citizenry. In 1959, Raghavan was appointed a member of the Central Sanskrit Board, formed to evaluate schools and their curricula. Subsequently, he was named president of the Central Sanskrit Institute at Tirupati, and chair of the board's Publication and Examination Committees. Raghavan was also active in India's emerging mass media. Since 1946, he had been a programming consultant and occasional presenter on All-India Radio. In 1964, he was asked by the minister of education (then Indira Gandhi) to deliver the prestigious Patel Lectures. The series was broadcast by All-India Radio and published by the Ministry of Education under the title *The Great Integrators: The Saint Singers of India* (1964).

23. Raghavan's term for this transformation was "Sanskritization" (1956, 1963). He first proposed this argument in the August 1956 issue of the *Far Eastern Quarterly* as a companion piece to the often cited formulation of Sanskritization by Srinivas (1956). Raghavan departed from Srinivas in asserting that Sanskrit's usage promoted cultural equilibrium rather than social mobility. Although Srinivas often used Sanskrit as a metonym for other political and socioeconomic processes, Raghavan understood Sanskrit's role in more literal terms, arguing that integration depended on actual communication in Sanskrit. Raghavan maintained that India's cultural integration was tied to the production and circulation of Sanskrit texts and that reading, writing, speaking, and hearing Sanskrit produced subjective transformations.

24. With the work of the Committee on Emotional Integration (1962), that expression had been outfitted with public policy implications. In its report, the committee (of which Raghavan was a member) offered that "our approach to these problems [national integration] has perhaps been almost purely intellectual and our appeals directed only to the intelligent self-interest of the nation. We

have failed to give emotions the attention they deserve. . . . [For the purpose of the present movement for national integration] we should employ something like the technique of the psychiatrist. The hidden causes of the malaise are to be laid bare and removed by recourse to reason seasoned with sympathy" (1962, 1.2–1.3).

Acknowledging that there had been assaults on national unity because of communalism and regional secessionism (Dravidianist political parties were explicitly mentioned here), they denied that the fault lines of caste, class, sect, region, or language were inherent structural features of Indian society. "A deep respect for all faiths and compassion for all creatures characterised the Indian spirit. Such a spirit naturally leads to patience and tolerance. . . . It was this spirit of tolerance which made it possible for various religions to find a home in India on equal terms with other citizens" (1962, 1.12). Finally, the medium by which emotional integration produced national consolidation was identified as Sanskrit, the "national link language" (1962, 1.17), and recommendations for greater accommodation of Sanskrit education at the secondary level were included (1962, 5.24).

3

The Moral Etiquette of Everyday Hinduism

In Chapter 2, I contextualized the discourses on domesticity that were produced by cultural debates on nationalism, especially since the turn of the twentieth century. The chapter closed with Raghavan's assertion from the mid-1950s that the upper-caste home served as a site of and a model for Sanskritization. The Great and Little Traditions, as well as tradition and modernity, were sutured in these contexts. This representation of the domestic realm differs little from earlier nationalist images; like them, it was a source of ongoing tension. Raghavan himself acknowledged this, for elsewhere he expressed doubt about people's willingness to adhere to the prescriptive tenets on which the idealized upper-caste home rested. These disjunctions are worth attention because they capture the dilemmas that are still voiced by upper-caste urban elites. The following paraphrased remarks, made in 1955 by the (then) Shankaracharya of Kanchipuram, speak to ideologies of upper-caste domestic life as well as its unresolved conflicts:

> Ten years ago there was hardly one post-puberty marriage, now there is hardly one pre-puberty marriage. . . . This is really more important than the abolition of untouchability. Wherever one goes he will encounter these polluted girls who have married after puberty. And girls who are sent to colleges are not permitted to absent themselves for the three days in each month when they should stay in the house and not see any one. Practically all houses are now impure. (Singer 1955, 5)[1]

The Shankaracharya's comments were made during an interview with Milton Singer, in response to Singer's question about the challenges that the Shankaracharya anticipated for his successor.[2] In this conversation, during which Raghavan provided translation, the Shankaracharya characterized modernity in terms of contagion. He attributed this to government actions taken earlier in the century—raising the age of consent, abolishing Untouchability, and expanding the opportunities for female education and employment. These measures were harmful, the Shankaracharya contended, because they had led to a relaxation of female body discipline. In his field notes, Singer recorded Raghavan's response to the Shankaracharya's words. Raghavan had offered "additional insights" into the issue of pollution during a private conversation with Singer after the audience:

> He told several stories which indicated his own attitude pretty well. . . . He himself had found some fresh blooms in his garden faded, and asking his wife about it found that she had walked near the flowers while she was menstruating. These effects, he thought, were probably chemical, and needed more scientific study, but it was evident that they were disturbing both to others and to the woman herself. The three days isolation imposed on her every month was a good way to minimize the disturbances. . . . Dr. R[aghavan] described how one courageous educator in P. insisted that each of the girls in his college stay away from school three days each month, because these would not be good days for "brain work."
>
> If a girl did not marry just before puberty, she would become a "danger" as she approached puberty. She would be "dangerous" to those around her and a victim for any Don Juan that came around. If she married after puberty she would already be polluted. (Singer 1955, 17–18)

Singer added that Raghavan continued in this vein, pointing out that avoidance on account of pollution was a functional necessity, but it did not diminish the affection between husband and wife. Raghavan noted that this same situation informed the relations among castes. "In the past, the best feelings and mutual respect prevailed between untouchables and Brahmins. Now new ideologies have disturbed and misinterpreted these relations" (Singer 1955, 18).

Claims like Raghavan's continue to be reiterated and used hegemonically. Twenty years after Raghavan's conversation with Singer, the Committee on the Status of Women in India (1974) described, with alarm, women's consent to containment of the sort prescribed by the Shankaracharya, underscoring women's "conservatism" and "traditionalism." Feminist critics of *pativrata* or *pativratādharma*[3]—the terms they used to denote the ensemble of religious attitudes and behaviors undergirding women's submission to patriarchal authority—have suggested that these values continue to be asserted (Chakravarti 1990; Sunder Rajan 1993). Militant, ethnicized forms of religious nationalism, such as the Rashtriya Swayamsevak Sangh's (RSS) espousal of Hindutva and the neotraditionalist defense of *satī* (prominent nationally in September 1987 after the death of Roop Kanwar in Rajasthan), emphasize female containment, with domesticity as the site for and expression of their religiosity (Das 1995, 55–83; Hawley 1994, 100–103; Sarkar and Butalia 1995, 6–9).[4]

This chapter examines the ways in which prescriptive discourses on femininity are translated into everyday domestic practices, and it considers how these practices contribute to the cultural production of caste and class. Upper-caste women are by no means confined to the domestic arena—they participate in the labor force in growing numbers and are educationally advantaged. In addition, they are active as social service providers through voluntarism. Yet women of all ages consistently defined themselves as women through their domestic activity and relations, which were grounded, in turn, in notions of Hindu propriety.

The centrality of domesticity in south Indian women's lives is reiterated in Hindu public culture. Devotional films depicting the earthly exploits of goddesses and their amelioration of the tribulations of ordinary pious women are popular across the entire caste/class spectrum.[5] Some, like "Jai Santoshima" and "Māriyamma<u>n</u>", offered appealing depictions of women's devotion to regionally based deities and led to certain local styles of women's worship being adopted transregionally (Das 1981).[6] During the last decade, certain styles of goddess worship and certain shrines have enjoyed a surge of popular interest. This is typified in women's participation in a ritual vow taken to Durga, which I witnessed often during 1987–1988 and again in 1996 (Cattiyanatan 1985). Women gathered at local shrines on Tuesday afternoons during an inauspicious period known as *rākukālam*,[7] often having fasted during the day. They lit small lamps fashioned from limes and placed them in front of the goddess shrine.[8] A temple priest then performed *pūja*, his Sanskrit prayers accompanied by the women's devotional songs. Though the elements of the ritual were familiar, the use of limes and the scheduling of group activity during Tuesday's *rākukālam* were innovations that had not been described prior to the mid-1980s.

Though the audiences of these films and devotional forms cross caste, class, sectarian, and regional lines, their message was reshaped in the course of upper-caste consumption and appropriation. As early as the 1930s, upper-caste women were encouraged by the reigning Shankaracharya to gather at goddess temples for group recitations of Lalitha Sahasranāmam (1,000 praise names of the goddess) and to sing other prayers that he himself had set to music. This I learned from an elderly woman who had participated in these groups in the late 1930s and continued to lead such a group in the 1980s, when she was well into her seventies. In the 1950s, the same leader issued a general directive advising women to form cross-sectarian *bhajanas* for Mārka<u>l</u>i (mid-December to mid-January) performances of prayers honoring the goddess Āṇṭāḷ.[9] His stated intention was to form a cross-sectarian constituency among upper castes in the hopes of undermining anti-Brahman, "rationalist" goals of Dravidianism. These sorts of goals have also been espoused by that leader's successor, Jayendra Saraswati. Many women whom I knew during the 1980s had received personal instructions detailing the format for specific types of public, collective ritual from both leaders. *Tiruviḷakku pūja* and special *pūja*s marking full-moon days *(paurṇami pūja)* were most common. In 1987, the current Shankaracharya launched a nationalistically oriented social service movement, Jaṉ Kalyāṇ, using group performances of lamp *pūja* for publicity and recruitment (Hancock 1995b).

People's reactions to my interest in women's ritual revealed that domestic ritual was often a matter of conflict, despite its popularity. The position taken by Raghavan in the excerpt above resembled the kinds of reactions that people in Chennai had to my research. They made assertions about the traditionalism of the home and women's attachment to Hindu ritual traditions. I was offered extensive lists of dos and don'ts associated with domestic ritual, and some people furnished me with family ritual calendars detailing what festivals occurred, when, and why. Cheap and easily available ritual pamphlets and instructional audiotapes reiterated women's role in upholding Hindu tradition in their formulaic introductions: "All of the greatness of our land shines through our women. It is our country's great asset that women continue our traditional practices despite the rapid advance of civilization."[10]

Although all of the innovations mentioned above were approved in the sense of being endorsed by Smārta leaders, their execution was enmeshed in delicate family negotiations—especially between women and their husbands and in-laws. A woman's expertise in a domestic ritual might be seen as a challenge to patriarchal authority, particularly if she pursued it without her husband's approval. Although domestic rituals were touted as residues of an idealized past, for those of a self-consciously modern and cosmopolitan bent, they were uncomfortably close to superstition. This came through in the "we don't do *that* anymore" reaction that my questions sometimes elicited. The implication was that some rituals belonged to the past and to the countryside, though whether the rural past was better or worse than the present was a matter of debate. People who instructed me to carefully transcribe ritual sequences and utterances and described women as traditional sometimes apologized about the haphazardness of their own everyday practice. At other times they adopted an ironic distance from these same activities.

The objectification of orthodoxy and heterodoxy, as well as the accompanying feminization of tradition and its connotations of a rural past, is related to Smārtas' historical positions as cultural brokers. In this chapter, I consider domestic mediations of these discourses, asking (1) what these formulations of Hindu "tradition" mean in terms of everyday cultural practices of upper-caste women and (2) how gender as part of a larger system of identity and difference is reproduced in these contexts.

Everyday Hinduism

In Chapter 2, I described a public ritual held to commemorate the Shankaracharya's birthday, which I had witnessed in 1987. The organizer of that event, Purnima, was a woman in her fifties whom I came to know well. She had never been employed formally, though she had received both primary and secondary education. She was a respectable married woman, but hardly a stay-at-home one. Her three adult children were all married, two with children of their own. Her husband owned an automobile repair shop that was located on the ground floor of their residence (they lived on the upper floor). Besides her work for TAMBRAS, she was active in several other groups, performing what people described (using the English expression) as "social service." She sat on the boards of a private preschool and a women's cooperative milk distribution center; she coached a neighborhood girls' sports club; she was a marriage broker. Her wisdom was highly regarded, and she counseled many women about domestic difficulties and other personal matters. At the hub of all these activities was her own devotional practice. She had an elaborate and lovingly cared for *pūja* room, an alcove of the sort found in many houses. It contained deity images (figures, *vigraham*, and pictures, *paṭam*) of Minakshi, Murukan, Krishna, Renuka, Lakshmi, and Ganesha, as well as other ritual accoutrements. The focus of worship was Minakshi, her *iṣṭa teyvam* (chosen deity), to whom Purnima was personally attached. She worshiped daily, and every Friday she performed a special *pūja* for this goddess, assisted by her husband, Bhaskar. The care that she took was well-known, and people regarded Purnima herself as a person saturated by the goddess's grace—specially blessed and thus worthy of deference. They sometimes joined her as an audience for these events. I came to know her through a friend who was a neighbor of Purnima's. My friend insisted that I visit Purnima to learn about domestic ritual from one whose own piety was genuine and, more importantly, to seek Minakshi's blessing on my work: "It's she who will pave the way for you."

As soon as she learned about my research, Purnima invited me to join her on Fridays when she performed a special, elaborate *pūja* for Minakshi. Bhaksar sometimes assisted her, but he joked that he was just an extra hand and pointed out that Purnima was really in charge. "She tells me what to do." Purnima's authority derived from several different sources. In the first place, she had been initiated to Śrī Vidya, a system of esoteric knowledge and ritual practice derived from Adishankara's teachings and based roughly on Tantra. Within the Śrī Vidya system, Shakti, the goddess-consort of Shiva, was worshiped foremost; Minakshi as bride of Sundareswarar (a form of Shiva) is regarded as a form of Shakti. Second, many of the objects in the collection had been owned originally by Purnima's father and her grandfather before him, both of whom had been initiated as Śrī Vidya adepts. It was her grandfather, a colonial civil servant, who had commissioned many of the silver and bronze images, including the figure of Minakshi, which was about six inches in height and was made of an expensive alloy of gold, silver, copper, lead, and iron called *pañcalōkam* (five-metal). They had been bequeathed to her after her elder brother had declined them because he felt he lacked the ritual expertise and dedication to worship them properly. Finally, Purnima's emotional attachment to Śrī Vidya stemmed from an earlier trauma—the death of her daughter in a fire. Her daughter had been married and was the mother of an infant son; the fire had been a kitchen accident.[11] In her grief she had sought solace through devotion to Minakshi and had developed the fairly elaborate ritual repertoire that I encountered.

One Friday in June, I joined her for the first time. When she had invited me earlier that same week, she had explained that I should be sure to bathe *(kuḷi)* before joining her. She meant that, in addition to having washed, I should not be menstruating—a condition considered to be polluting. When I arrived at her house, she asked if I had bathed. Then she led me to the bathroom and asked me to wash my feet and hands.

That day's *pūja* was to be a special observance—Purnima had bought a necklace that she intended to offer to Minakshi. Normally, after preparing the family's meal, Purnima normally changed into a nine-yard silk sari to perform the *pūja*. That day, she decided to wear a wedding sari. Most Tamils considered its distinctive maroon color attractive as well as auspicious. Her husband set up the cassette player, and Purnima selected the music—some tapes by the famous playback singer Yesudas—that would accompany the ritual. *Bhajan*s filled the room as she and her husband set out the items they would need—cups, trays, incense sticks, cubes of camphor, sandalwood paste, and more. They then began the *pūja* by propitiating Ganesha, the elephant-headed "lord of beginnings" (Courtright 1985, 172–187). All rituals begin with this action. Then they enacted an elaborate *apiṣēkam,* a ritualized bathing of the deities' icons. On other days she did this by simply sluicing the figures with water and milk. This day, a Friday and a full-moon day, was dedicated to the goddess, however, so the formula was much more involved. She poured milk, honey, rosewater, lime juice, turmeric paste, and clarified butter on each deity and then anointed them with sandalwood paste and sacred ash (see Figure 3.1). The figures were then rinsed, clothed in small pieces

FIGURE 3.1 Domestic Performance of *Apiṣēkam* By Purnima and Her Husband, Bhaskar, 1987. Photograph By Author.

of silk, daubed with vermilion and turmeric paste, and finally decorated with flowers. Minakshi's image received additional attention of the sort that mimicked the patterns of temple ritual. These gestures, Purnima assured me, were the same ones that had been performed by her father and grandfather. Purnima's collection included jewelry made of gold and gemstones; most had been commissioned by her father and grandfather, though Purnima herself had furnished additional pieces. The newest was the necklace of freshwater pearls that she was presenting to Minakshi that very day. She selected several pieces from a case and then covered the small figure with pieces of silver armor *(kavacam)*. Finally, she placed Minakshi on a lotus-shaped dais framed by a small arch *(tiruvāṭci)*, a replica of the throne on which the goddess presides at her temple in Madurai, the Minakshi Sundareswarar temple.

These gestures were followed by *arrcaṉai,* the recitation of the deity's praise names accompanied by offerings of flower petals, saffron-coated rice grains, or lotus-embossed coins. For this, Purnima selected a new audiotape, one featuring Sanskrit praise poems that had been manufactured by a local priest for this kind of home usage.[12] She then offered fresh fruit, flowers, and the cooked food prepared earlier (and slated to be served as a meal later that day). More offerings followed—additional food, incense, and finally a coconut as a sacrifice. Purnima concluded the *pūja* with *āratti,* waving a plate of burning camphor before the deities. This, she explained, protected them from the effects of envy or ill-will *(tiruṣṭi).*[13] (The reassembled shrine with its fully adorned images is pictured in Figure 3.2.) The last gesture was redistributing among participants the substances used to sluice and anoint the deities during *apiṣēkam* and portions of the food offerings. These "leftovers," *prasadam,* are regarded as having been transvalued through physical contact with the deity; they transmit the deity's blessings to those who ingest them, including people who may not have been physically present during the ritual.

I was struck by the affection for the goddess that permeated Purnima's ritual performance and her explanations of her actions. She talked about Minakshi in a way that suggested an ongoing relationship between a mother and a doted-on child. She told me that she chose Minakshi's clothing and adornments in response to the goddess's own wishes. Sometimes, Purnima said, Minakshi appeared to her in dreams and let Purnima know her preferences. Moreover, the relationship was multigenerational, having been initiated in the past and transmitted to Purnima through her male ancestors. The attentions that had been lavished on the goddess over time had congealed in the *vigraham*—adding weight, luster, and warmth to it. Purnima's husband told me that had they neglected this goddess—by not providing enough food or attention—she would languish, losing both volume and value. Bhaskar used the Tamil word *tēy* (meaning to become thin or worn out) and then glossed it in English: "She would starve."

Once I asked Purnima about the particular substances she used in *apiṣēkam* because I was curious about what she viewed as their effects. Her reply alluded to the familial qualities that I had already noticed. Echoing conventional explanations of *apiṣēkam,* she told me that the substances used were beneficial—that they were cooling and thus necessary to insure the thermic balance of a powerful and hence heated deity. She then recast these generalities in her own way:

> When a woman gives birth to a child, she wants to feed it well, to keep its skin healthy and clean, and to dress it well. It pleases the parent to be able to feed and care for the child. In the same way, I want to keep the *ampāḷ*[14] in per-

FIGURE 3.2 Domestic Shrine Following the Completion of a *Pūja*, 1987. Photograph By Author.

> fect condition—for her welfare, for my satisfaction and happiness, and for the blessings that she bestows. *Apiṣēkam* is healthy for the deity's body. . . . it makes Minakshi cool and happy. Honey is very good—it purifies the heart. All the sweetness and beauty of those flowers is in the honey. Curd and lime are also good for the skin. Humans use them to smooth and lighten their skin; for the deity it is a brightener. It makes the figures more lustrous. All of the substances used for *apiṣēkam* do that. (Field notes, August 13, 1987)

The practical creation and consequences of this—and its familial setting—were illustrated in another anecdote that Purnima told me.

> A friend was disposing of some old kitchen vessels, including a small figure of Krishna. She brought these things to the shop [to sell them to the shopkeeper], and there the shopkeeper scratched it and put some acid on the leg [to determine its composition]. Just then, my friend changed her mind and decided that she would not sell it. Instead, she came to our house to inquire if I wished to buy it from her. I could not buy it because I did not have the money with me. Later, my friend's daughter returned [home] from school with boils on her leg. When my friend told me of this, I knew that the boils had come because of the shopkeeper's putting acid on the figure of Krishna. I told her to do milk *apiṣēkam* daily in order to cool the god, and this only relieved her daughter. (Field notes, August 13, 1987)

These anecdotes and Purnima's own style of ritual performance illustrate the privileged place of ingestion and vision in ritual transactions. This, as many have observed, is generally the case in Hindu ritual, be it domestic or temple (Fuller 1992, 57–82). Lawrence Babb (1987, 205–225) has argued that these types of sensory engagement are central features in Hinduism as currently practiced. Purnima's case illustrates Babb's assertion and shows how the bodily transactions of worship generate a sense of familial relatedness. Through the sensory transactions of worship, people create a sense of belonging and connection (among family members and between persons and deities, but potentially among larger collectivities). This "us-ness" is grounded in morally laden, material transactions and is critically linked to cultural representations of femininity. Considered in terms of substantialization, worship is both homologous with and dependent on commensal acts—storing, preparing, serving, and eating food. The following sections concentrate on the spatial and material sites of these transactions. I describe, in detail, the characteristics of domestic spaces of worship and commensality—their architectural markers, their material inventories, and their associated practices. Considering domestic space as (1) locus for and (2) engendered by these actions enables me to address how the boundaries of caste, class, and gender are substantialized.

The Domestic Interior

Tamil speakers condensed the meanings of "house" and "household" using the term *vīṭu,* which refers to both a physical dwelling and the coresidential family group. When speaking among themselves, Brahmans preferred a different term, *akam,* which subsumed the notion of a dwelling within the broader rubric of interiority. A place to begin a discussion of domestic life, then, is with the notion of interiority itself. Though glossed as "interior," the variety of contexts and genres (poetry, in particular) in which the term *akam* is used point to its complexity and its semantic density. *Akam* denotes any relational "inside" *(uḷ),* a house (*vīṭu or manai,* which is also the root word for wife, *manaivi*), the mind or self *(manam),* and the earth *(pūmi).* In poetics *akam* describes the classical genre of love poems, about which Ramanujan has written, "the interior world is archetypal, it has not history, and no names of persons and places, except, now and then, in its metaphors" (1985, 235). As a description of Brahman domestic space, *akam* is an indicator of the cultural value and semantic density of interiority. It is a kind of space critically associated with females and femininity, and it is defined by experiences such as eating, dressing, washing, and sexual relations that are the cultural mediators of personhood. It suggests that domesticity is valued as a kind of interior world in which persons and relatedness among persons are generated and boundaries between categories of persons are delimited.

Interiority is defined against that which is exterior, *puram.* Lexically, *puram* is glossed as "side" or "area" *(pakkam)* and "outside" *(veḷiyē).* Those described as *purattar* are "outsiders" of one sort or another, and certain exterior parts of a dwelling can be modified with *puram,* such as a "rear door" *(purakkatavu).* The *puram* genre of classical Tamil poetry comprises elegies, panegyrics, invectives, and poems about wars. In architecture, the paired aesthetic principles of *akam* and *puram* inform monumental construction. The spatial interior of the Hindu temple, the shrines and *maṇṭapams* within its walls, are categorized as feminine and interior in contrast to masculine and exterior parts such as the *kōpuram* (tower above the main entryways).

The architectural boundaries between dwellings and their various exteriors were varied. The visual accessibility of dwellings was often limited. For example, until the mid-twentieth century, when flats and bungalow-style houses became common as middle-class residences, windows tended to be small and few in number. The walls surrounding house compounds were obvious examples of these boundaries, also. Such walls often featured details such as small recesses in which a deity figure, usually Ganesha, was placed to invoke divine protection. Less benign boundaries were the shards of rock and glass embedded in walls to prevent people from climbing them.

Boundaries were created behaviorally as well as architecturally. People entering a home removed their footwear and placed it near the wall of the compound or at the threshold of the house. Transactions with outsiders—vegetable or fruit vendors, repair people, or drivers—were often conducted at the boundary between the house and its adjacent public passageway. *Kōlam*s were commonly used to mark the edges of domestic spaces. *Kōlams,* as shown in Figure 3.3, are geometric designs drawn on floors, walkways, or ground surfaces adjacent to gates and/or doorways. They are made by women, using rice flour or chalk. On festival days, colored powder might be used to make a type of *kōlam* called *rangoli. Kōlam*s are drawn in the early morning and again in the evening, after the areas near the thresholds have been swept and washed. Though many families felt that only female family members should draw the house's *kōlam*s, some women delegated the task of drawing the outermost *kōlam*s to maids. This preserved their feminine association but created gradations among domestic boundaries and linked those gradations to caste and caste differences.

The strategies informing the placement of *kōlam*s are indicative of the contrasts between interiority and exteriority that existed *within* domestic space. Interiors comprised kitchens, shrines, and—increasingly for the middle classes—bedrooms for individuals and married couples. Exteriors might include verandahs, balconies, or living rooms (Tamil, *kūṭam;* the English word "hall" is also used for the latter). They were located in front areas of the house; like compound walls, they mediated between the space of the home and the street. Verandahs and living rooms were sites for informal interactions between family members and outsiders, such as friends, coworkers, or salespeople. The growth of middle-class consumerism has seen the elaboration of these spaces. They have become showcases for consumption that are furnished with sofa sets, cushioned chairs, sideboards, and consoles for televisions, radios, and videocassette players. In some households, *pūja* rooms, previously located in sequestered interior regions of the house, have been moved to front areas, thus signaling the extension of consumer culture to ritual praxis. People have also begun to collect and display discarded kitchenware and ritual utensils, treating them as antiques.[15] It has long been common for families to discard durables periodically and re-outfit their households, for example, when a woman marries into a family. In the past, these discarded metal goods were melted down and recrafted into similar pieces; now they are remarketed as souvenirs or antiques to affluent Indians whose taste for crafts has grown, as well as to foreign collectors (Breckenridge 1986).

FIGURE 3.3 An Elaborate *Kōlam*, a Design Made of a Flour-And-Water Paste and Applied to the Floor Near a Threshold, 1988. Photograph By Author.

Furnishings and decorations of this sort confirmed the family's wealth, prestige, and transnational networks. A sofa set could be translated bluntly into rupees; it might offer evidence of a marital connection with a "good" family. In a more nuanced way, it conveyed cosmopolitan tastes and experiences, sometimes by exoticizing South Asia's past. Embossed plaques and figurines, decorated metal and ceramic ware, or a set of ceramic dishes and cups might be placed in a cupboard within easy view of visitors. They too were cosmopolitan artifacts, testifying to trips throughout India and abroad and to gifts from affluent relatives and friends. Similarly, they signaled commitment to negotiating social identity and class privilege through domestic consumption and display. A family might seek to transmute wealth into moral worth, for example, by investing large sums in its household shrines. The changing use of front rooms in middle-class homes was an index of the growing significance of consumption. Twenty years ago, it was not uncommon for middle-class families to keep a few folding chairs, a chest, and rolled-up bedding in the hall, with more elaborate furnishings in kitchens and *pūja* rooms. The front rooms, despite their lack of furniture, accommodated a wide range of functions, including food preparation, entertainment, studying, visiting, and sleeping. This situation existed in a minority of the homes I visited in 1987–1988, and even fewer in 1996. The functional elasticity of individual rooms has declined as consumption has become a more important avenue for status negotiation.[16]

Though interiors were the core spaces of family life, people considered exteriors (verandahs and halls, for example) important sites for domestic activity. One friend had recently moved from a second-floor flat without a balcony to one with a balcony. She had complained endlessly about the old flat. "No one [in the family] was content there; we were unhappy and tense. Without a balcony, it was like being in a prison." She pointed out that the new apartment was well ventilated because of the balcony; she herself enjoyed watching, and sometimes chatting with, people as they passed on the street, finding it a relaxing respite from her busy schedule as a teacher. She still regretted her new flat's lack of a verandah: "There is no place to meet people or to leave our chappals." I encountered such sentiments often. As more and more flat complexes replace bungalows and courtyard houses, especially in the older sections of the city, there are fewer noncommercial places along streets that invite people to pause for casual conversation.

Interiority and Its Spatial Practice

Though the term *akam* did not designate particular rooms within the house, there were certain parts of Brahman homes, notably spaces for worship and for cooking and eating, in which forms of social and spatial exclusion were more elaborately developed. These etiquettes derived from cultural understandings that were shared by most Tamil Hindus but used differently as groups sought to fashion social identities and boundaries of varying degrees of inclusion and exclusion. My visits to kitchens and *pūja* rooms introduced me to the Smārta etiquettes of inclusion/exclusion that both governed and were reproduced in these spaces. I learned that women's labor was a crucial feature in defining these boundaries. The constellation of cultural meanings of upper-caste femininity came into being in these spaces through women's action. Like the strategies of display and boundary making already discussed, these etiquettes relied on and produced intimate grammars of identity and difference. This was not just a matter of prescriptive discourses about identity; it entailed the ways that sensory experiences and aesthetic judgements worked to create, sustain, and blur differences of caste, class, and gender.

The innermost spaces of the house were those used for worship and cooking; they tended to be inaccessible to culturally construed outsiders. The latter could include unrelated persons or relatives. The spaces were made inaccessible by their distance from the main entry *(talaivācal)* and by the presence of barriers. In most households, kitchens were discrete rooms, recessed and often physically separated from other house areas by doors or curtains. Although the interiority of *pūja* rooms and kitchens was sometimes compounded by the use of sections of the kitchen—alcoves, cabinets, or wall sections—as spaces for worship, *pūja* rooms have become more accessible as they have become more significant sites for status production.

It was not only location that set kitchens and *pūja* rooms apart from other domestic spaces. Compared to the front rooms, which communicated directly with space outside the house and accommodated diverse functions, the spaces used for cooking and worship had limited uses and functionally specific furnishings.[17] In the pages that follow, I describe these spaces, their associated inventories and behaviors, and the cultural values with which they were imbued.

The Pūja Room

Domestic Ritual Practice. In most upper-caste households (Smārta and other), ritual activities were regular parts of family life. Domestic rituals included *pūja*s and life cycle ceremonies, known collectively as *samskāra*s.[18] Individuals, of course, varied in the attention that they paid to these undertakings. Performing certain domestic rituals was normally the duty of a household's eldest married couple, but in fact the roles could be taken on by others and were. But duty was not the only consideration; as Purnima's example illustrated, people also acted on their own desires in performing domestic ritual (cf. McGee 1992). There was also considerable room for improvisation in the enactment of ritual. Shortcuts, as well as personal embellishments, were not unusual.

Regardless of who actually performed rituals and how often, most homes contained a space that served exclusively as a shrine. It was described variously as *cūvami uḷ* (the god's room) or *pūcai uḷ* (*pūja* room), with the term *uḷ* highlighting the interiority and boundedness of that space. Other collective areas of the house might be adapted for ritual use on special occasions, such as life cycle ceremonies. The latter often included a Vedic-style *hōmam* (fire sacrifice) and rarely took place in the family's shrine.[19] Instead, a temporary altar was constructed on which a priest kindled a fire and, with Sanskrit recitations, poured clarified butter and other substances into the fire as sacrificial offerings.

Purnima's performance was of the type known generically as *pūja.* Rituals of this sort were performed regularly in all Hindu temples and in many Hindu homes, regardless of caste. Domestic versions of *pūja* were modeled loosely on temple ritual, the formats for which are prescribed in several Sanskritic manuals. It is the presence of the deity's image—a picture or a figure made of metal or stone—that distinguishes *pūja* from *samskāra*s. Chapter 4 contains a discussion of *samskāra*s; in this chapter I focus on *pūja* because of its role in defining domestic interiority, spatially and materially. *Pūja,* more than life cycle rituals, shaped domestic habitus because of its frequency, its material presence, and what I felt was its greater popularity and accessibility. *Pūja* could be performed without a priest, most rituals being learned from relatives or friends; instructional pamphlets, magazines, and audiotapes; and even movies.

Pūja was conceptualized as an interaction between persons and deities in their embodied forms. Through these actions, the worshiper showed deference, devotion, and attention to what she understood as the needs of the materially embodied deity. *Pūja* comprised a flexible series of self-contained acts of adoration directed to a deity's image. The acts that *pūja* included were described collectively in Sanskritic ritual manuals as *upacāram.* This term is usually glossed as hospitality and modeled on prescribed acts of deference toward royalty (Diehl 1956; Fuller 1992, 67). Sixteen or more separate acts could be included, all of which fell into four broad categories: prayer or *stōttiram* (the praise names of deity), food offerings or *naivēttiyam* (fruit, milk, or cooked dishes), and *prasadam* (redistributed food offerings). *Āratti,* performed by waving a lighted piece of camphor in front of the deity, closed the *pūja.* Song, dance, and instrumental music were sometimes included in elaborate versions.

I was told that the most perfect rituals were those done simply for the sake of worship. That, however, was difficult for many to do consistently, given the emotional trials and inexplicable tragedies of daily life. *Pūja,* therefore, was often done with some goal in mind—to fulfill a vow made to a deity, for relief from illness or financial insecurity, or with a desire for children or a better job. It might also be performed as a component of a ritual cycle, for example, as a weekly observance during the six-week period of fasting *(maṇṭalam)* that precedes some major pilgrimages.

Domestic Ritual Space. Many flats had been built with alcoves or small rooms designed as *pūja* spaces. One architect told me that it was not uncommon for buyers to request such accommodations from builders. In homes that lacked such spaces, kitchen shelves or closets might be used. The *pūja* room usually included some kind of concealing device that enabled people to control who saw or touched the collection. For example, *pūja* things might be kept in small cabinets that Smārtas called *maṇṭapam*s (the same word was used to describe the pillared halls in large temples). Before any ritual was performed (usually daily), a female family member drew a *kōlam* in the space in front of the *pūja* room. As noted earlier, *kōlam*s were also drawn at house thresholds and marked the boundaries between various kinds of interior and exterior spaces, with the shrine constituting the most interior space, the "home" within a home. The uses and meanings of *kōlam*s illustrated the ways in which domestic shrines could be thought of a "social spaces": *kōlam*s occupied certain kinds of spaces even as they defined those spaces (LeFebvre 1991, 77). *Kōlam* making was one portion of a series of ritualized action that sacralized space and created boundaries that defined domestic interiority. In the paragraphs that follow, I elaborate on the everyday practices of which *kōlam* making was a part.

Boundaries of ritual space were encoded socially in the categories by which legitimate users were identified. All family members could enter a household's *pūja* space, but few did so regularly, whether to perform or to participate. Among Smārtas, both men and women were entitled to perform *pūja,* though women's autonomy in ritual contexts was said to be more curtailed than men's. Both men and women cited the menstrual cycle as the specific reason for women's inherent unfitness to be ritual performers. They noted that women might take up *pūja* after menopause, but younger women's periodic avoidance of household shrines made continuity in performance impossible. Women also said that their housework and jobs limited their opportunities for engaging regularly in domestic rituals. Many women, however, negotiated around these limitations, for example, modifying ritual schedules or having their daughters substitute for them so that their menstrual cycles would not interfere. The reasons for making these efforts included the concrete benefits that women hoped to gain for themselves and others through ritual. Fertility, health, prosperity, and long life for their husband were most often sought. Over time, I came to understand that women derived great pleasure from these activities—emotional and aesthetic satisfaction, equanimity, the friendship of other women, and sometimes a reputation for piety. Given the range of interests that performers brought to ritual, as well as the negotiability of authority in this realm, women had scope for competing as adepts. Consequently, boundaries of ritual space were not reckoned according to gender, though gendered difference informed these social spaces and was expressed in them.

Boundaries were made and unmade in ritual, as well as in the preparation of these spaces for ritual use. The space-time of domestic ritual was also marked by women's bodies and their work. The regular preparations for *pūja* involved actions intended to remove potential sources of pollution from the area. Insofar as these pollutants (saliva, blood, sweat) were all products of life processes, the effect was to create a space-time defined by the absence of the mutability and decay associated with ordinary life. Bathing, the first step in preparing to perform *pūja,* thus signified more than the removal of dust, sweat, or other dirt. In order to retain the bodily condition that bathing brings about, clothing that was clean in the sense denoted by the term, *maṭi,* was donned after bathing.[20] To be categorized as *maṭi,* the clothing, in addition to ordinary washing *(tuvai),* must have remained untouched during the processes of its washing, drying, and storage. Persons who adhered to these norms often washed their own clothes and kept them folded and stored on bamboo rods suspended near the ceilings of houses. These garments were handled using special wooden sticks. On some occasions, the clothing was dipped in water immediately before dressing, which also satisfied the requirements of noncontact.

The material composition of a garment could also promote or detract from cleanliness. Some people only wore silk clothing when doing *pūja*s at home. Silk *(paṭṭu)* was the fabric of choice because most regarded it as impervious to contamination. Because of its intrinsic cleanliness, silk did not need to be washed between wearings to maintain its *maṭi* condition. Cotton and synthetics, on the other hand, were thought capable of transmitting contaminants between persons, and their *maṭi* condition was dependent on washing.

Maṭi, used with reference to ceremonial purity, implied that garments possessed a certain kind of impenetrability rather than an infusion of some "pure" substance. Though it referred to moral imperviousness, it could not be divorced from its mechanical or material aspects. Water erased from the cloth the accumulated residue of the body's presence and so nullified the material traces of decay. In more abstract terms, washing halted or reversed the moral trajectory of ordinary duration and substituted a positive, auspicious moral trajectory of ritual space and time.

Like the body, the space used for *pūja* was prepared by cleaning. Women did most of this work, which consisted of daily sweeping and washing.[21] This preparation graded into the initiation of the ritual. *Pūja* was opened by actions intended to create the heightened cleanliness of ritual purity *(paricuttam).* Typically this involved sprinkling the area and images with water in which cow dung had been soaked. Purification was also contingent on the utterance of *mantirams* (the Tamil version of the Sanskrit term that is usually transliterated as *mantra*), phrases that are viewed as harnessing divine power or *shakti* and are considered to have transformative, sacralizing powers. The images and the ritual space were then sprinkled with that water—an action that defined the beginning of ritual time and the boundaries of ritual space.

The final gesture that was both preparatory and initiatory was the illumination of oil lamps. This act welcomed the deity in the same way that lighting lamps in the home conveyed that the dwelling was inhabited and that those who entered would be treated hospitably, pointing to a common idiom of rituals of worship and domestic action. The particular types of lamps (see Figure 3.4) used for *pūja* were worshiped, on some occasions, as forms of the goddess Lakshmi, who safeguarded prosperity, health, and domestic harmony. In addition to being visual metaphors of femininity, such lamps were also the property of women. They were, along with kitchen goods, jewelry, and saris, requisite items of the trousseau provided by her family. In the context of *pūja,* the performer lit the lamps to begin the ritual, thereby taking a relationally feminine (and subordinate) status with respect to the deity. According to the model of hospitality, the performer was the welcoming host, and the deity was the honored and indulged guest.

The control of contact exemplified in preparations and access rules did not negate the tendency to use ritual as part of status production. *India Today,* a national biweekly, ran a feature article in 1991 entitled "Decking Up the Deities," which described several household shrines in New Delhi, emphasizing their ostentation and cost. It bears comment that such articles are staples in *India Today.* They seek out the elusive domain of Indian "tradition" with a cosmopolitan gaze that is both ironic and nostalgic. But the article included a vivid description of something that I had witnessed often. The extravagant furnishings, architectural detail, and decoration of the *pūja* rooms were contrasted with the modesty of the homes in which they were found, and glossy color pictures illustrated the article. Through these mass-mediated images, families invited the appraising glances of distant audiences. Domestic space was thereby projected as a form of public culture.

FIGURE 3.4 A Set of Oil Lamps *(viḷakku)* Displayed for *Navarāttiri*, 1996. Photograph By Author.

These mass-mediated and commodified displays had something in common with some long-standing uses of domestic space. In his research on the Radha-Krishna *bhajana*s that became popular in Chennai around the turn of the century, Singer learned that the earliest participants had hosted large gatherings on a regular basis in their homes.[22] Such forms persist. In the mid-1980s, I knew several families who sponsored devotionally oriented gatherings in their homes. One family, followers of an internationally known figure, Sathya Sai Baba, hosted a weekly *bhajan* group. Each session was opened by a short *pūja* that was held in the living room, using the household's ritual accoutrements. In another household, the *pūja* room was situated in the kitchen. The wife, a singing teacher, hosted a fortnightly *bhajan* honoring the god Krishna and his consort Radha. She moved some pictures, figures, and utensils into the front room and, with her students (mostly local housewives), sang devotional songs praising the deities and performed an elaborate *pūja*. In another house, an unmarried daughter had persuaded her family to allow her to host regular sessions in which she read from the Bhagavad Gita and commented on it.

I also knew people who did not belong to formal groups but invited neighbors and work associates to their homes to celebrate special occasions, like the completion of a private ritual cycle or the initiation of a pilgrimage. Visitors, who may or may not have been close friends or relatives, were invited to view the family shrines. This conflated the meritorious practice of *darshan*—the act of seeing and being seen by the deity—with the appraisal of household wealth. Indeed, it was the material transmutation of family piety that was on display.

Ritual and Value. The actions and social spaces of *pūja* conflated moral and material values. Ritual involved sensory engagement. It was the bodies of human devotees and of deities (as images) that engaged in and were affected by the material transactions of worship. This connectedness was spoken of in ways that signaled its physical-moral qualities and its multivalence, *oṭṭu,* which meant to stick or attach, could describe the attachment of sin *(pāvam)* to people, the attachment of friendship, and the contagion of disease. Similarly, *paṟṟu* could mean to attach (the way that rice might attach to a plate or cooking pot), to be devoted, or to be bound to another.[23] Bodies could become repositories of blessings or divine power (like Minakshi) or, like the offended Krishna, they could be material metonyms of danger. Hence cultural understandings about materials, their properties and propensities, were critical features of a ritual's efficacy.

The collections of objects found in shrines included deity or saint pictures (lithographs, drawings, photographs) and/or figures. Oil lamps, stone or metal utensils (such as tumblers, incense burners, spoons, trays), and photos of deceased relatives were also kept there, as were instructional pamphlets, audiotapes, and handwritten instructions.

The deity images and associated utensils were composed of silver, *pañcalōkam,* brass, stone, and occasionally other alloys. In general, costs varied with the integrity and purity of the metal. Culturally, these attributes were considered indicators of stability, that is, relative impermeability in transmitting the physio-moral qualities of the substances that they held. The most desirable (and most expensive) were those considered best able to withstand the contagion of "uncleanliness" *(acuttam).* Unalloyed silver was more expensive than other metals; it was also viewed as being more stable, thus desirable for *pūja. Pañcalōkam* could also satisfy the desires for purity because, depending on its source, it contained greater or lesser proportions of gold and silver. Pure gold, though appropriate in principle for deity images, was costly, and images of gold possessed elaborate requirements pertaining to the conduct of worship, to the quality and amount of offerings, and to the condition of worshipers. Images of brass and bronze were the most numerous in domestic collections. Many were inexpensive, ready-made figures that had been purchased in shops specializing in utensils for ritual and in local craft emporia geared to the tourist trade.

The choice of material took account of the fact that the needs and desires of deities were involved. People wanted to minimize the possibility of contagion and maximize beneficial and honorific transactions. Several attributes were critical, first, the luster or shine *(pirakācam).* Shine connoted cleanliness and monetary value, although it was understood also as a materialization of the worshiper's devotion and the deity's *shakti.* Objects were thought to absorb and to be transformed by the worshiper's attentions, in some cases becoming warmer and shinier. The verb *eri* "to set aflame" was sometimes used in descriptions of this sort of transformation. Purnima, for example, had inherited from her father a gold *cakkaram,* an important object in Śrī Vidya ritual. A small, usually flat metal tile, the *cakkaram* is made of gold or copper and is etched with complex geometric designs. The designs were aniconic images of the goddess, though their designs also condensed esoteric instructions, the interpretation of which changed as the initiate moved through successive stages of sacred knowledge. Purnima was very keen on having me take a color photograph of the *cakkaram.* She specified that it be taken after she had done *pūja.* Then, she explained, its power was greatest. When I presented her with the photo, she admired it and then invited me to hold the *cakkaram.* She wanted me to feel its weight *(kaṉam)* and its warmth *(cūṭu),* both of which, she maintained, had increased over the years in which she and her ancestors had kept it. That same day, Madhu, a mutual friend, told me that Purnima herself "shined" because of her dedication to Minakshi. This echoed an observation that I heard about other adepts. People felt that both the worshiper and the deity image expressed the blessings and power that accumulated in worship. The verb *eri* was used to describe how energy exchanges in worship infused the deities' images and human devotees with power. Such transformations were revealed in the lustrousness of their appearances. The Sanskrit term *tejas* was used to describe the glow that emanates from the face of such a devotee. Brahmans sometimes characterized this radiance *(kaḷai)* as distinctively Brahmanic.

Another attribute that affected the quality of interactions between humans, deities, and objects was described through electrical metaphors. Color combinations such as red and green or green and gold were often used when dressing the images because their opposed polarities were thought to be energizing. I often heard that copper was preferable for water-bearing vessels because it imparted beneficial minerals to the water and because it was a "conductor." The English term "conductor" was used in Tamil sentences in these contexts, as were the words "negative," "positive," and "current." People argued that the transmission of divine energy, or *shakti,* was facilitated by the use of copper. In contrast, iron was regarded as inappropriate for *pūja.* Affluent and orthoprax persons usually avoided using stainless steel for worship because of the amount of iron it contained. Those who did use it claimed it was a temporary compromise.

Substantializing Practices

Though it comprised formal acts that could be completed easily by rote, *pūja* was for many an emotionally intense and highly personalized transaction with a deity. It could be more like the ongoing drama of family life than an abstracted act of worship. Like Purnima, many people claimed an *iṣṭa tevyam:* a deity to whom they felt personally drawn and on whom they lavished special attention. Even though almost all the objects used, including the deity images, were mass-produced commodities, they were appropriated in ways that singularized them—through decoration and with narratives about their acquisition and use that emphasized the compatibility of a deity and her devotee. Some steps in *pūja* allowed for greater expression of these sensibilities, for example, Purnima's bathing and anointing of the images and her attention to Minakshi's particular tastes and needs. A worshiper's choice of food offering may also reflect such considerations. Some goddesses were thought to have a liking for mixed rice dishes—yogurt rice, lemon rice, and coconut rice—which were considered to have cooling effects on the deity's *shakti*-laden heat.

The devotee who furnished these treats acted more like an indulgent mother than a dependent child. This underscored, again, the implications of deities' embodiment. They were handled with the respect and honor due to the deities themselves. At the same time, as materialized bodies, they had needs—for food, clothing, and cleansing—and relied on substantive and sensory transactions with human worshipers to fulfill those needs.

The materials from which ritual objects were composed were matters of some importance and were subject to socially rendered distinctions regarding their moral qualities, their material value, and the suitability of the match between deity and worshiper. The composition, design, and weight of ritual objects were closely scrutinized by those who purchased, used, and received these objects. Moreover, the capabilities and tastes of devotees had to be balanced against the needs and desires of deities. When a *pūja* room was revealed to persons outside the family, it was value in this composite and substantialized sense that was displayed and put into play as a part of status production. Monetary value thus served as an indicator of moral and aesthetic value; wealth (and the types of class privilege it stemmed from and fostered) was thus naturalized by being related directly to qualities attached to substantive, sensory transactions.

Commensality

The effects of mixing substances were at once physical and moral, and they were not restricted to worship contexts. This reflected the ways that acts of worship were threaded in and dependent on other everyday actions. The concerns of domestic worship both depended on and mirrored those of everyday familial interactions, especially those of commensality.

Kitchens *(camaiyal a̱rai or camaiyal uḷ)* were equipped with small double- or single-burner gas ranges, electric grinders, water filters, and refrigerators. Most houses had running water, and kitchens usually had at least one tap, though people preferred to have two water taps. The tap away from cooking and food storage areas was for washing utensils and sometimes clothing. Water from the other tap was used for drinking and cooking. Metal, ceramic, glass, stone, and wooden vessels were used for storing various provisions and for cooking and serving food. Further, the space within the kitchen was organized to segregate different kinds of foodstuffs and utensils, and adherence to these categorical distinctions was essential for cleanliness *(cuttam)* as it was culturally constituted. Food offerings for *pūja* were prepared with attention to this cleanliness, as were meals and snacks.

The preferred materials for cooking and storage vessels varied with foodstuffs. This was explained in terms of the effects of certain metals on the stability and taste of foods, as well as in terms of the health and moral benefits (or dangers) of contact between some metals and foods. As in ritual contexts, metals were valued for their relative resistance to "mixing" *(kalappu)*. Containers of brass or more usually "eversilver" (the English term was used by Tamil speakers, and it had no common Tamil equivalent), a type of stainless steel, were used for rice, sugar, dals (dried legumes), and other dry substances. Eversilver has become increasingly popular in all parts of India during the past couple decades, replacing utensils of bronze and bell metal.[24] Its retail price was cheaper (cost per weight) and its lower production costs have made it readily available, both from shops and street vendors who often exchange new eversilver for old cloth (especially cloth with gold or silver threading). It was also durable and easy to clean, and it retained a luster, which people found aesthetically appealing. By contrast, glass and ceramic containers, which have been available for a much longer period, were far less desirable for serving or storing foods other than spice powders and *ūḻukāy* (fruits or vegetables soaked in oil and spices, and eaten as condiments).

Heavy stainless steel pots and, more recently, teflon-coated pans were the most common cooking vessels, though other materials—soapstone, tin, and bell metal—were preferred for some dishes. For example, bronze vessels were desirable for the preparation of the sweetened rice *(carkkaraippoṅkal)* eaten at the annual festival of *poṅkal*, and *racam* (a thin soup flavored with tamarind, lemon, or tomato) was thought to be tastier when prepared in vessels made of a tin-lead alloy called *īyamcempu*. Iron skillets were used for frying, though they were avoided for preparing milk- or water-based foods, particularly rice and some dishes ordinarily eaten with rice, such as *kuṭṭu* or *cāmpār* (both of which are dal and vegetable stews). Water was regarded as a more permeable medium than oil, and mixing iron and water-based preparations was disliked, both because of the taste *(raci)* and because the cleanliness of the food would be compromised. These concerns were paralleled by people's avoidance of iron utensils for ritual.

Eversilver plates and serving dishes were also common. Each member of a Smārta household usually had an eating plate made of eversilver.[25] The importance of individual plates grew out of the concern with the "unclean" *(acuttam)*, hence polluting, effects of saliva *(eccil)*; separate plates ensured that no one would come into contact with someone else's saliva or with food residues that might carry saliva. Saliva was considered a medium that transmitted substance between people and as such could cause potentially dangerous mixing of incompatible substances. The word *eccil* connotes pollution, and it was considered too crude to be used in conversation. This was not a matter of following an explicit rule but was instead tacit, a matter of habitus. One friend, a Smārta woman close to me in age who was quite critical of the social exclusivity of "Brahmanism," told me that even the thought of sipping water from a tumbler used by another person was revolting. She said that she knew that "there was no harm in it" but could not overcome her own repulsion, a reaction she considered involuntary and hence natural.

Some families augmented their everyday utensils with an additional set of silver *(veḷḷi)* that they used for festivals and life cycle rituals. Silver was considerably more expensive than eversilver, but Smārtas desired it for moral and aesthetic reasons. According to some, silver was more stable than eversilver, meaning that there was less propensity for foods served in silver vessels to absorb elements from their containers that could affect the eater adversely. For the same reasons, those who performed elaborate household rituals preferred silver accoutrements. Others used a different rationale to justify silver's value, contending that the quality of food served in silver utensils was enhanced by the minute particles of silver that the food absorbed through contact.

Few Brahman households were without utensils designated for serving children and guests. These might be eversilver tumblers and plates, but frequently they were plastic, glass, or ceramic ware. These kinds of utensils were introduced during the colonial period and were acquired by elite Indians who adopted Euro-Western styles of dress, eating, and so forth. Yet despite the availability of such commodities and their modern cachet, they have not become generally popular as eating or serving utensils among upper-caste elites. Plastic, glass, and ceramics remain problematic because of their greater capacity to absorb and then transmit substances, in comparison with eversilver or silver. Consequently, though many acquired and displayed these items, fewer used these utensils themselves. These concerns about use were incorporated into household etiquette and labor. Hospitality dictated that guests be served some kind of refreshment—coffee, tea, or some other beverage, and perhaps a snack. Deference and avoidance were combined in the use of trays to offer the foods, and in the reliance on servants (or lower status women of the household such as daughters-in-law) to collect the used cups and plates. Not surprisingly, as the home has become the site for status production, for example, by entertaining guests, the inventories of dining and serving ware made of glass, porcelain, and plastic have grown.

Concerns about cleanliness deriving from notions of the permeability of bodily boundaries informed the etiquette of storing, serving, and eating food. These cultural understandings were made tangible in the spatial organization of kitchens, and they were reiterated in everyday, mostly tacit practice. For most people, ideas about pollution were matters of bodily praxis rather than objectified concepts, and commensality was the arena in which it was worked out. This involved an acute awareness of the physical-moral boundaries of one's own body. People ate most things with their hands, and the most scrupulous (and orthoprax) avoided touching their mouths with their fingers when eating. This was commonly done by rolling the food into a compact ball and using the thumb to push it into the mouth. People also avoided touching utensils with their lips—pouring beverages from tumblers or bottles into their open mouths.

For all Tamils, regardless of caste, sect, or class, the presence of plain boiled rice defined a meal *(cappāṭu)* as opposed to a snack *(palakāram),* which might include foods like *toca* (savory crepes) or *iṭli* (steamed cakes) made with rice. People expected that courses in individual meals would be served and eaten in an order thought to be most conducive to taste, digestion, and health. Although the particular order varied among families, it generally involved consumption of rice with vegetable and lentil dishes, followed by more rice and *racam,* and (for anyone who could manage to eat more) a third portion of rice eaten with yogurt or buttermilk, sometimes accompanied by a spicy pickle. Such dishes were pretty much the norm for Tamil south India. Brahmans often noted that in addition to their vegetarian diets they preferred less spicy, cooling foods. One friend, Mani, asserted this and maintained that buttermilk was an essential part of Brahman meals because it was cooling. Some interpreted a vegetarian diet as one that excluded garlic and onions, though this was more common among Vaisnavite Brahmans.

Food was constitutive of persons morally and materially. In their decisions about what and when to eat and in their analyses of their own taste, people considered the compatibility between their bodily constitutions and the qualities of the food. When Brahmans distinguished themselves from non-Brahmans, they did not appeal to legalistic abstractions; rather, they understood their own social identity (and thus difference) in substantialized terms that centered on bodily experience. They were more concerned with demarcating us-ness and did so by appealing to spatial boundaries (the interiors of domestic space), bodily constitution and tastes, and styles of cultural knowledge and performance. Sudra-ness, which could encompass any non-Brahman group whose behavior fell outside what Brahmans considered "clean," was characterized by a non-vegetarian diet and the preference for hot (spicy) foods. Some styles of dress and cosmetic use, such the use of bright reds, could be deemed as representing "Sudra-taste." There were also subtle differences of dialect that were most developed in the vocabularies of worship and commensality.

For Smārtas, awareness of the effects of foods carried with it the expectation that women would be hyperattentive to these matters when preparing food. As cooks, women monitored their own actions as well as the actions of any others present, especially servants. They tried to avoid preparing meals prior to bathing. To prevent their own saliva from coming into contact with the food, they avoided tasting it while cooking, and some would not talk. Because most middle-class households had servants, the interiority of kitchens was less a matter of architecture than praxis. The boundary between domestic interior and public exterior was reinscribed in kitchens through interactions with servants and, with that, class and caste differences were spatialized. Servants and low-status female family members cleaned dirty dishes at the tap reserved for that purpose, but unless Brahman themselves, they were not generally allowed to handle foodstuffs prior to or during cooking.[26]

Boundary making of a slightly different order took place at meals. People expected to be served food by the cook from utensils that she alone had handled. This usually amounted to married adult women serving other family members. Men (husbands, fathers-in-law, sons) were served first along with any guests, followed by other females and children; women ate their own meals last. Serving order enacted hierarchical principles, with social superiority or moral precedence marked by being served first and decreasing status marked by subsequent servings, with the receipt of "leftovers" (contaminated leavings from another's portion) the marker of lowest status. Food prepared for a meal but not entirely consumed during that meal was considered "old" *(paḻacu).* Some things might be eaten at a later meal, but these leftovers were normally given to servants or beggars. Here, as in cooking, the practices that produced cleanliness and propriety—notably the servant (or low status female) cleaning used dishes and disposing of or consuming leftovers—enact and naturalize the relations of power that informed gender, class, and intrafamilial status.

Although the act of eating together marked the "us-ness" of a family, differences of status and power among family members and between family and servants were rendered both tangible and strategic. The stylistic range of these actions, and the many variations in serving order, quantity, and so forth, were the means by which these intimate hierarchies were practically constituted—manipulated, reworked, and undermined.

Kitchens As Engendered Spaces

Among Tamil Brahmans (as well as Tamils generally), there are dense associations between women and the domestic realm, particularly the kitchen. The array of objects with which Brahman kitchens were outfitted were often part of in-marrying women's marriage settlements.[27] It was incumbent on a woman's birth family to provide her with kitchen utensils, ritual accoutrements, and, sometimes, other appliances and furnishings for use in her husband's household. This was not only because women spent much of their time in the kitchen but because these were forms of property in which women retained substantial material interests subsequent to their marriages. These interests could be expressed in terms of ownership (and thus the right of alienation) but were more often phrased in terms of entitlement to use.

The most ubiquitous and semantically dense objects—oil lamps *(viḷakku)* and metal containers *(cempu, pāttiram, pāṉai)*—were associated with women who used them on a daily basis in utilitarian and ritualized contexts. The metaphoric associations among these durable objects, feminized divinity, and women were apparent in the array of women's domestic rituals that used such objects. The oil lamp, for example, was treated as a deity image (the goddess Lakshmi) in *tiruviḷakku pūja.* This common ritual was performed by married women to preserve the health and prosperity of their husbands and families, as well as by unmarried women seeking husbands. Among the daily duties prescribed for married women was lighting oil lamps; it signified ordinary hospitality as well as deference to the goddess Lakshmi.

The wealth of symbolic connections between women and domestic objects was fortified by Smārta notions of appropriate uses and users of these objects. Most of the work of food preparation and service fell to the women of the house, though this was a matter involving negotiation of space, authority, and power with female servants. Women not only did kitchen-based work but were defined by these actions, as were class- and caste-related differences among women. Bearing in mind the sorts of knowledge and action deployed in food preparation, women explained their activities as cooks as their primary moral responsibility. They also recognized that these actions were sources of moral power with which they were able to foster dependence on themselves. The decisions that they made about food combinations, cooking vessels and preparation techniques, the types of personal cleanliness that they observed, and the care with which they served meals and snacks were all thought to affect the health, well-being, and biomoral identities of their husbands, children, and other kin. By extension, this private etiquette was the raw material on which reputation was based, with women as its labor and its emblem.

The behaviors associated with cleaning and with food preparation were predicated on categorical distinctions that the Tamil term *pattu* encodes. Although the word objectified their categories to some extent, much of what it denoted was tacit, working knowledge maintained by women. Women used certain cues or associations as ways of classifying foods but never offered a conceptual framework when I spoke with them about *pattu* foods. Foods that were prepared by boiling or soaking in water were categorized as *pattu,* though many women also used the presence of salt as an index, meaning that *pattu* foods were those prepared with salt or eaten with salted foods. The term *pattu* is derived from *parru,* a verb with a range of meanings including "to adhere" and "to be devoted" (V. S. Rajam, personal communication). *Pattu* foods were superficially sticky, and the fact that they were prepared in water—regarded as an effective medium for transmitting substances between persons (Marriott 1976)—made them "sticky" in a biomoral sense. Because of the high degree of cleanliness required in handling them, they were potentially the most pure; by the same token, they were also the most permeable and thus were liable to gather contaminants. Awareness of *pattu*-based distinctions also dictated great care in storage. Raw or uncooked foodstuffs designated as *pattu* were stored in specially designated containers of brass or eversilver and were segregated spatially from that which was not *pattu.*

Pattu, as I understood it, referred to the permeability and catalytically induced instability of foods prepared in water. Plain boiled rice was the definitive *pattu* food, and dishes consumed with rice became *pattu* as a result of that contact. The sticky texture of boiled rice was both a representation of and a medium for the potentially harmful mixing of categorically distinct substances that can happen in the course of cooking, serving, and consuming food, as well as in the handling of leftovers and used vessels. Rice, however, was also synonymous with food in southern India; as an offering in *pūja,* it marked the most elaborate rituals. Because of its permeability, however, the most life-sustaining food was also the most dangerous. Avoiding these dangers was only possible by eating among like persons, those of one's own family and caste, which, in turn, heightened the family members' sense of belonging and identity. This was the source of some Brahmans' reluctance to eat food prepared outside their own home; yet it was an issue around which there was room for negotiation. As restaurant dining has become a more popular component of middle-class consumerism, networks of restaurants that advertise themselves as *caivam* and are owned by, and targeted to, Brahmans have expanded. These ranged from large establishments serving both snacks and meals to a sizeable number of private houses whose residents (sometimes with additional employees) prepare foods to be carried out or eaten on the premises.

Knowledge about cooking, eating, and worship was reiterated in microtechniques of bodily discipline, most emphatically among adult women. Though women were responsible for maintaining physical-moral cleanliness of the household through labor and through self-discipline and self-monitoring, they themselves could threaten these conditions. On the one hand, women whose bearing was modest, whose hair was neatly plaited, who were attired in silk, gold bangles, and wedding necklace *(tāli),* as well as ornamented with a *poṭṭu* (the dot applied between the eyebrows) and daubs of *kuṅkumam,* were "Lakshmi-like" *(laṭcumikaramāka).* As married women with living husbands, *cumaṅkali*s, they embodied auspiciousness *(maṅkalam)* and with their actions enhanced this quality. On the other hand, women's bodies could be transgressive because of menstruation. During their menstrual periods, Smārta women, like other orthoprax Hindu women, were expected to avoid the kitchen and thus did not engage in any work connected with preparing and serving food. They were also expected to avoid temples, including the family's shrine room. Brahmans referred to the contaminating qualities of menstruation with the term *tīṭṭu,* an expression that also described the temporary impurity associated with death and childbirth. Menstruating women were described euphemistically as being "away from the house" *(akattukkuttūram)* or "not in the house" *(akattil illai).* This categorical separation was reiterated pragmatically. Not only did women avoid cooking and serving food; in orthoprax households, they were prohibited from taking meals with the family and from receiving portions of foods prepared for the family. Separate meals were made for menstruating women, and their utensils were cleaned by servants. Some version of this also existed for postpartum women. When they explained this to me, women stressed their own weakness and contagion: Women's vulnerability made them more susceptible to germs, and they themselves were sources of harmful substances.

The forms of seclusion, however, differed among families and among individuals—from nuanced gestures, like putting a screen in front of the *pūja* space, to formal, elaborate measures such as those described above. This suggests that Raghavan's concerns, discussed earlier, are not dead, though I found that women's nominal adherence entailed creative negotiations and, like other strategies of substantialization, yielded a practical logic of caste and class. Menstrual "seclusion" could justify a restaurant meal. It might allow women to reduce the amount of household work—often by relying more heavily on servants or on other female members of the household. Servants' roles, in turn, substantialized the "uncleanliness" attributed to Sudras—they were the ones who buffered the contact between the women and their families by serving food and washing clothes—and this circular logic naturalized class and caste difference.

People also expected that others, regardless of caste or religion, would follow this etiquette when visiting. Friends discreetly pointed this out to me and asked that I adhere to it when I was in their homes. I asked one of my closer friends about this and she described it in English as a "precaution." If I were wearing cotton or polyester, the "germs" could be transmitted, especially if I sat on cloth-covered furniture or touched the clothing of another person. Conversely, most of my Brahman friends politely refused any refreshment other than coffee or milk when they visited me. Their concern about contagion was exacerbated by the unknowability of the practices and sensibilities of others—especially in a city in which people interacted with numerous anonymous others on a daily basis. One friend told me about her mother-in-law's insistence that she change into a clean sari after returning home from work because she may have come into contact with menstruating women unknowingly—by sitting on a bus seat previously occupied by a menstruating woman or touching the sari of one on a crowded bus or train.

Whether these boundaries were anachronistic was a matter of debate among Brahmans. For example, it was not unusual for speakers to embed the English term "hygiene" in Tamil sentences. This served to gloss some local practices and tastes—hygiene being invoked to justify avoidance of eating in and traversing public areas. Hygiene was also offered as a reason for retaining use of the banana leaf for serving meals, as justification for segregating different categories of food (specifically those designated as *pattu* from non-*pattu*), as a warrant for vegetarian diets, and as a reason for insisting on menstrual seclusion.

Significant too was the transcription of these styles of domestic habitus in a popular household manual and cookbook, *Camaittuppār* (English version, *Cook and See*), authored by a Smārta Brahman woman, S. Meenakshi Ammal (1976). The book was not geared only to Smārtas, though Smārta tastes were reflected in the recipes and in the ritual procedures it outlined (Appadurai 1988a, 14–17). The dishes preferred among Smārtas and their ritual calendar were the norms, with other communities and regions presented as variants. Many Smārta friends owned or used Ammal's book and considered it indispensable as a reference. I noticed that there were marked continuities between the objectified written form and the tacit, orally communicated knowledge about cooking. It objectified the middle-class Smārta commensal styles, though it did so for a transnational audience of Indian women. The author explained that this was necessary because of the present-day dispersal of families. In earlier generations, a woman learned to cook for the household under the tutelage of her mother-in-law. The book was a substitute, in effect objectifying knowledge that had previously been mediated in daily practice within joint families. Like many of the material and practical innovations discussed so far, the manual was self-consciously modern and cosmopolitan, though differentially so. It appropriated pieces of Euro-Western knowledge and resituated them within matrices of local knowledge and practice.

The effect of these discourses is one of finessing Euro-Western modernity by demonstrating that Indian practice is traditionally hygienic. At the same time, this sustains the exclusionary etiquettes of caste, class, and gender under the banner of modernity. Homes were sites for deploying these concepts, and women both used them and were interpellated by them. Indeed these concepts were means by which spatial and semantic boundaries of the domestic realm were fixed and domestic identities were substantialized.

Conclusion: Cultural Logics of Consumption

Substantialization

The domestic world was pragmatically centered on transactions intended to manage the permeable boundaries among persons, between persons and things, and between persons and deities. The principal arenas for this, housework and ritual, were located in the domestic interior and were constitutive of it. The practical logic at work was not peculiar to Smārtas; the centrality of ingestion and visualization resonated with broadly shared Hindu concerns. However, it was their applications in the production of Smārta "us-ness" that I find worthy of attention, as well as their interpenetrations with class ideologies and modern consumerism.

Khare (1976) has written definitively about the cultural construction of Hindu domesticity in northern India, showing the semiotic centrality of commensality in the making of Hindu persons. Appadurai subsequently drew on Khare's work to analyze the ways in which these interiors were reproduced in the daily life of Tamil Hindus—in their gastro-politics (1981) and in their uses of domestic space (1985). Appadurai distinguished the interiority of the Hindu home from "privacy" as it was understood in Euro-Western contexts (1985, 5). There the notion of privacy was based on the capability of persons to set themselves apart—legally, spatially, and emotionally—from the claims of others; privacy, in practice, was expressed in the privilege of having one's own room and legally and philosophically in the sense of moral primacy and autonomy accorded "individuality." The Hindu house offered a contrast in that it was collectively managed to meet the needs of a particular kind of grouping, with its definitive and innermost spaces dedicated to worship and cooking. These activities, in turn, have become significant elements of India's public culture as vernacular and regional cookbooks and restaurant cuisine have objectified and gentrified commensal practice and made it a site for the appropriation and expression of hybrid modernities and assertions of class privilege.

What Appadurai pinpointed were cultural technologies of substantialization—the practices that naturalized collective and personal identity. With this in mind, I have treated domestic space and practice as sites that generate systems of privilege and inequality. At the heart of the cultural practices that make interiors and generate difference is cleanliness: *cuttam.* Contact, spatial and social, were managed to preserve or create cleanliness. It was cleanliness that yielded the semiotic substrate and moral etiquette by which caste, class, and gender differences were reproduced, reworked, and resisted.

The expression *cuttam* referred to the kind of physical cleanliness that resulted from bathing *(kuḷi)* or from washing an object with water *(tuvai).* It connoted other qualities as well. Luster, brightness, beauty, and moral propriety could, in different ways, be causally related to cleanliness. Desires for cleanliness underlay a variety of strategies for controlling contact with persons and things deemed "other." These differed among families, though most people explained particular strategies as principles to which they, as Brahmans, adhered. They used the term *ācāram* to summarize these normative dimensions. *Ācāram* could be used interchangeably with terms translated as "ritual purity" (e.g., *maṭi* or *paricuttam*), though it had broader uses. As "right action" (consistent with *dharma*), it encompassed ordinary actions such as cleaning one's person, clothing, utensils, and home. It also glossed scrupulous attention to the manner in which food was prepared and served, both in ritual contexts and in everyday meals. As Smārtas explained, *ācāram* described morally and socially appropriate actions and attitudes; *ācāram* thereby marked persons socially as Brahman and sustained their reputations, most critically among other Brahmans. Appealing to this reasoning, some people insisted that the designation Sudra was not used with reference to caste *(jāti)* but described people whose habits were "unclean" *(acuttam),* a condition stemming from nonvegetarian diets. This was not simply a matter of behavior but reflected a propensity that I heard described as "Sudra taste." In this way, non-Brahmanness too was substantialized. Such naturalistic accounts of difference at times accompanied other markers of class distinction (education, occupation, income, property) but in other cases were independent.

Aesthetics As Everyday Practice

Discursive elaborations of cleanliness shared a practical logic that is best described as aesthetic. In the first place, it denoted sensory perception. Second, and more familiarly, aesthetic can also be understood as pertaining to the critical judgement and appreciation of beauty. Worship and cooking in Smārta households, as elsewhere, were matters of seeing, hearing, tasting, touching, and smelling. Underlying these actions were aesthetic meanings, emergent in the possibilities and effects of sensory engagement among persons and between persons and embodied deities.

Thus it was in terms of aesthetic practice that the interiority of domesticity and the sense of us-ness were negotiated. By the same token, this generated and transformed the cultural meanings of gender, caste, and class inequalities.

This aesthetic logic can be apprehended by returning to the connotations of beauty that attach to cleanliness. For Smārta Brahmans, beauty *(aḻaku)* designated a desirable physical-moral state—one of illustriousness, equanimity, bodily well-being, and in some instances, wealth. In ordinary usage, beauty referred to comeliness, though it is inseparable from the paired conditions of happiness and bodily well-being that the Tamil term *cukam* conveyed. Beauty might also be aligned with illustriousness and tokens of material wealth *(celvam)* such as jewelry and silk clothing, which contributed to a person or object's being judged "beautiful." Beauty relied on embellishment with materials that in some ways induced and in other ways augmented the physical attraction that a person exuded. Jewelry, cosmetic unguents, and silk clothing exemplified such materials. They did not merely improve or enhance one's appearance. Rather, because of the permeability exhibited by all substances to varying degrees, beautiful clothing and jewelry positively transformed and refined the wearer's own bodily substance. Conversely, transactions with categorically unclean substances could detract from this. Hence there were anxieties about buffering the domestic realm from the effects of interactions that family members might have outside the house; similarly, anxieties existed about how to manage interactions within the house with servants and with friends or relations who were not Brahman.

Beauty was thus an other-directed emanation, an energy beam. In this respect, it was like *darshan,* the meritorious visual transaction between deity and devotee,[28] or *tiruṣṭi,* the malevolent gaze. Beautiful persons and things shined *(pirakācam),* thereby touching the sense awareness of others. Most of the objects and conditions described as beautiful shared this quality of lustrousness—recall the desirability of lustrous surfaces in *pūja* and kitchen goods. *Cīr* referred to wealth and its lustrous emanation: the glimmer of gold or silver, the glistening facets of diamonds, or the glossiness of silk cloth; it referred also to women's wealth, the objects included in a dowry or trousseau. Similarly, the visually perceptible emanation of a purified, thermally balanced, and adorned person was gathered together in what some Smārtas called a Brahman look—*kaḷai*—manifest in a person's face and eyes.[29]

Beauty depended on everyday actions such as bathing, grooming, and eating, and as such it necessitated women's labor and the self-discipline and monitoring that surrounded it. The womanhood so invoked was modeled on Lakshmi, and female appreciation for this model was never far from the surface of daily life. One friend, a married Brahman woman, commented on the pleasure she experienced when she saw elderly *cumaṅkali*s. She referred specifically to the beauty of their faces, the clarity of their eyes, and the luminescence of their skin, as well as to their dress, jewelry, and comportment. Her own style of grooming, like that of most married Brahman women, incorporated a similar set of aesthetic diacritics—oiled, plaited hair, diamond earrings, gold bangles, a carefully tended marriage necklace, toe rings, a modestly tied sari. Such an appearance earned the compliment that a woman was "Lakshmi-like." With its imagery of tying and binding,[30] it also aestheticized the multiple and subtle relations of force and resistance (see also Reynolds 1982). Through the practices of being *cumaṅkali*, patriarchal relations of force and dependency, as well as systematic inequalities of caste and caste, were encountered, regenerated, and/or resisted. These relations of force could have concrete expression in everyday acts of physical and emotional violence, and in the threat of such action. More pervasive (and ambiguous) were restrictions on women's movements and everyday activities, such as menstrual restrictions, applied as often by other women as by men—in-laws, parents, siblings.

Substantialization drew on the existing sense of caste identity/difference and reconfigured it. It did not generate a systematic ritualized hierarchy that was generally applied or adhered to; rather, it produced a system of identity and difference that was manifested and sustained by domestic sentiments, habits, and orientations concerning consumption, personal cleansing and grooming, eating habits, clothing, speech styles, spatial organization, and ritual praxis. The dispositions and desires can be summed up as taste,[31] and they produced a moral etiquette[32] of domestic life. This etiquette comprised a grammar according to which caste, class, and gender distinctions were expressed, reproduced, and reconfigured. The persistence of this grammar must in some measure be linked to nationalist interventions in discourses on domesticity, domesticity being seized as a critical site for appropriating and resisting modernity. It continues to operate in cultural mediations of class privilege, particularly in arenas of consumption and status production. Women's agency was located in the moral etiquette that continuously reinscribed these contradictions through disciplinary practices. Women thereby sustained the boundaries of domestic habitus but confronted their own otherness with each iteration.

Notes

1. Milton Singer. 1955. "A Sacred Center in a Polluted World," page 5, folder 2, box 17, Robert Redfield–Ford Foundation Cultural Studies Papers, Department of Special Collections, Joseph Regenstein Library, University of Chicago.

2. These were statements made orally and later transcribed by Singer and deposited in the Robert Redfield–Ford Foundation Cultural Studies Papers, archived in the Department of Special Collections, Joseph Regenstein Library, University of Chicago.

3. On the basis of its etymology, Paul Courtright interpreted *patrivratādharma* as meaning "moral action *(dharma)* that is rooted in vows *(vrata)* undertaken for the protection and well-being of the husband or lord *(pati)*" (Courtright 1995, 186).

4. This occurs despite the obvious nondomesticity of some women leaders and activists within the RSS and allied organizations, such as Uma Bharati and Sadhvi Rithambhara (Sarkar 1995).

5. One of the most popular Tamil chief ministers of recent years, M. G. Ramachandran, relied on his popularity as a film star to gain political power. His film persona, which was deliberately crafted as his political identity, was a Robin Hood–type defender of women whose virtue or piety had been assaulted (Dickey 1993).

6. A Tamil instructional pamphlet (*Śrī Cantoṣimātā Pūjaiyum Kataiyum,* by Ji. E. Ramacantira Castirikal and Em. En. Raja, 1978) outlined the procedures, prayers, and songs that were part of the *pūja* associated with "Jai Santoshima."

7. Tuesdays and Fridays are dedicated to the goddess. Tuesday's Durga *pūjas* were scheduled during the *rākukālam* as a way of accentuating the devotee's need for the goddess's intervention, and hence amplifying the blessings that accrued from that ritual act.

8. Limes, like coconuts and gourds, are sacrificial offerings. Limes, moreover, have special and complex uses in the worship of volatile goddesses. Because their effects are considered cooling, they may be used in food offerings (as whole fruits, juice, or in other preparations) that are designed to soothe or appease the goddess, whose concentrated *shakti* is heating. Limes thus offered may be redistributed to devotees, who may consume the fruits for their healing or other beneficial effects. Limes can also be used in ritual to absorb and deflect the dangerous energy of *tiruṣṭi* (the malevolent or envious gaze), whether it emanates from malevolent spirits such as *pēy* or from other people. After being cut, those limes are discarded outside the living space of the afflicted person, usually at a crossroads. David Scott (1994, 212–213) described comparable uses and meanings of limes in the context of a Sri Lankan Buddhist healing ceremony.

9. An instructional pamphlet, *Tiruppaḷḷiyeḻucci Tiruvempāvai Tiruppāvai,* published by Giri Traders in Chennai, was in its third edition in 1987.

10. *Tiruviḷakku pūjaiyum tuḷasistōttaramum,* 3d ed., no. 31 in the Gita Series, published by Giri Trading Agency, Madras and Bombay, 1986. See also Cattiayanatan and Cami Aiyar (1978) and "Castiri" (1977).

11. The incidence of death and injury from kitchen fires among women has increased in recent years. This has been attributed to the stronger emphasis on dowry in marital negotiations among a larger portion of population. This in turn relates to the greater availability and desire for the consumer goods that dowries currently include. These "dowry deaths" occur when women either kill themselves or are murdered by affines, usually after a period, before and after marriage, of escalating harassment by in-laws for additional dowry goods or money.

I never learned whether Purnima's daughter had died in such circumstances, but I was aware that relations between Purnima's family and her former son-in-law were exceedingly strained.

12. The availability of such cassettes grew during the 1980s as part of the larger diversification and decentralization processes that were ongoing in India's music industry (Manuel 1993, 116–120).

13. Fuller (1992, 68) attributes a more encompassing significance to *āratti:* "In the final analysis, the camphor flame, as the culmination of worship, stands synecdochically for the entire ritual."

14. A term used by Brahmans to refer to Sanskritic goddesses.

15. To my knowledge, Carol Breckenridge (1986) is the only scholar to have analyzed this phenomenon in Tamil Nadu. Studies analyzing elite consumption of handicrafts elsewhere in India have been published by Greenough (1995), Nag (1991), and Tarlo (1996).

16. See work by Ifeka (1987) and Parmar (1987) for comparative materials dealing with other parts of India.

17. Between 1985 (the year of my first visit to India) and 1996 (my most recent visit), I noticed that, with the explosion of flats and the types of room arrangements they offered, more people had specially appointed bedrooms. In 1985, it was not uncommon for people to sleep in front rooms or verandahs, rolling out mats and bedding as needed and putting those things away during the day.

18. *Samskāras* are defined as acts undertaken for purification during an individual's lifetime. About twenty-one *samskāras* are observed, and they are clustered into groups celebrated at birth, puberty, marriage, pregnancy, and death. The principal Sanskritic references for these practices are found in the Grihya Sutras (Das 1977, 17; Pandey 1969). The expression *samskāra* is a multivocal Sanskrit term. Besides denoting Brahmanic life cycle rituals, it can also mean "purification," "refinement," or "recollection." It is sometimes glossed as Sanskritic "high culture" (Ramanujan 1978, 139).

19. The formal differences between *pūja* and *hōmam* have historical referents, though they do not have discrete origin points. The sacrificial fire is the form of worship described in the Vēdas, a collection of hymns recorded sometime around 1000 B.C.E. after having been transmitted orally for several centuries (Thapar 1966). Vedic praxis, which is focused on the self-consuming sacrificial fire rather than on deity images, is regarded by many Hindus as the earliest and most orthoprax style of worship. *Pūja* consisted of adoration through praise, offerings, and the redistribution of offerings among participants (Diehl 1956). It appeared during the Puranic period (ca. 300–700 C.E.) and was contemporaneous with the rise of temple building on the Indian subcontinent.

20. The same expression, *maṭi* (which used as a verb can mean "to fold" or "to be folded"), described the lap made when a person sat or squatted; in some instances it referred to a woman's abdomen, the section of the body that "folded" when she sat. Finally, *maṭi* was also used to gloss the pouch made by gathering a portion of the sari and tucking it into a waistband. The semantic range of this term is discussed further in Chapter 4.

21. The preparation of ritual space also involved collecting the remnants of prior performances—flower petals, incense sticks, ash, and so forth. These things

were discarded outside the house, and some people specified that they should be dropped in a well or in the ocean. In practice, people who had wells sometimes cast the remnants of past *pūja*s there, though more often the debris was left behind their houses in a place away from other garbage, which was ordinarily burned. People preferred allowing things that had been transvalued by having been offered to the deity to rot or disperse.

22. Milton Singer, "Bhajan Interviews" and "R-K Bhajans," box 34, Milton Singer Papers, Department of Special Collections, Joseph Regenstein Library, University of Chicago.

23. Sumathi Ramaswamy (1997, 4–9) discussed its semantic range in her analysis of the passionate devotion to language, *tamiḻppaṟṟu,* that has infused Tamil cultural nationalism.

24. This alloy was described by Breckenridge (1986) as "high tin bronze."

25. This was common in most affluent Hindu households.

26. These boundaries could be marked architecturally. Homes commissioned by affluent families sometimes included multiple taps, arranged so that some were more accessible for servants and distant from those used by family members.

27. The term *stridhana* is used in Sanskritic sources on law to denote women's property such as this. The Tamil expression *cītaṉam* is also used to refer to marital prestations. Other trousseau items included vessels for preparing, serving, and eating food, jewelry, saris, and ritual accoutrements.

28. Some people described *darshan* in terms of the beauty of the deity's image, emphasizing its attractive force and meritorious effects.

29. Simmel's writings on the sociological significance of adornment capture the same dynamic of self-other implicit in Tamil Brahmans' notions of beauty. He observed that "the aesthetic phenomenon of adornment indicates a point within sociological interaction—the arena of man's being-for-himself and being-for-the-other—where these two opposite directions are mutually dependent as ends and means" (Wolff 1964, 339).

30. Another term to refer to *cumaṅkali* was *kaṭṭukkaḻutti,* a woman "tied" *(kaṭṭu)* to her husband through marriage.

31. The verb *raci* glosses the acts of relishing or enjoying foods or artistic performances. *Racam,* a noun, refers to the emotional response that, according to Sanskritic philosophical writings on aesthetic forms, is generated by artistic performances or visual arts. (The same word glosses fruit juices as well as a commonly eaten soup.)

32. I am indebted to my late friend and colleague, Thomas Zwicker, for bringing the expression "moral etiquette" into the discourse on caste boundaries. Zwicker (1984), following Sabini and Silver (1982), defined moral etiquette as "morally coercive logics of interaction and of relation to others." Though Zwicker's concern was with the reproduction of hierarchical inter*jāti* relations, the notion of etiquette, connoting a pervasive and in some respects tacit system of practice, can and should be extended to the consideration of the issues of difference and sameness that arise in intra*jāti* relations.

PART THREE

The World in the Home

4

The Ritualization of Womanhood

> A woman's first guru is her husband. . . . Women are never given the full power to make decisions in the house. The primary tasks are done by the husband with the wife's assistance. Even if a *pūja* is done with all the formalities, there will be no benefit from it if the husband does not approve. The relation of husband and wife is like that among the *varṇas*. The Brahmans perform, the Kshatriyas assemble the necessary items and ensure that the ritual can proceed. Vaisya merchants provide the necessities and Sudras produce those things. Below them are the laborers who support all of the others. All those below the Brahmans are *karmayogis*—their *dharma* is in providing all that the Brahmans need. (Field notes, August 31, 1987)

I was told this by Janaki, a Smārta woman in her fifties. She was married and lived in an extended household consisting of her husband, an adult (unmarried) son, a young foster son, her widowed mother-in-law, and a divorced sister-in-law. Her family was, as far as I could tell, quite well-off and possessed rural landholdings. Her husband and son were successful chartered accountants.

I had come to know Janaki, as I had come to know quite a few women, through the informal networks of ritual activity and information in which many urban women participated. Janaki's comment about the relationship between husband and wife was made in response to a question that I had asked about her role in the family's daily *pūja*. She firmly placed these activities within the boundaries of domestic space and relations. She had begun by outlining the *pūja*s that her husband's parents' families had done in the past, emphasizing that continuity was a crucial element in a ritual's effectiveness. Once a *pūja* cycle is begun, she observed, it should be performed regularly; otherwise, the deity will be displeased and some harm may come to the household. She asserted that this need for continuity made women important members of the family, for they were the ones who were emotionally attached to the *pūja* and to the family. They would guarantee that the ritual cycle would remain unbroken.

In her account of the household's organization and the relations among members, she repeatedly invoked their Brahmanness, emphasizing family members' adherence to what she understood as shastrically grounded moral, aesthetic, and behavioral codes. She noted that her mother-in-law's asceticism was congruent with shastric prescriptions for widowhood. She fasted regularly and performed rituals of atonement, wore only unbleached cotton saris, and shaved her head. Shastric directives were also realized in her husband's performance of daily rituals (assisted by Janaki and their son) associated with the Brahman householder, the second of the textually inscribed life stages for "twice-born" males. Janaki described the foster son as the child of a "poor Brahman family." The boy was expected to assist with housework and in return was fed, housed, and educated in ways consistent with shastric norms. Janaki saw these duties as derived from her family's Brahman identity and the performance of them as a public reiteration of it. Defining and caring for the "deserving poor" consolidated the Brahman community across class lines. Only the divorced sister-in-law interrupted Janaki's harmonious construct of family and community. In describing her sister-in-law to me, Janaki focused on her rejection of *cumaṅkali*hood (i.e., her divorce) and her avoidance of household duties, which she ascribed to mental illness.

With those observations—in which her household was reckoned as both instantiation and boundary marker of an idealized Brahman household—she girded her own authority to speak and act. At the same time, she described the contradictions of being a Brahman woman. As a Brahman, she occupied a position of privilege within the moral landscape of *varṇa;* as a woman she was subordinated and likened to the other *varṇa*s as a *karmayogi.* She, like other Brahmans, men and women, attributed women's subordination to the polluting effects of menstruation and childbirth. With one motion, she both established and disavowed her authority to speak.

In the months that followed our first meeting, I read through my notes often and never failed to find her recapitulation of the Laws of Manu[1] disturbing. I had come to admire her capable manner and her intelligence, and I was warmed by the hospitality that she always showed me. My unspoken wish, however, was that she would refuse to buy into this world of orderly inequality, and I combed my notes for some hint that this might be so. I found no trace of subversion, however, and no evidence that her compliance to the coextensive moral and material orders of *varṇa* shielded a "hidden transcript" of resistance (Scott 1990). For her, this was a terrain inhabited and sustained by different categories of beings *(jāti),* each of which possessed characteristic desires, abilities, and physico-moral substances. More to the point, she evidently consented to occupying one of these slots.

The system that she outlined, with its distinct, bounded, and hierarchically organized categories, corresponded to the image of Hindu South Asia found in Dumont's elegant work *Homo Hierarchicus* (1970). The consistency between her words and Dumont's synthesis point to the implicit but unmarked positionality in *his* argument—the textually inscribed stance of the Brahman male. With this observation, I echo some of the well-known criticisms of Dumont's work. Khare (1984), Mencher (1974), and O'Hanlon (1986), for example, identify internal critiques of the principle and practice of hierarchy in the worldviews of Dalits, Muslims, and laborers (see also Bailey 1957; Berreman 1967; Beteille 1965; and Eisenstadt et al. 1984). Inden (1990), taking aim at Orientalism in South Asian studies, faults Dumont's favoring of "holism" over "history" and the essentialism that results.[2]

Taking a cue from those criticisms, I take Janaki's words as traces of hegemony, as artifacts of the relations through which power is constituted and deployed. Hegemonic power operates in a dispersed way, affecting both the formation of personal identities and the organization of social institutions. Ritual practices have been characterized as products of and vehicles for hegemonic power, as well as sites for resistance to hegemony (Asad 1993; Austin-Broos 1997; Bell 1992, 69–93; Boddy 1989; Comaroff 1985; Kelly and Kaplan 1990). With this in mind, I offer in this chapter a close reading of the processes that Brahman rites of passage entailed, using the rubric of ritualization.

Catherine Bell (1992) provided a helpful review and programmatic description of ritualization as an analytic category. She argued that acts glossed as rituals differed in degree from non-ritually-marked action, but not in kind. Like other practices, ritual acts were situational and strategic. They fostered participants' misrecognition of some ritual goals, and they reproduced and reconfigured visions of sociomoral order, termed "redemptive hegemonies" by Bell (1992, 81). Ritualization described the strategic employment of formality, fixity, and repetition in action. Bell contended that these were the mechanisms that warranted analytic attention because their socially and culturally situated uses produced acting subjects, structured and structuring contexts of action, and relations of power, as well as locally understood oppositions between ritual and nonritual action. Following the arguments made by Bourdieu (1977, 1990) and Comaroff (1985), Bell noted that the "strategies of ritualization [were] particularly rooted in the body, specifically, the interaction of the social body within a symbolically constituted spatial and temporal environment" (Bell 1992, 93; see also Lewis 1986; Munn 1986; Schieffelin 1985).

Bell's programmatic contribution to ritual studies is important because of her attention to the embodiment of power relations and to the questions of agency and subjectivity that such processes imply. Despite recognizing the salience of these questions, however, her analysis does not develop means for investigating human agentive capacities or consciousness in ritualized contexts. These have become central questions in many recent works in the anthropology of ritual (and performance, more generally), but Turner's early contributions are worth mentioning. In a passage from his essay "Betwixt and Between," he provided an important entry point for current arguments about ritual and hegemony:

> Liminality breaks the cake of custom and enfranchises speculation. . . . The communication of sacra both teaches the neophytes how to think with some degree of abstraction about their cultural milieu and gives them ultimate standards of reference. At the same time, it is believed to change their nature, transform them from one kind of human being into another . . . for a variable while [during the liminal period] there is an uncommitted man, an individual rather than a social persona, in a sacred community of individuals. (Turner 1967, 106, 108)

Turner's own exploration of "enfranchised speculation" led to an interest in the critical (and even revolutionary) capacities of *communitas.* Taking the ideas of enfranchised speculation and the uncommitted man—and *woman*—seriously opens up a space for probing the indeterminacy of what often appears to be the normalizing practices of ritual. Applying these insights to Hindu practice, Ramanujan (1973, 32–35) suggested that "counter-structural" communities, such as *bhakta*s, might be among the social outcomes of these experiences of ambiguity. This argument has merit, but it misses the social ambiguity of counter-structural forms. *Bhakti,* for example, has been used oppositionally as well as hegemonically.

In this chapter, I am interested in pursuing this line of argument from the marginal positionality of the female subject in the contexts of Hindu orthopraxy (rather than its counter-structural alternatives), which, I argue, has contradictions and indeterminacies at its heart. I show that in ritual the moment of inscribing gender and sexuality is also the moment of being outside those categories of identity—of contemplating oneself as a gendered and sexed being. For female participants, this entailed engaging with hegemonic representations of womanhood *(peṇmai),* figured often as idealized types of women and/or goddesses. Most prominently it was the figure of the *cumaṅkali*—the chaste married woman who honors her husband as her first lord and is invoked as a cultural ideal of auspiciousness. In this chapter and the next, I explore women's encounters with these normative images of femininity, considering the prescriptive and practical boundaries of womanhood that were enacted in women's ritually mediated relations with other women and with men, and how these actions produce subjects who embody social relations of power but recognize and at times question those relations.

Ritual Time

How is womanhood ritually fashioned? And in what sense are ritual processes dependent on women's actions and on the imagery of femininity? Ritual is a means of making worlds and establishing subjective orientations to and in those worlds. These intentional worlds are constructed, interpreted, and ruptured through practice. At the same time, it is only in terms mediated by intentional worlds that doers and knowers—whether conceived as agents, persons, subjects, or individuals—are delimited and defined, and agency circumscribed. Rituals, I would argue, are major sites for the formation of intentional worlds insofar as they mark and make bodies and the space-time infrastructures of human action.

The threads among ritual practice, femininity, and temporality are complex, and they reveal critical features of ritual's semiotic capacities and hegemonic functions. Generally speaking, Hindu rituals are conceived as discrete phases within more extensive cycles. They mark critical calendric and life cycle transitions. Ritual practices and utterances also construct the durational matrix in which ritual itself is located—representing duration in terms of a gendered landscapes of the macrocosm and of the body.[3] In so doing, ritual practice constructs an intentional world in which time, space, and the gendered body are constituted as categories of perception, cognition, and experience. Canonical Hindu ritual constitutes womanhood as a marker of sexuality and sexual difference, as well as an index of qualitative and quantitative distinctions among durational categories.[4] In the next sections I review Hindu notions of duration and draw on ethnographic observations and secondary literature to identify major temporal cycles, qualitative emphases, and gender associations.

Cycles

Hinduism's syncretism and heterogeneity notwithstanding, there are broadly agreed-upon principles pertaining to the cosmological frames of individual action (Fuller 1992). Individual lives are thought of as emerging against a grandly proportioned moral and cosmological backdrop. According to the theories developed in Puranic literature (a body of Hindu mythology and historical narrative compiled between 300 and 700 C.E.), duration is conceived cyclically, as well as linearly. Maximally, duration comprises recurrent sets of four discrete, named ages *(yūkam)*. Each of the four ages is many thousands of years in duration, and each successive age is thought to be more decadent morally than its predecessor. According to this scheme, humankind is presently enmeshed in the fourth and most depraved age—*kaliyūkam*. However, the termination of this period will serve as the initiation of the next cycle of four ages, beginning with the golden era of truth, *satyūkam*.

Within these macro-ages are repetitive cycles. The Tamil calendar records solar days *(nāḷ)*, solar and lunar months *(mātam)*, and years of twelve or thirteen lunar months *(varuṣam)*. These compact cycles provide space-time maps of everyday life. They are represented synoptically in Gregorian-style calendars and in the special almanacs *(pañcaṅkam)* used for scheduling rituals and casting astrological charts.[5] Almanacs are redrawn annually, and each year has a Tamil name that recurs cyclically. Years are calculated with respect to both lunar and solar cycles; years are normally divided into twelve (but occasionally thirteen) months whose durations vary from twenty-eight to thirty-two solar days.[6]

Each leaf of the *pañcaṅkam* is a visual record of a Tamil month as it is described by variety of temporal indices. The primary indices are *naṭcattirams* (a series of 27 stars and constellations that recur along the moon's monthly path), *titis* (lunar phases, numbering from 28 to 32 per month), *karanam* (half a *titi*), *yōkam* (period when combined motions of the sun and moon are increased at identical rates), *vāram* (the week of 7 solar days). Each of these pages is like a page of an orchestral score. Just as the rhythmic patterns of sound and silence produced by individual instruments are usually recorded on horizontal lines, read from left to right and beginning at the top of the page, the *pañcaṅkam* leaf comprises vertical columns for each of the indices noted above. The columns are crosscut by rows marking the succession of solar days *(nāḷ)* during the month.

Kinds of Time

Imagine a straight vertical line crosscutting the horizontal instrument lines on a musical score. That harmonic moment, a distinctive pattern made by the different sounds of each instrument, is like the unique arrangement in space, of celestial bodies, that defines a single instant of time as described in the *pañcaṅkam*. The effects of celestial bodies on human activity and cosmological order are conceived as qualitative, that is, they produce different *kinds* of time—good or bad, auspicious or inauspicious. The qualities of duration, derived from the arrangements of macrocosm, are also represented as the products of their association with certain deities and physical elements. These properties of time influence the scheduling of actions, especially ritual. For example, a given solar day, Tuesday *(cevvāykiḻamai)* is associated with a celestial body (the planet Mars, *cevvāy*), an element (copper), and a deity (usually the form of the goddess known as Durga, though Murukan is sometimes associated with this day). Friday (*veḷḷnikiḻamai*) is associated with the moon, with silver *(veḷḷi),* and with the goddess Lakshmi.

Each of the seven days is divided into segments of about one and a half hours. each called *lakkaṉam.* Due to the changing alignments of celestial bodies, each *lakkaęñam* is auspicious or inauspicious. For instance, the period just before dawn has generally auspicious connotations, but there are inauspicious periods of each day, *rākukālam,* that recur at different points. These are considered bad times to begin projects or to undertake risky ventures, though some rituals, particularly those to propitiate volatile goddesses, are specifically scheduled to coincide with the *rākukālam* of certain days. Shrines dedicated to Durga, for example, are filled on Tuesday afternoons during that day's *rākukālam* by women who have made vows to that goddess in seeking a long life for their husbands. Similarly, Friday's *rākukālam* draws women to temples to propitiate Lakshmi.

Just as days consist of alternating good and bad periods, each month and each year is divided into auspicious and inauspicious periods, times of positive or negative moral trajectories. The time of the waning moon is a period of inauspiciousness, whereas the waxing moon signals auspiciousness. The "bright half" of the year comprises the six-month period between January and June, when the sun travels northward in relation to the equator; the "dark half" of the year marks the sun's six-month southward course.

Representations of femininity and women's practices figure prominently as temporal markers because of the association of auspiciousness with the *cumaṅkali.* Although these patterns are discussed in detail later in the chapter, a few observations are in order here. The shift from the dark cluster of solar months to the bright cluster at the beginning of the Tamil month of *Tai* (mid-January—mid-February) is marked by ritual attentions to *cumaṅkali* status. The goddess in her wifely form (Lakshmi) is worshiped and living *cumaṅkali*s are honored. The birth of a named year at *Cittirai* (mid-April—mid-May) is similarly marked.

The commencement of the dark half of the solar year comes with *Āṭi* (mid-July–mid-August). The intrinsically inauspicious elements of this transition are managed, again, by invoking feminine auspiciousness but also by ritual management of the creative energy (*shakti*) associated with sexuality. Celibacy causes such energy to accumulate, and certain deities are distinguished by this sort of power, notably goddesses without male consorts and gods described as bachelors or renunciants. At these times, some devout Hindus observe ritual prohibitions on sexual intercourse, and fasting and other bodily disciplines are stressed in women's rituals.

The conclusion of the dark part of the solar cycle comes with the termination of *Mārkaḻi* (mid-December–mid-January). Again, this transition is managed by women through ritual cycles involving prayer, fasting, and sexual restraint. In anticipation of the beginning of the year's bright half, however, the paradigmatic images of femininity that are invoked imply nascent rather than restrained sexuality. The aim of rituals performed by women during this month stresses the auspicious possibilities of femininity, these aligned with the year's bright half.

The auspicious possibilities located in femininity serve as a synecdoche for the moral trajectory of macrocosmic time. Women's auspiciousness, constructed and appropriated through calendric ritual, feeds back into the space-time macrocosm itself. Feminine auspiciousness ensures that time will be "good"—that action will yield positive results. The auspicious potentialities of femininity, and the auspiciousness of particular women, are enhanced by the ritual positioning of women at the critical macrocosmic transitions that calendars mark.

The Life Course Imagined

Samskāras

Among upper-caste Hindus, the culturally managed transitions of the life cycle were bracketed as the rites of purification or refinement known as *samskāras*.[7] Through the performance of *samskāras*, Smārtas (and other Hindus) articulated paradigmatic forms of personhood and created a world in which these paradigmatic figures were integral features. Priests, who were the only persons officially empowered to perform them, cited the *shastras* and the Vēdas as the foundational texts for these practices. Devout Smārtas described these rituals as "musts." Because performance could involve substantial financial outlay, however, their observance was often compressed or modified. The exegeses that nonspecialists and priests provided reiterated the notion that these acts were constitutive of persons and of the domestic sphere, defining each in terms of the other.

An elderly Smārta Brahman priest with whom I spoke extensively about *samskāras* described the relation between individual persons and the macro-orders of society and cosmos as that of ritualized debt or obligation *(muṟaimai)*. He put it this way:

> Once born, regardless of sex, each person has three sets of primary obligations to discharge. These duties are to the saints *[rishi]*, ancestors *[pitirkaḷ]*, and gods *[teyvam]*. Each person fulfills his obligations during each of the successive stages *[āśrama]* of his life. (Field notes, January 19, 1988)

Though he asserted that the condition of indebtedness was gender neutral, he specified that the fulfillment of obligations was achieved by Brahman men acting on behalf of all others. The practices of the *samskāras* were thus gendered and engendering.[8] He numbered the life cycle rituals at twenty-one (while indicating that some priests thought that the total was higher), and he clustered them into three sets, each of which corresponded to one of the major stages of the normative male life course. Each set of rituals fulfilled one of the three sets of obligations, and he explained them as follows.

Discharging the first debt, the debt to the saints, necessitated chanting the Vēdas. Initiation into the second stage of the idealized (male) life cycle entitled a man, as a *brahmācāri,* to learn the Vēdas through apprenticeship to a guru. Entry to this stage was marked by a rite known as *upanayaṉam,* the sacred thread investiture.[9] The second debt, the debt to the ancestors, was fulfilled by paternity and thus depended on marriage, conception, birth, and the rituals that marked those events. The status of householder, *grhastha,* fulfilled both the second and the third debt. The latter, the debt to the gods, was fulfilled by the householder's daily performance of the fire sacrifice. The fulfillment of this third debt also necessitated men's propitiation of deceased male ancestors on the yearly anniversary of their death. Women who died as *cumaṅkali*s were propitiated along with their husbands on these occasions.

The paradigmatic male life course had prescribed variants and was not limited to householder status. Between marriage and death, a man might enter successive life stages—*vanaprastha* and *saṉṉyasa*—in which detachment from family and caste was morally sanctioned. Though esteemed by orthodox Hindus, these life stages were not requisite for a morally coherent life.

The nature of the obligations and their fulfillment established the normative parameters of the Brahman male life course. These duties also established the male as the universalized and unmarked subject of the *samskāras* and of the other shastric rituals associated with *samskāras*. In the intentional world that was constituted through these rituals, actions undertaken by Brahman men fulfilled the moral obligations of all humankind. For example, the chanting of the Vēdas was restricted to men. These verses in their spoken form were described as giving life to the universe.

In terms of the dominant (i.e., textually encoded and authoritative) ideology of the *samskāras*, women were "muted" (Madan 1987; Ramanujan 1986).[10] In the context of ritual performance, women's bodies were present. Ritual syntax made it clear that men's action in ritual depended on the creative energy associated with womanhood. It was a man with a wife *(illāḷaṉ)* who was empowered to perform the most highly valued ritual acts.

This principle was represented iconically in the opening moments of the major life cycle rituals. The performer's wife was positioned as the conduit through which the sexualized, feminized energy of *shakti* was passed to her husband. As the seated husband faced the sacrificial fire, his wife stood behind him, resting a spear of *darbha* grass, which she held in her right hand, on his right shoulder. The priest whom I quoted above explained that the wife drew cosmic energy to her husband through the grass and that this power enabled the man to conduct the fire sacrifice that served as the ritual's core. As a metaphor she was like Parvati, the consort of the god Shiva; as a metonym she was an extension of creative energy of *shakti.* The embodiment and control of sexual difference, in terms generated from a male position of enunciation, was thus found in the imagery of the *samskāras* as well as among their goals (see also Smith 1992).

This construction of femininity in terms of sexualized energy was made additionally salient for Smārta Brahmans because of the place it held in past and present teachings of the Kanchipuram *maṭam.* Smārtas, though not a sect, expressed their collective identity in terms of a generalized adherence to the precepts of *advaitavēdanta* as they were propounded by the *maṭam,* and most Smārtas regarded the Shankaracharyas seated at Kanchipuram as their spiritual leaders. The current Shankaracharya and his predecessor were renowned as devotees of the goddess, and the *maṭam* controlled a large goddess temple through which it has sought to attract the participation of non-Brahmans (Mines and Gourishankar 1990). The Shankaracharyas have also authored songs, prayers, and a variety of ritual forms in honor of the goddess and have urged their followers to incorporate these elements into their own practice (Hancock 1995b). Throughout the past few decades, they have sought more publicity for goddess devotion. Their devotional attention to the goddess is matched by their endorsement of the values of *cumaṅkali*hood. The patriarchal values of these representations of femininity are clearer when viewed in conjunction with other positions the Shankaracharyas have espoused. They condemn family planning and birth control, and they have spoken out against women's property rights and have advocated ritual restrictions on widows.

Engendered Dilemmas

Samskāras were embedded in a highly variegated system of "shoulds" that allocated capacities for action appropriate for particular situations and for each kind of paradigmatic person who was envisioned in Sanskritic Hinduism. They mapped difference from the apical (though unmarked) position of the Brahman male. The system appeared, on the one hand, to have no "outside," that is, it generated an expandable map of physico-moral difference on which all forms of life and action could be located. On the other hand, it placed women ambiguously, as both inside and outside its classificatory reach.

The irony of this situation was apparent in Janaki's words as quoted at the beginning of this chapter. Womanhood was an essential part of a morally ordered world and the life cycle rituals that sustained it, but the canonical version of *samskāras* did not include practices that made or marked womanhood, independent of male intervention. Womanhood comprised different and unequally valued statuses. Most esteemed was the *cumaṅkali,* the wife who regarded her husband as her first lord. A woman became a *cumaṅkali* with marriage.[11] Prior to marriage, women were *kaṉṉi* (virgins), potential or nascent *cumaṅkali*s. Widows (*vitavai*) were *amaṅkali* "inauspicious women." The ritual boundaries of *cumaṅkali*hood—its initiation and conclusion—were inscribed on women's bodies and subjectivities in ceremonies in which the Brahman male was the focal figure.

Marriage, pregnancy, and childbirth, though central to women's lives, were treated within the canonical discourses on *samskāras* as transitions in the male life cycle. Though women were understood to be necessary to those transitions, they were not treated within textual accounts as the principal agents of transformation. This was conveyed to me explicitly by the priests with whom I spoke; it was also reiterated in the textual sources I consulted. As a *samskāra,* marriage transforms a man from a "student" to a "householder," a male identity that implies the presence of a wife. Women were declared to be *cumaṅkali*s when the bride was blessed following the *Sapta-padi* (rite of seven steps), the legally binding event during the ritual. The *samskāras* of pregnancy and childbirth culturally transformed a fetus into a human infant; priests asserted that they may please the mother, or in the case of childbirth, contain and eliminate the pollution *(tīṭṭu)* that she emitted. But those effects were not the primary goals of the rites. A woman only relinquished *cumaṅkali*hood with her husband's death, and ritualization of that transition was incorporated into the funerary observances for the man. By all accounts, this transition was one of euphemized violence directed on her body. At the conclusion of a man's funeral, his son (or another close male relative) was expected to remove the woman's marriage necklace, toe rings, and bangles. Her head was then shaved and she was given the unbleached cotton sari that would be her uniform thereafter. Most of the women and men I knew spoke disparagingly of this practice and eschewed it, the same people regarded widowhood as a less auspicious state than wifehood.

Thus, though so much hinges on *cumaṅkali*hood (for women and for men), its ritualization was more developed outside the contexts of *saṁskāras* in practices known collectively as *nōṉpus*.[12] *Nōṉpus* were ritual cycles that included bodily disciplines such as fasting and acts of worship. They were performed by women to obtain marital felicity and husbands' longevity, though some women performed them to attain more specific goals, such as a child's academic success. They were always described to me as parts of longer cycles with durations that could range from six weeks to several years. *Nōṉpus* used as charter myths Puranic stories about deities' life histories. The stories were allegories about the rewards of exemplary devotion; they also anchored the *nōṉpus* format. Its prescribed actions were often condensed recapitulations of the events that the narrative recounted, and the *nōṉpu*'s instrumental aims were mirrored by the story's outcome. Some *nōṉpus* were scheduled to coincide with the major transitions of the calendar—amplifying the auspicious qualities of certain times and mitigating the inauspiciousness of others.

Nōṉpus constituted *cumaṅkali*hood in an ongoing, quotidian sense. The stories that framed them were well-known, mediated by oral transmission and by popular devotional films and comic books. They were done without priests' interventions—instructions for their performance were shared by women, orally and in pamphlets and on audiocassettes. Their formats were adjusted by performers according to their own needs, desires, and convenience. Their schedules and styles differentiated them from *saṁskāras*; another difference was that *nōṉpus* were not caste specific. Most available evidence indicates that women of all caste and class strata knew about and performed *nōṉpus*, although details of form varied (Reynolds 1982). Indeed, *nōṉpus* spoke to a universalized image of Hindu womanhood characterized by patience, auspiciousness, and chastity. They reiterated the importance of the creative, femininized energy of *shakti*, and they defined womanhood in those terms.

As practiced by Brahmans, however, *nōṉpus* generated the positive value of the *cumaṅkali* through and against the negative value of the widow. *Nōṉpus*' instrumental aims were the husband's well-being and longevity; as a corollary, women, desiring auspicious deaths as *cumaṅkalis*, prayed that they would die before their husbands. Considered in this light, *nōṉpus* both defined and destabilized the images of womanhood that their performances conveyed.

Nōṉpus were popular among Smārta women, and there were continuities between the actions *nōṉpus* included and those performed outside ritually marked contexts. Women's commitment to their practice suggested to me that women were always aware of the precariousness of their identities as *cumaṅkali*s. *Nōṉpu*s framed *cumaṅkali*hood as an object of desire and were the means with which women reinscribed themselves as *cumaṅkali*s. Women's attention to *cumaṅkali*hood—its value and the dangers of its loss—were illustrated in what an elderly Smārta woman, Anandaveli, told me about her husband's illness and death. He had passed away shortly after she had organized the purchase and donation of a necklace made of gold coins to the Kamakshi temple in Kanchipuram:

> A: He [her husband] collapsed [in January 1986]. . . . he had suffered from high blood pressure and heart trouble. I visited him in the hospital; then I went to the Paramacharya[13] to seek his guidance. . . . He gave me some turmeric powder and told me to put it on my skin each day when I bathed.
>
> MARY: Why did he give the turmeric to you, when it was your husband who was ill?
>
> A: It's *cumaṅkali*s, only, who apply turmeric to their bodies, to their faces and their hands. Haven't you seen this? [I nodded, and she continued with the story] . . . [after] he recovered and was released from the hospital . . . I went again to Kanchipuram, bringing along jaggery, rice, turmeric, a *dhoti*,[14] and a sari to donate to Kamakshi. When I got there, Paramacharya told me to give these things to all those who were present. It filled me with joy to be able to do so. On the following Wednesday, March 13, he [her husband] died. That was Kamakshi *nōṉpu*s It could be said that the husband's dying on that day was a bad sign. . . . Paramacharya's presentation of the turmeric to me so soon before his [her husband's] death was also difficult to understand. . . . But I think that all that happened was Kamakshi's will to keep me as a *cumaṅkali* in order to present the necklace to her. (Field notes, October 9, 1987)

To be a *cumaṅkali*, potentially or in actuality, was to occupy a positively valued and totalizing subject position that persisted even after death. Despite this, the *cumaṅkali* was always casting backward glances at the widow. The death of Anandaveli's husband imposed widowhood on her; that moment was one of abjection (after Kristeva 1982). Her words betrayed her hesitation in acceding to this state of affairs. As a Brahman, she was bound to interpret her husband's death as the result of some "sin" *(pāvam)* that she had committed, either in her present life or in a past life, despite her unceasing efforts to embody *cumaṅkali*hood. She also knew that the prescribed life of a widow was one of asceticism, devoid of what she understood as beauty and auspiciousness. Not only were the conventional markers of *cumaṅkali*hood (e.g., jewelry, cosmetics) proscribed, widows were in principle prohibited from participating in any auspicious ritual events.

Anandaveli's hesitation was evident not merely in her words but in her gestures and appearance. She did not conform entirely to orthodox directives in her dress and behavior, though she did refrain from adorning herself in ways that signified auspiciousness. She did not wear jewelry or *kuṅkumam,* but neither did she shave her head or wear an unbleached cotton sari. Nor were her tactics unusual; I knew other widows who had worked out similar compromises.

Whatever resistance to widowhood I might have inferred from this, however, was carefully hedged by Anandaveli. The fact that she did not refuse widowhood outright was revealed when she told me that her husband's death caused her to feel "shame" *(veṭkam),* whereas her son's death was a source of "grief" *(tukkam).* In those comments I read a profound ambivalence about widowhood and about womanhood. She was repelled by cruelty toward widows, but she realized that the widow's inauspiciousness was the flip side of the *cumaṅkali*'s auspiciousness. Together, they defined womanhood. If she had resisted widowhood outright, she would also have repudiated her past with its ritually textured valuation of *cumaṅkali* identity. Such a repudiation seemed unlikely, given the enthusiastic detail with which she recalled the many *nōṉpu*s, some with performance cycles of five years, that she had observed as a younger woman.

It is possible to see the workings of hegemony in the ways that rituals of the life cycle naturalized gendered relations of power and authority, and re-created caste. There is, nevertheless, an unevenness in their hegemonic power stemming from a lack of resolution at the heart of ritual action itself. This unevenness may be uncovered by examining life cycle rituals from the perspective of female participants. The ritually mediated subjectivities of Brahman women were predicated on a series of entangled contradictions. Through *samskāra*s, they as Brahmans occupied the unmarked (albeit male) space of action, and they assumed authorship of the systems of difference generated from that position. Janaki's rehearsal of the principles of *varṇāśramadharma,* with its devaluation of female action, exemplified this. At the same time, however, womanhood was culturally crafted in the performance of *nōṉpu*s, ritualized acts that lay outside the canonical directives of the *samskāra*s but were no less compelling. Anandaveli personified this contradiction. She was caught in the untenable position of being asked to reaffirm the value of *cumaṅkali*hood with her own abjection, by consenting to be the boundary marker who reminded other women of the fragility of womanhood.

Negotiating Normativity

Like Anandaveli, Janaki was also quite reflective about Brahman *cumaṅkali*hood and wished to be seen by others as scrupulously adhering to those values. How I met her reveals something about those values and about how they were constituted in women's actions. Through a friend, I had heard about a women's *maṇṭali* (association or sodality) that sponsored and conducted elaborate *pūja*s at a small temple in Mylapore. My research assistant, Minakshi, was curious as well, especially because that temple had a shrine for Kamakshi, her own *iṣṭa teyvam.*[15] Upon arriving, we found a group of married women assembled at the Kamakshi shrine. Parvati, the woman leading their performance, was a Smārta Brahman, though the group included women of other castes. Most were from lower-middle-class households.

The women sang devotional songs as a Lingayat priest (a temple employee) performed *apiṣēkam* for the *mūrtti* (a figure of Kamakshi) housed in the shrine. Once this was finished, Parvati announced that a woman living nearby (Janaki) had invited all of them to her home. To fulfill a vow she had made, she had invited groups of *cumaṅkali*s to her house on several occasions and presented them with small bundles of turmeric roots. They described the event to me as *maṭimañcaḷ* and told me that the name denoted both the turmeric *(mañcaḷ)* and the way in which the gifts were received (*maṭi*).[16]

About twenty of us set out together. Our destination was a large two-story house whose occupants were obviously quite affluent as well as quite religious, if the many pictures of deities and saints hanging on the walls were any indication. The woman who had invited us, Janaki, had us sit in her front hall while she, with the assistance of a servant, assembled each woman's gift (known generically as *tāmpūlam*), which consisted of chunks of turmeric along with a few betel leaves and areca nuts *(veṟṟilpākku).* The actual presentation was made by Janaki. As she stood in the center of the room, the women one by one (beginning with the Parvati) took a seat on small bench and faced Janaki. Each woman held out the edge of her sari, and Janaki placed the gifts in it. Janaki then held out a small tray with *kuṅkumam,* and each woman took a pinch and daubed her forehead and the center part of her hair with it. Those women who were younger than Janaki prostrated themselves in front of her, although those like Parvati who were older did not. After giving *tāmpūlam* to all of the women, Janaki distributed sprigs of fragrant jasmine to everyone.

This ceremony was well-known among the women who participated in it. Most of the older women I knew had either attended or sponsored a similar event on more than one occasion. Several women described it similarly to me. The cycle was initiated by a *cumaṅkali* with a vow to distribute a *lakh* (100,000 pieces) of turmeric over some specified period of time. She herself made up and distributed the *tāmpūlam* packets, perhaps by taking them to a temple when women are expected to be there. Or she might invite women to her house for a series of ceremonial distributions, as Janaki did. The gifting is an act of deference to *cumaṅkali*s (and to *cumaṅkali*hood), a way of giving honor or respect *(mariyātai)* and thereby obtaining their blessings for general welfare or for some specific end.

Similar gestures and desires were incorporated into an event known as *cumaṅkali pirārttaṉai,* which can be a propitiation of women relatives who have died as *cumaṅkali*s, in which case it is performed in conjunction with the observance of the death anniversary *(sraddha)* of deceased male relatives. Some women also used the expression *cumaṅkali pirārttaṉai* to describe ritualized obeisance to older *cumaṅkali*s. Kamala, a Smārta woman slightly older than I was, had a twenty-year-old daughter and wished to arrange her marriage. She told me that she had been advised by an astrologer to complete a five-week cycle of *tiruviḷakku pūja,* initiating it with a *cumaṅkali pirārttaṉai.* She described the event to me after it had taken place, saying that she had invited five elderly *cumaṅkali*s—women, she specified, who were members of her "community" (i.e., Smārtas) and with whom she ordinarily exchanged Navarāttiri visits. When the women arrived at her house, the daughter, for whose marriage this was done, washed their feet using water in which turmeric had been dissolved. The women were then served a sweet and presented with *tāmpūlam* packets of flowers, *veṟṟilpākku,* turmeric, a comb and mirror set, a piece of cloth (suitable for a blouse), a banana, and a case for holding *kuṅkumam.*

The *tiruviḷakku pūja* that Kamala had initiated with the *cumaṅkali pirārttaṉai* was another practice that the Hindu women whom I knew considered emblematic of *cumaṅkali*hood. This *pūja* (discussed in Chapter 2) was very popular among women of different castes and classes, perhaps because it did not make stringent demands on time or material resources. Written instructions for its performance could be found in cheap pamphlets, though women also shared information orally. It was supposed to be done on a weekly or daily basis, and it could be done for an indefinite period or for a specified duration (e.g., 42 days). In the *pūja,* an oil lamp[17] was worshiped as an iconic form of the goddess Lakshmi. Like other *pūjas*, it consisted of onomastic praise, offerings of food and other auspicious substances, and the redistribution of those offerings, usually to family members and neighbors. Lakshmi was praised verbally in the words of the prayers and gesturally through circumambulation of the lamp and *arccaṉai* using *kuṅkumam,* flower petals, or copper coins.[18] It was common for women to fast on the days they performed this *pūja.*

Women who did this *pūja* (and I knew few who did not) marked and preserved their own *cumaṅkali*hood by propitiating Lakshmi, the consort of Vishnu. Lakshmi represents femininity in its wifely, docile form; she also signifies wealth, propriety, and domestic order. *Tiruviḷakku pūja* linked women's own *cumaṅkali*hood with those attributes, as their metaphor and their cause, and so made family wealth, status, and honor the responsibility of women. With its gestural economy and its bodily disciplines, moreover, the *pūja* inscribed *cumaṅkali*hood on women's bodies, as habitus.

The accounts of *tiruviḷakku pūja, maṭimañcaḷ,* and *cumaṅkali pirārttaṉai* that women offered revealed the subtle and multiple techniques by which femininity was objectified. Their accounts also hinted at the ways in which some kinds of objects and conditions were themselves engendered. Lamps, turmeric, and *tāmpūlam* were iconic representations of femininity. Ritual transactions mediated by them both typified and constructed *cumaṅkali*hood. The ritual lexicon offers a case in point.

The expression used to described the ceremony that I witnessed, *maṭimañcaḷ,* is semantically dense. *Maṭi* can refer, colloquially, to ceremonial cleanliness (as discussed in Chapter 3). In the contexts described above, however, other meanings were foregrounded. *Maṭi* as a verb can also gloss the act of folding things such as clothing or in compound forms the reception of alms in the folds of one's clothing (a gesture like the one that I observed). As a noun, *maṭi* refers to a person's lap, a "fold" in the body created by sitting; it also refers to a woman's pelvis or abdomen. In Minakshi's exegesis of the ceremony we attended, she emphasized the latter and suggested that the gifts of turmeric were like the "filling" of a woman's abdomen during pregnancy. The receiving of turmeric in this way could be seen, she offered, as a means of seeking a *cumaṅkali*'s blessings for something specific (e.g., conceiving a child) or for general auspiciousness.

Turmeric has culinary, medicinal, and cosmetic uses, which I described in Chapter 3. These values are distinct in English but are conflated in the commonsense Tamil understanding of turmeric. For example, turmeric is added to the cooking water with dal to impart cleanliness and flavor, and a woman applies turmeric paste to her skin to both cleanse and beautify it. These uses, in conjunction with its place in ritual, are indicative of its gendered associations. Though it can be offered to both male and female deities in *pūja,* it is women who use it cosmetically and give and receive it, as in gestures of hospitality that recur in ritual and other settings. When applied to the skin, turmeric causes a temporary yellowing, and this is thought to impart beauty and luminescence. It is considered visually appealing, as well as beneficial in a physical-moral sense. Its yellow color has a wide range of positive connotations, suggesting gold and the sun. These in turn are associated metaphorically with purity, beauty, illustriousness, and prosperity. The cosmetic and ritual uses of turmeric by women appropriate and feminize these desirable qualities.

The semiotic connections among objects , women's bodies, and conceptions of womanhood were reproduced and reconfigured in the course of everyday life—in special events like *maṭimañcaḷ* and in ordinary actions associated with hygiene and cooking. Gendered identities and differences are made in the ritualized textures of everyday action.

Temporality and Womanhood

In all of the women's rituals with which I was familiar, particular representations of femininity and action sequences (e.g., gift exchanges) recurred. These patterns of sociality—their scheduled occurrences and their durations—marked time and also made time, semantically and experientially. They created contexts by providing the temporal architecture of a world of desire, sociality, and meaning. In my conversations with Smārta women, I found broad agreement about gendered qualities of major transitions during the annual cycle, as well as shared understandings about the importance of ritualized practices focusing on and/or enacted by *cumaṅkali*s in managing these transitions. *Nōṉpu*s, in particular, were actions that marked and gave gendered meanings to space and time because many *nōṉpu*s recurred annually in conjunction with important macrocosmic transitions, in addition to being scheduled in accordance with women's personal needs and desires.

The Birth of the Year

The year's bright half began with the Tamil month of *Tai* (mid-January–mid-February). In the accounts given orally by men and women, and in the written versions found in instructional pamphlets and other manuals, *cumaṅkali*s were assigned major roles in initiating this auspicious month. The prior month, *Mārkaḻi* (mid-December–mid-January), commemorated the period during which Āṇṭāḷ (a Tamil saint) prepared for her marriage to the god Vishnu. In December 1987, I was awakened before dawn by women singing at a nearby temple. When I inquired about the women's actions, a neighbor told me that she and other local women were completing a month-long *nōṉpu* with daily visits to a local goddess temple. They sang verses describing Āṇṭāḷ's visualization of the lover she had yet to meet and of the wedding to be celebrated. Since 1954, these observances, which earlier had been common mostly among Vaishnavite women, have become standardized and more broadly enacted. The then Shankaracharya of Kanchipuram was instrumental in this, pitching it as a cross-sectarian and cross-caste form of ecumenism intended to counter

been em-
ever. Un-
month in
e similar
ve … neal per
day … predawn temple visits) was a typical part of this *nōṉpu.*

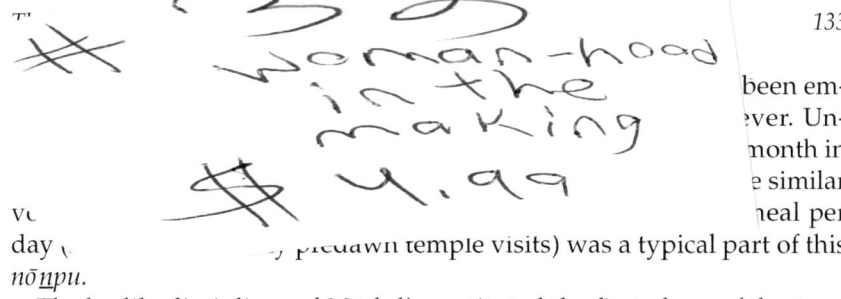

The bodily disciplines of *Mārkaḻi* constituted the first phase of the transition from the dark half to the bright half of the year. The conclusion of *Mārkaḻi* was marked with an observance, *poki paṇṭikai,* when used or "old" *(paḻacu)* household objects were burned. Those items were "old" in the same sense that leftover food was "old"—they had accumulated the residues and impurities of those who had used them. These actions were accompanied by women's creation of auspicious thresholds. They drew *kōlam*s called *paṭikōlam*s outside house doorways. Women, married and not yet married, took oil baths, and on the first Friday of the new month, *cumaṅkali*s invited other *cumaṅkali*s to their homes for meals in accordance with vows taken during *Mārkaḻi* month. The official beginning of *Tai* was observed with Poṅkal. This festival has rural origins, and it marks the first harvest of paddy. It was named for the rice dish *poṅkal,* which was made from the new yield and offered as *naivēttiyam* during *pūja.* To prepare it for offering, the special pot (containing the cooked rice) was prepared by whitening its surface with a mineral lime paste and decorating its rim with dots of vermilion and turmeric. A fresh turmeric plant, with the root attached, was tied around the vessel's neck. Brahmans, who characterized Poṅkal as a "village" festival, felt that they observed the occasion less elaborately than non-Brahmans. Despite distancing themselves from the festival's origins, however, Brahmans' versions prescribed the patterns of women's action and retained the feminine imagery that together evoked the *cumaṅkali*'s auspiciousness as the metonym and synecdoche of the macrocosmic qualities of that temporal transition.

The Dark Half of the Year

The shift from the bright half to the dark half of the year was marked by women's action, in this case seeking the protection of powerful but unpredictable deities. The Tamil month of *Āṭi* marked the entry into the dark half of the annual solar cycle, and in Tamil Nadu it was strongly associated with goddesses such as Māriyammaṉ, who lacked male consorts. Ritual attention to these goddesses acknowledged the physicomoral risks immanent in the sun's recession. These *ammaṉ* goddesses are mothers, as their names suggest, but they are mothers with powers to destroy as well as create. Because they are non-Sanskritic (and are at times propitiated with animal sacrifices), some scholars have assumed that they lacked Brahman devotees. I did not find this to be the case. Brahman women were among those who regularly worshiped these goddesses, though they did so with an awareness that they were negotiating a physico-moral boundary. This negotiation had hermeneutic and behavioral dimensions.

Brahman women interpreted these goddesses as representations of the phases of sexual detachment in the cycle of lives of a Sanskritic deity (e.g., Parvati). The significance of their restrained sexuality, in contrast with nascent sexuality, was rooted in the general Hindu view that the suppression of sexual activity (in either men or women) fostered *shakti,* the internal concentration of energy and desire. *Āṭi* was therefore a time of the goddess's greatest volatility and power. This energy, because of its concentrated and heated nature, was viewed as unpredictable and unrefined.

During *Āṭi,* women propitiated *amma<u>n</u>* goddesses with cooling offerings for thermic balance and with obsequial attentions to mollify a powerful but unpredictable figure. During *Āṭi* (as during *Tai*), Fridays were especially important. On those days, women of differing caste and socioeconomic background filled the temples of the more popular goddesses, often in fulfillment of personal vows. Certain genres of ritual practice were associated with these occasions. One, *māviḷakku,* took its name from its principal object, a shallow lamp *(viḷakku),* made from wheat flour *(māvu),* jaggery, and ghee. The lamp was then offered and distributed as *prasadam.* Sweetened rice, *carkkaraippoṅkal,* prepared in a special bronze pot, was another common offering.

Brahman women participated in these forms of worship, though their encounters with the goddesses and other devotees were carefully negotiated in recognition of the risks they perceived in the interactions with other bodies and substances that such visits entailed.[19] Many worked this out by following the common practice of preparing their own offerings on the temple grounds and thus controlling what they distributed and ingested as *prasadam.* Some—hesitant to "mix" with non-Brahmans, especially in a goddess temple (in which animal sacrifices were reputed to take place)—relied on their non-Brahman maids as intermediaries and had them visit the temple and perform the necessary acts of worship.

During *Āṭi,* Smārta women also propitiated Sanskritic goddesses in the more controlled environments of their homes. On the last Friday of the month, a popular *nō<u>n</u>pu* in honor of Varalakshmi was celebrated by Smārta *cumaṅkali*s.[20] It has become enormously popular in recent years, and there are a variety of manuals describing its performance. Taped cassettes are available that offer both instructions and recorded recitations of

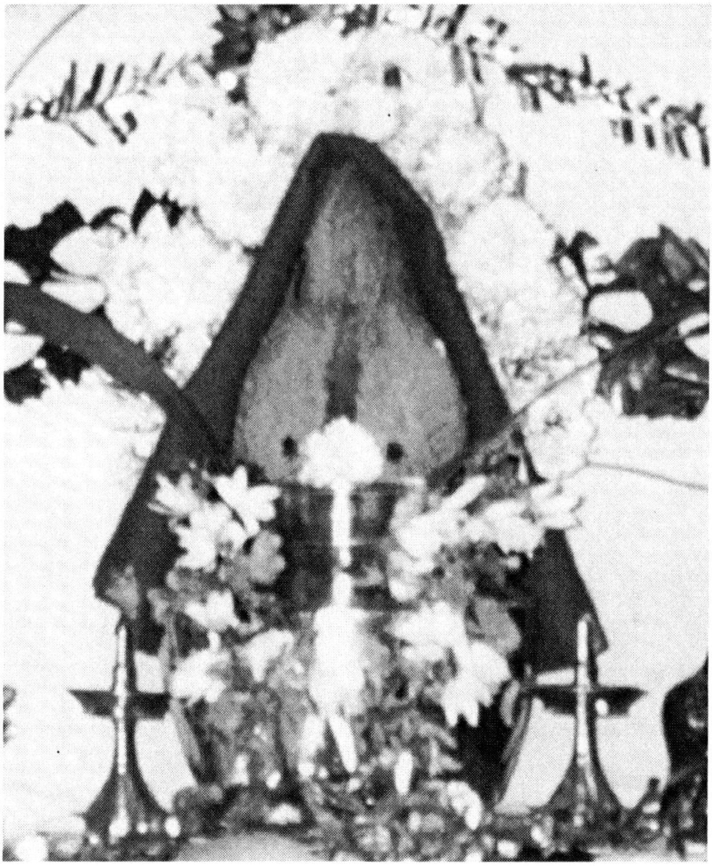

FIGURE 4.1 A *Kalacam,* a Water Pot Decorated As an Image of the Goddess, 1996. Photograph By Author.

the accompanying prayers. Performance of the *nōṉpu* required a special material inventory, the most important object of which was a masklike face *(mukam),* preferably of silver, of the goddess Varalakshmi.[21] The goddess icon, a *kalacam,* was made by attaching the face to a coconut and decorating it with jewelry, *kuṅkumam,* and flowers (see Figure 4.1). The coconut "head" was then set atop a "body" made of a silver water pot. The pot's rim was lined with mango leaves, and *veṟṟilpākku,* mineral lime paste, gold jewelry, and a coin were placed inside. A piece of cloth was draped around the vessel as a "skirt."

The objects of which the *kalacam* was made signified femininity metonymically, and the format of the *nōṉpu,* like others, emphasized feminized relations of hospitality. The week-long *nōṉpu* was initiated by placing the *kalacam* outside the house doorway and inviting the goddess, in that form, to enter. Once brought back inside, her icon was placed on a banana leaf or a tray at the base of which raw rice was kept. Women then performed *pūja,* first for turmeric-paste figures of Ganesha and then for Varalakshmi, offering her special foods, *tāmpūlam,* and pieces of yellow string. Women completed that *pūja* by distributing the strings among female relations; elder women offered the string to younger women and the younger ones reciprocated with *tāmpūlam.* Women might invite other *cumaṅkalis* to visit and receive *tāmpūlam.* The *kalacam* was usually dismantled the following day, but the silver *mukam* was put into the bin in which raw rice was stored. A week later, a sweetened pudding was made, using the rice on which the *kalacam* had sat and the coconut to which the *mukam* had been attached. The pudding was then offered in another *pūja* and distributed as *prasadam.*

Women's Times, Women's Things

In the rituals that marked the transitions between the year's bright and dark halves, a familiar family of objects appeared. Betel leaves and areca nuts, fruits, milk (and derivative products), raw rice, turmeric, vermilion, cloth, strings, lamps, gold jewelry, and silver vessels served as representations of deities, instruments of worship, offerings, and gifts. These objects, as well as others, appeared in many ritual contexts and connoted auspiciousness. What my discussion emphasizes is that those meanings emerged through their multiple uses but especially in *nōṉpu,* in which they were employed to adorn and refine women's bodies and to signify womanhood. Lamps, vessels, jewelry, turmeric, strings, and vermilion stand for *cumaṅkalis* and the relationships that define *cumaṅkali*hood. But for participants, the relations between signifier and signified were neither arbitrary nor unmotivated. Rather, these articles were always connected to women's bodies by being ingested, absorbed, worn, and positioned as conduits for relations among women and between women and deities. These actions placed the signifiers firmly in the intentional world that mediated reality. For women who performed and participated in *nōṉpus,* the meanings were self-evident, embodied, and pragmatic; they were not esoterica but matters of a shared common sense. The initiation and execution of *nōṉpus* were designed to take advantage of qualities associated with particular temporal intervals, though they also reinforced the feminine associations of those moments. In these ways, *nōṉpus* were sites for the production of a spatio-temporal architecture in which women came to recognize femininity as part of a naturally established cosmic order.

Conclusion: Womanhood's Contradictions

By dealing with ritual as an engendering process, with the uncommitted woman at its center, I have tried to reveal the contradictory and underdetermined aspects of actions and imagery that appeared traditional. This approach undermines the closure that an Althusserian treatment of ritual as interpellation would imply by searching out cracks in the subject-constituting practice of ritual, beginning with its construction of femininity as both center and margin. Women, especially those with the deepest commitments to orthopraxy, were compelled through ritualized practice to reimagine and improvise their identities as *cumaṅkali*s, to reposition themselves as uncommitted, and to reengage contradictory images of femininity. The reproduction of *cumaṅkali*hood was part of the moral etiquette of domestic life and entailed frequent compromises and negotiations. Patterns of hospitality and deference, embodied in ritualized gifting, feeding, and bathing, connected women as friends, kin, and ritual partners. At the same time, these practices constituted the *cumaṅkali* as a person defined through her deference to the needs and desires of her husband and family, and through the familial status that accrues as a result of her efforts. As a consequence, women were often caught between these contradictory pulls on their affections, desires, and practical capabilities.

To engender themselves as *cumaṅkali*s, women negotiated relations with other women through the medium of ritualized practice. But their husbands, who were the foci and beneficiaries of these activities, often restricted such pursuits, disparaging them as "superstitions." This was especially prevalent when women's activities took them into non-Brahman domains, such as *amma<u>n</u>* temples. Men's criticisms of the religious interests of their wives and daughters sometimes centered on the fact that those activities took women outside the home and thus outside male surveillance, making them unavailable to attend to husbands and families. Women often told me how difficult they found it to set aside enough money from their household funds to finance elaborate ritual cycles. They were keenly aware that the time available for such activities was limited, and they completed domestic rituals and visited temples, spirit mediums, or gurus while their husbands were at work. They endured their husbands' displeasure and anger—describing even that silent suffering as an inscription of *cumaṅkali*hood. And always, the *cumaṅkali*'s double—the widow—stood at the edge of women's images of womanhood.

The everyday practices of patriarchy thus positioned Brahman women as improvisers on, as well as negotiators of, womanhood. The contradictions that they confronted were expressed in the ways that they participated in both *nōṉpus* and *samskāras*. Together, the canonical *samskāras* and noncanonical *nōṉpus* secured an imagined and ahistorical world of moral order and orthodoxy *(varṇāśramadharma)* that hinged on patriarchy and caste privilege. These rituals bracketed that world as traditional and situated it in the space of the home, in the bodies of women, and in the community of Brahmans. These representations of tradition have allowed some interpreters to infuse Hindu ritual with nationalist sentiment, thus investing ritual with the capacity to create nationalized, Hindu subjects. These ways of negotiating personal and collective identities, however, rested on practical grammars and were subject to unmaking. Women negotiated womanhood in the ways that they ate, dressed, and cleansed themselves; womanhood was written on their bodies as they menstruated, had sex, and gave birth; it was imagined in the speech, silences, gestures, and accoutrements of ritual. As they encountered normative images of womanhood, women were asked to consent to an encompassed, domesticated subjectivity—to consent to an abjection that sustained the moral order of tradition. However, the contradictions of womanhood and the experimental nature of each woman's negotiation of femininity could and did destabilize the processes of consent. In the next chapter, I turn to these transgressive possibilities.

Notes

1. The Laws of Manu state that a woman "must not seek to separate herself form her father, husband, or sons; by leaving them she would make both (her own and her husband's) families contemptible. She must always be cheerful, clever in (the management of her) household affairs, careful in cleaning her utensils, and economical in expenditure. . . . No sacrifice, no vow, no fast must be performed by women apart (from their husbands); if a wife obeys her husband, she will for that (reason alone) be exalted in heaven" (Buhler 1964, 195–196).

2. Though the positions taken by the Subaltern Studies Collective are not directly engaged with Dumont, the thrust of their critique of Orientalist and colonialist historiography can be read as a criticism of Dumont's writing of South Asia from a Hindu/Brahman/elite stance, and of Dumont's privileging of "ideology" (defined after De Tracy, rather than Marx) as a central analytic category (Guha 1989; see also Dirks 1992). See Nandy (1983) for a non-Marxist critique of Orientalism and colonialism, based on alternative, anti-Enlightenment universalisms.

3. See Munn's (1992) excellent review of anthropological studies of temporality.

4. See Logan's (1980) similar argument, based on her extensive analysis of women's ritual practice in the city of Madurai in southern Tamil Nadu.

5. See Merrey (1982) for a thorough review of these systems.

6. The most commonly occurring Tamil months and their Gregorian equivalents are *Tai* (mid-January–mid-February), *Māci* (mid-February–mid-March),

Paṅkuṉi (mid-March–mid-April), *Cittirai* (mid-April–mid-May), *Vaikāci* (mid-May–mid-June), *Āṉi* (mid-June–mid-July), *Āṭi* (mid-July–mid-August), *Āvaṇi* (mid-August–mid-September), *Purattāci* (mid-September–mid-October), *Aippaci* (mid-October–mid-November), *Kārtikkai* (mid-November–mid-December), *Mākaḻi* (mid-December–mid-January).

7. Life cycle rituals are elements of Hindu practice that cross caste lines. However, the centrality of the four-phased male life cycle in the rituals, as well as the use of the term *samskāra* (thereby alluding to their "refining" effects and their Sanskritic mediation) to refer to the rituals collectively, are indicators that the rituals are constitutive of the paradigmatic life cycle of "twice-born" males.

8. The priest's description of *samskāras* was consistent with that of Pandey (1969).

9. The threads are replaced yearly in a ceremony known as *Āvaṇi aviṭṭam* and after a man's father dies.

10. By this I do not mean to argue that Hindu orthodoxy attributes women's status *entirely* to men's action. Women were accorded moral agency in Sanskrit moral treatises; wifely virtue depended on women's enactment of domestic ritual and other markers of propriety; these in turn were said to guarantee her husband's well-being (Courtright 1995; McGee 1992). I am making a more limited claim about the presence of women in Smārtas' performance and everyday understanding of *samskāras*.

11. Pandey (1969, 220) noted that the final part of the wedding ceremony, following the blessing of the bride, was known as *sumangali*, the Sanskrit version of *cumaṅkali*.

12. Tamil *nōṉpus* were structurally similar to the ritual cycles known as *vrats* (see Reynolds 1982; Wadley 1983). Mary McGee (1992) glossed these as "votive rites" and described them as worship performed unconditionally; she contrasted them with contractual rites, *navas*, performed if and when a desired result had been obtained. She also noted that although textual sources described *vrats* as optional, their performers considered them to be fulfillments of the obligations of womanhood. By contrast, the everyday understandings of *nōṉpus* that women communicated to me seemed to encompass features of both *vrat* and *navas*—they were motivated by both practical and unconditional aims; they were also regarded as essential for the maintenance of *cumaṅkalihood*.

13. The deferential term of reference by which the (then) eldest Shankaracharya at the Kanchipuram was known.

14. A man's garment consisting of a large piece of cloth that is worn folded and tied at the waist.

15. The genesis of this group (which was about four years old) and the actions that its leader, Parvati, had employed in "colonizing" some of the shrines in that temple form the subjects of Chapter 5, so I will not open up those issues here.

16. The *Tamil Lexicon* lists the verb form, *mañcaṭkuṅkkumattukkalai*, meaning "to invite womenfolk, on an auspicious occasion when saffron, red powder, betel, etc. are given" (5: 3007). The term *lakṣamañcaḷ*, referring to the total quantity of turmeric (100,000 pieces) that was distributed, was also used.

17. The lamp used is usually one of the tall, standing variety *(kuttuviḷakku)*, with a bowl for oil, in which wicks are laid, near the top.

18. The coins were used because of their copper composition and because they were stamped with a lotus flower design, a flower iconographically associated with Lakshmi.

19. My Brahman friends were concerned but not surprised when I contracted paratyphoid during *Āṭi*. "You went about in so many of those places [*amma<u>n</u>* temples]," one said, "that [my illness] will always happen."

20. Because Tamil months fluctuate in length from year to year, Varalakshmi *nō<u>n</u>pu* can fall in either Āṭi or Āvaṇi. In 1987, it occurred during Āṭi.

21. *Mukams* were usually given by women to their married daughters as gifts (often part of trousseau) if the latter had married into households in which Varalakshmi *pūja* was performed.

5

The Uncertain Subject(s) of Womanhood

Meeting Janaki had spurred me to probe feminine normativity and its contradictions. Another group of women, also goddess devotees, encouraged me to consider the boundaries of that normativity and the ways that women drew on its idioms to reinvent womanhood.

I had been in Chennai for two months, and like all fledgling anthropologists, I had a pencil that was poised to record whatever shards of data fell my way. In my eagerness, and in faltering Tamil, I accosted anyone capable of speech for nuggets with which to fill my newly acquired, Lakshmi-embossed notebooks. My neighbors complied with what they genially regarded as my eccentricities, though most shrank away, deferring to unnamed "priests" and to that omnibus of authoritative knowledge, the "shastras." I was ill at ease, therefore, when Ramanujan (an affluent Brahman engineer) inquired in English, "Are you making any progress?" My vague response encouraged him to enlarge upon the flaws of my approach. "You must go only to the *maṭam* for authentic information. Those temple priests are crooked, and ordinary people don't know the real meaning behind the rituals they do."

He continued, "I do *pūja* daily, but it is only recently that I have begun. It's for my own peace of mind, and it's not at all elaborate—it's for my *iṣṭa teyvam,* Murukan. It was my mother's devotion to Murukan that drew me." This was all beginning to sound like transcribable data to me, so I encouraged him by offering that I had noticed many women being very active as ritual performers. He agreed, "Yes, that's so" but went on dismissively, "so much of it is just one cult or another—they've picked up things here and there; some have come in from the north." By this point, he had become exercised, stating with conviction, "Women are not fit to do *pūja*—in our house, I do *pūja,* not my wife! Once you have started a *pūja,* it must be done daily, but for women, daily *pūja* is impossible."

Sensing my confusion, he added, "Several days out of each month they cannot bathe, so you see, it's the men who must do."

In the months that followed, I amassed a shelf full of notebooks crammed with scribbling—much of it recording those very "cults" that Ramanujan had dismissed. Still, his cautionary words stayed with me, particularly because they effectively recreated the contradiction in which South Asian women often seemed caught. As *cumaṅkali*s, and especially as mothers, women were extolled. Among the core images of both Hindu and Dravidian nationalism, was the mother, often a mother goddess.[1] By contrast, restrictions on women's actions and subjectivities were often underwritten by broadly framed cultural constructions of female sexuality. Associations with blood, interiority, and desire made it at best the site of volatile possibility—a manifestation of the feminized power of *shakti*—though more often women's sexuality was associated with uncleanliness, danger, and even death. Both orthodox and popular understandings of menstruation, widowhood, and female chastity confirmed this. Femininity was simultaneously margin and center, and women's everyday lives, though mediated by the structural inequalities of caste and class and by specificities of domestic politics, were negotiated at this junction.

In this chapter I address the expression of these contradictions in the social interactions and interpenetrating narratives of four specific women, one of whom, Minakshi, was my research assistant and friend. Three were middle-class Brahmans, and the fourth was from a formerly Untouchable *jāti* and had become prosperous in her forties. My questions were shaped by my observations of the ways that their subjectivities, and their interactions with each other, were mediated by ritual practice and by talk about those activities. Through ritual, they fashioned complex and nonunitary identities—they encountered, merged with, and argued with goddesses, they negotiated complex and precarious relations with other women, they reconfigured their sexuality, and they rewrote ritual syntax.

The first part of this chapter is organized around a series of fairly long narratives. All are translations from Tamil originals (with exceptions as noted) and all were prepared with the help of my assistant, Minakshi. As will soon become clear, Minakshi was a key figure in the group discussed in the chapter. The narratives included here are based on detailed notes that I took during my conversations with these women. I present these accounts in the order of their original delivery to emphasize that the stories that these women told about themselves and each other were delivered over time. Although they described a process—a life history anchored by ritual practice—they also were events that shaped the process. The variegated (and somewhat choppy) result reiterates, formally, a point having theoretical import that I explore in the second section of the chapter. The stories are biographical records and sites for agency. They are themselves modes of action and intervention in social life.

The content of this chapter, as well as its form, are intended to problematize female subjectivity in a manner that extends the arguments of the previous chapter by probing the edges of normativity. My aim is to show the uneven, unfinished process of disclosure in which I was positioned as instigator, interlocutor, and observer. I hope that this will provide an opportunity to conceptualize subjectivity—as negotiated by and coded in ritual—as dynamic, contingent, and intersubjective. This will further disrupt the imagery of culturally sealed personhood that anthropological studies of life cycle rituals often convey, and in so doing disrupt the tendencies to see both caste and gender as overdetermined dimensions of identity.

The Goddess and Her Servants

Let me begin by introducing the women who are the subjects of this chapter. All resided in Chennai with their husbands and children—at the time I knew them, two (Saraswati and Minakshi) lived in nuclear households and two (Sunithi and Valli) lived with extended families. Though all four had had direct encounters with the goddess, only Saraswati, Sunithi, and Valli were mediums. Each had developed client networks, and the primary sites for their public ritual performances were shrines located in their homes. All fell within the broad range of what constituted the middle class in India, though they were not equal in terms of household income and consumption levels, educational attainments or occupational status. They ranged in age from their middle thirties to late forties, and three (Sunithi, Valli, and Minakshi) had passed menopause. Minakshi was the only one to have been educated beyond the secondary level and to have had formal employment experience.

The youngest, Saraswati, lived with her husband and young son (he was about 14 at the time) in an apartment in an old bungalow-style dwelling that had been divided into rental units. She was not employed, and I never learned the extent of her education. Her husband was employed by the city's Municipal Corporation. Their income and consumption levels put them in the middle class, but their material circumstances were precarious and unstable. Like many middle-class families in Chennai, they were at risk of losing that status, and material security depended on careful provisioning, frugality, and luck.

Minakshi, who was in her mid-forties, was my research assistant and my friend. Minakshi had graduated from college and had worked in a variety of professional jobs. She lived with her husband and three unmarried children in a flat in Mylapore. Minakshi was very gregarious and smart and had a sharp sense of humor; she considered herself a devout Hindu. When I met her, she was self-employed as a private tutor. She was keen to help me out, for she saw it as an extension of the kind of work that she already did. And the salary she received was a welcome supplement to the household income.

Sunithi lived in a flat in a modern apartment building with her husband, son, and widowed mother. Her husband and son were professionally employed—her husband was in the central government service and her son was an accountant. Their combined income gave Sunithi's family considerably more wealth and security than either Minakshi's or Saraswati's households. When I met them, Sunithi's mother had been living with them for several years. I was told that she had resided previously with Sunithi's brother and his wife, but a dispute with them had caused her to join Sunithi's household.

Valli lived in a joint household with her husband, unmarried children, married children and their spouses, and grandchildren. Though the house was large and comfortably appointed, it was located in a *cēri* (the colloquial term for a poor neighborhood). The family had been extremely poor until Valli became a medium for the goddess. Subsequently, they acquired wealth from devotees' donations, though her husband and sons were employed as drivers and contributed to the household's income. Saraswati and Sunithi also accepted devotees' donations, though they had been mediums for a shorter time than Valli and had smaller client networks; their families, therefore, were primarily supported by men's earnings.

Sunithi

July 9, 1987. I had visited a temple with Minakshi and had run into Viji, one of Minakshi's sisters-in-law. Viji was a neighbor of Sunithi, and she told us about Sunithi's elaborate *pūja*s. She also asserted that "the goddess had come to" Sunithi *(amman̲ vantatu)* and that miracles had occurred. A few days later, we went to visit Sunithi. We arrived in the late afternoon and were greeted by Sunithi and her mother. We introduced ourselves and explained why we had come—mentioning our encounter with Viji. Sunithi offered to tell us more about her experiences and invited us into the room in which the household shrine was displayed. There were no furnishings in that room except for the things that made up the shrine itself: framed and garlanded pictures of deities and saints (including Sathya Sai Baba), small figures of deities, trays, bowls, and other utensils. The centerpiece (shown in Figure 5.1), displayed on a raised platform, was a small image of the goddess Karumāriyamman̲'s face, surrounded by fresh flowers.

FIGURE 5.1 Decorated Image of the Goddess Karumāriyamman̲ in Sunithi's Shrine, 1987. Photograph By Author.

Upon entering, Minakshi immediately approached the shrine and prostrated herself before it in a gesture of deference. With some uncertainty, I followed. Sunithi then spoke briefly about her childhood and her marriage at the age of seventeen, followed by a description of her first encounter with the goddess:

> After we married, I did not do any *pūja*s, nor did I take vows or keep fasts. I did not even go to the temple regularly. I put no trust in omens; I went for rational explanations. If something broke, it was because of clumsiness, not the *rākukālam*. . . . Things changed when I was thirty-five. I had been unwell—experiencing heavy, painful menstrual periods—so I went to an allopathic doctor who gave me medicine but did not wish to operate on me. But even before I had gotten that doctor's advice, the *tēvi* had told the same thing. It was like this: My servant knew of my problems and tried to persuade me to go to the Karumāriyamma<u>n</u> temple nearby. I saw no need for such things, but still she tried to convince me, saying that other Brahmans were going to that temple and having their problems solved. Still, I refused. You see, I had no belief in such things, and I was also not in the habit of going about in such neighborhoods [the slum where the temple was]. So that servant took things into her own hands and went to the temple and offered a lime to the *tēvi* on my behalf. At the temple, the *amma<u>n</u>* [Valli, who served as the goddess medium and temple priestess] told my servant, "Take that lime back to your mistress and give her its juice to drink." The servant did so, and I agreed to drink it. Once I did so, I felt that I must leave the house and go myself to that temple—this even though I did not know the way! My neighbors were astonished, but I had never before felt such a force. I had to go. Once I got to that temple the *amma<u>n</u>* with the tangled hair told me that my health problems would cease for the next five years and that no knife would cut me until then. This was told to me before I received the doctor's advice.
>
> Five years later, in 1981, my problems began again—just as that *amma<u>n</u>* had predicted. I went to the clinic, and the doctor there prescribed a hysterectomy. I went again to the temple, and the *amma<u>n</u>* said, "I [the goddess] will come to you during the operation. It will take only a half hour, and you will have no problems thereafter." It happened in just this way, but even then I did not begin to do any *pūja*s for the *tēvi*, but only kept some pictures and *vigraham* out for festivals. I only started doing *pūja*s for *tēvi* some time later. (Field notes, July 9, 1987)

At this point, a few other women entered the room. They were neighbors and clients and had come to pray and make offerings at Sunithi's shrine. They joined us and listened to Sunithi's narrative—occasionally confirming points made by Sunithi or asking for elaboration.

SUNITHI: During the first week of August in 1984, my mother, a Muslim friend, and I were sitting in our front room, and a beggar woman approached the door. . . . That woman was clad in a white cloth. She was quite dirty, and she had long, tangled hair that she had not tied or wound into a knot. It was around noon, and that beggar entered the house and just stood, staring at us. I said to my mother, "Just give her some money and send her off," but my mother said nothing. The beggar then said, "Stop, I don't want *iṭli,* I don't want rice, I don't want money." Then, "I've come to give *uttaravu.*"[2] She went on, "All under this roof have good hearts; whoever comes is fed and satisfied; there is no *tīṭṭu* in the house." All this was true, but I still felt some hesitation. I did not want to invite her in. This woman then asked for camphor and a match. I gave her the camphor only and sent her off. [To me, Sunithi said, "Would you give matches to such a person? I was afraid that she might start a fire."]

Later that same day, I went into our *pūja* room. I did not go to worship, but in my heart I asked whether that incident was a good event, an auspicious event. I saw on the picture of Kamakshi, *amirtam,*[3] and that, I knew, signified good. . . . Some days later, I saw that beggar woman again. . . . she repeated the words she had spoken here . . . and opened her hand to show that the camphor was exhausted. . . . That very night, while I was sleeping, I awoke to see a snake coiled around the clothesline in our house. . . . later I saw a young girl, well dressed and with jewels, carrying a basket that held a snake. . . . The next day, while I was resting, I had a dream. In it, I was walking through [the neighborhood in which the *tēvi* temple was located], and people along the road were speaking to me. There were Brahmans and Sudras among them, and they were trying to provoke me. One Sudra woman said, "There is some damage in my wall; I want you to repair it." I replied, "Are you kidding? Am I a mason? Ask someone else." That woman then took my hands into her own and said something that I cannot recall. After I awoke, my son arrived at home, and I suggested to him that we go to [that] temple. . . . When we got there, the *ammaṉ* with the tangled hair told us that the *tēvi* had told her [Valli, the medium] that we would come. Then, that *ammaṉ* spoke with the *tēvi*'s voice and told us, "I have come in different forms, and have called you. I want to speak with you. I came to your house, but you did not let me in. I called affectionately, but you did not come; so I had to scare you with the snake to make you come to me." The *ammaṉ,* still speaking as the *tēvi,* said, "I wore that dirty sari because I want you to get me a new one." As we left, Prakash [her son] commented that we should get her a sari but said that he did not know how much should be spent. I decided that about two hundred rupees should be spent.

We presented a sari to the *tēvi* on the first Friday of Navarāttiri. . . . Since then, however, I have not gone to that temple, but I continue to donate money. I also make *carkkaraippoṅkal* on the first Friday of each English month and have my servant take it to the temple as an offering."

MARY: Why did you stop going to that temple?

SUNITHI: [pointing to the small goddess icon, the *mukam* that was the centerpiece of her shrine] The *tēvi* is here. Once I welcomed her, there was no need to go to that temple. Here she is with her family—her husband, Shiva, and her sons, Murukan and Ganesha. (Field notes, July 9, 1987)

One of the other women present turned to Minakshi and me and told us that Sunithi performed a very special, elaborate *pūja* for the *tēvi.* She encouraged Sunithi to elaborate on this, which Sunithi did, describing the first three or four *apiṣēkam*s in detail. In her narrative, she concentrated on the progressive and conjoined changes in the forms of the rituals and in her subjectivity—emphasizing the gradual shift from performer to performer/medium.

Each ritual, she asserted, differed slightly from its predecessor:

One of our neighbors is a Marathi woman, and her friend's son came down with measles. . . . The Marathi woman came to me, asking what the boy's mother should do. I told her to pray with sincere belief and to keep the *tēvi* cool with *apiṣēkam.* I then told her that after the boy recovered, she should offer *carkkaraippoṅkal* to the *tēvi,* though I did not specify where or when.

That boy was cured, and his mother came along with my neighbor, and they asked me to do *apiṣēkam.* . . . I protested, and they argued with me. They would not take no for an answer . . . so I agreed. But I wondered what I would do—I had never done such a ritual, and I knew none of the formalities. The Marathi lady told me to just do it with belief and it would come. Then I had a dream in which a small girl asked me why I was worried, and told me that she would do everything. This made me calm. I then went out and bought all of the necessities for the *apiṣēkam* myself—limes, rose-scented water, sandal powder, turmeric, young coconuts, curd, milk, honey, ghee, and oil. This *apiṣēkam* took place in March of 1985. . . . Those present . . . were stunned by my performance. There was no hesitation on my part. . . . [a neighbor] swore that no one seeing it would have believed that I had never done it before. . . . The second *apiṣēkam* was done for another boy's school admission. . . . Archana [one of the women present with us] was helping me . . . but when I tried to speak to her, I was unable to talk. My concentration then shifted from the *apiṣēkam* to the *tēvi,* and I asked [the goddess] why I could not speak. It was only at the end, as I lit the lamp, that I

> was once again able to speak. With my own voice, I instructed Archana to light them. I then apologized to the *tēvi*, asking her to reciprocate the scolding I had given her. After everything was finished, I went to Archana's place for some tea. When I returned, I sat in the *pūja* room, and there I saw a small snake with the markings of a cobra. It was . . . near where the *apiṣēkam* had taken place. It slithered down the head of the *tēvi*'s face, formed a necklace, and then . . . disappeared.
>
> After the third *apiṣēkam* and up to the ninth or tenth, I spoke to no one during the performance. Since then, I have begun to speak [aloud] but I have no awareness of the outside world at those times, and I don't remember what has been said. (Field notes, July 9, 1987)

She explained that since the tenth *apiṣēkam*, she had been doing them about once each month, usually at the request of others. On those occasions the goddess came to her and she did the ritual, after which, she explained, the *tēvi* left and "allow[ed] me to go and rest before answering people's questions." Sunithi usually did the *apiṣēkam* between 3:00 and 5:00 in the afternoon, rested until about 6:00, and then from 6:00 to 8:00 returned to give advice and predictions: "At about 8:00, there is a knock, and that is the sign for me to stop." Normally, following that, the goddess came to her again, this time taking the form of a small girl: "I drink, eat, dance, and sing. People bring gifts for the child." She added that the *tēvi* also came to her on the first Friday of every English month. On these occasions she did not do *pūja* but only gave advice to the people who visited.

She attributed her ability to describe the performances to the fact that her family and followers regularly recounted the events to her. During the past year, her husband had also recorded some of the proceedings on audiocassette. (A few weeks later, she told me that she had acquired the ability to remember what had occurred during episodes when the goddess came to her. Shortly thereafter, following her son's marriage, the goddess's coming became more frequent, and often spontaneous.)

By this time, it was dark. We had stayed much longer than planned and so prepared to leave. Sunithi invited us to return the following day to listen to the continuation of her story. The other women also rose to leave. Before departing, each turned to Sunithi to receive her blessing. Sunithi applied *kuṅkumam* and *vipūti* (sacred ash) to each woman's forehead, then dropped some *vipūti* on each woman's tongue. The women then prostrated themselves before her.

July 10, 1987. When we arrived, Sunithi reopened the subject of her relationship with the medium at the local temple. She then returned to the first visit she had made to that temple. At that time the medium and her family were very poor, so poor that

> they did not have enough to maintain a buffalo and cow and still feed themselves. I asked *tēvi* why she did not improve that lady's life. The *tēvi* spoke [through the medium], saying that she could do it but that once done, the lady would become arrogant. Well, over time that lady did start to prosper . . . and she continued to give advice to people. I also continued to go to her. Then, one day, I went and found a poor couple waiting to see her. . . . That *amma<u>n</u>* invited me in, but she ignored those people waiting for her. I was shocked by her conduct. I approached the couple and offered them some money—they had spent all they had on travel. I then went to the entrance of the temple, and I announced that if such was the treatment given to devotees, then I would no longer come there. (Field notes, July 10, 1987)

Sunithi then told more anecdotes about miracles, visions (which she referred to as *darshan*) that had occurred. After listening to her for a while, I brought up the subject of her household shrine and, specifically, the goddess icon that was its centerpiece. "When did you get this *mukam*?" I asked. She explained that her mother's mother had given it to her in 1959, shortly after her marriage, to use in Varalakshmi *nō<u>n</u>pu*. This answer, however, expanded into a longer narrative describing how that object had been radically transformed by the goddess's entry into Sunithi's home.

The *mukam* had begun to change gradually and, according to Sunithi, miraculously. These alterations had the appearance of surface oxidation, and Sunithi's mother and some of her neighbors attributed the changes to a spontaneous emergence of *vipūti*. Sunithi was initially skeptical, thinking that their devotion had warped their judgment, but she was persuaded after Valli intervened.

> On the next Friday [about a month after the changes began], our servant went as usual to the temple to offer *carkkaraippoṅkal* to the *tēvi*. The *amma<u>n</u>* asked her whether any miracles had taken place in the house. Our servant told her about the *vipūti* on the *mukam,* and told her, as well, that I did not believe. The *amma<u>n</u>* replied in the *tēvi*'s voice, "I am there already, in spite of that she still refuses to believe. In four weeks time, I will make her believe in the power that exists and many people will start to visit me in that place."
>
> After that, we noticed gradual changes in the *mukam*. First, there was only *vipūti;* the next week, some spots of *kuṅkumam* were there. This news spread, and people started to come in, wanting to see this *mukam*. . . . One day, I put a betel leaf under her face and some *kuṅkumam* fell on it. I put some on my own forehead and then offered it to the people who were there. Those who took it did so with great devotion and brought it back to their homes. During the third week, there was a light rose tinge and the smell of sandalwood.
>
> By the fourth week, my doubts were gone, and I believed that there was *shakti* in our house. By then, our servant had informed us of another instruc-

tion from the temple *amma<u>n</u>*, "Do not touch my face; let me dress as I wish. I will change my appearance as I wish." So, I do not touch her face, I only decorate her by placing flowers around. (Field notes, July 10, 1987)

Before Minakshi and I left, Sunithi invited us to return the following Sunday for the *apiṣēkam* that she was going to perform for her son's twenty-seventh birthday. My July 19 field notes record,

When we got there, about five women in addition to Sunithi and her mother were sitting in the *pūja* room. . . . Sunithi invited me to sit immediately to the left of the shrine, where [she said] I would have a good view of the proceedings. This placed me optimally for eye contact with her as well. Sunithi pointed out Saraswati, a friend who had also had many "experiences" [in English] with the *tēvi*. Saraswati insisted that we visit her so she could tell us more about those things. . . . Minakshi observed that the red of the *amma<u>n</u> mukam* was stronger [than it had been on the previous day], that there was more *kuṅkumam* on the face. Also, later [during the *apiṣēkam*] Minakshi pointed . . . [to] the eyes of the *mukam*. . . . "You see, her eyes are open now" [in English]. [See Figure 5.2.]

People began crowding into the room, and by 3:00 it was packed. Sunithi's husband was seated in a far right corner near the door, had a tape recorder ready and a diary open. [Her performance] began promptly at 3:00. Sunithi turned to [her husband], asked, "Shall it start?" and he nodded. . . . She was wearing a red silk sari . . . and was seated, facing the shrine. When her husband nodded, she closed her eyes and began to sway slightly. After a few moments, she opened the eyes. . . . [As the goddess] she is flippant, making light conversation . . . and tak[ing] on a childlike . . . demeanor. . . . This is interrupted with more serious self-presentation at points; she gives *uttaravu* in the latter tone. . . . [Later, during the *apiṣēkam*] she told Minakshi . . . to continue with the work she was doing without expecting reward and despite any physical problems that arise. Minakshi took it as a [reference to] her work with me. . . . Sunithi also asked who I was, and Minakshi identified me as "my friend, Mary." Sunithi responded by pointing to me and then to the picture of [the Christian] Mary [kept in the shrine] and to the *Karumāriyamma<u>n</u> mukam* in her shrine, murmuring as she did that, "Mary, Māriyamma<u>n</u>." (Field notes, July 19, 1987)

Sunithi began the ritual by worshiping Ganesha and then performed *arcca<u>n</u>ai*, which ordinarily involved recitation of a deity's praise names while placing coins, flower petals, rice grains, or *kuṅkumam* in front of the image. Sunithi's version was different. With each praise name, she tossed a few grains of rice back over her shoulders so that they fell on the audience rather than in front of the deity. She then began *apiṣēkam*; she undressed the images and sluiced them with milk. Again, her version differed from performances I had seen elsewhere. Her assistants brought in

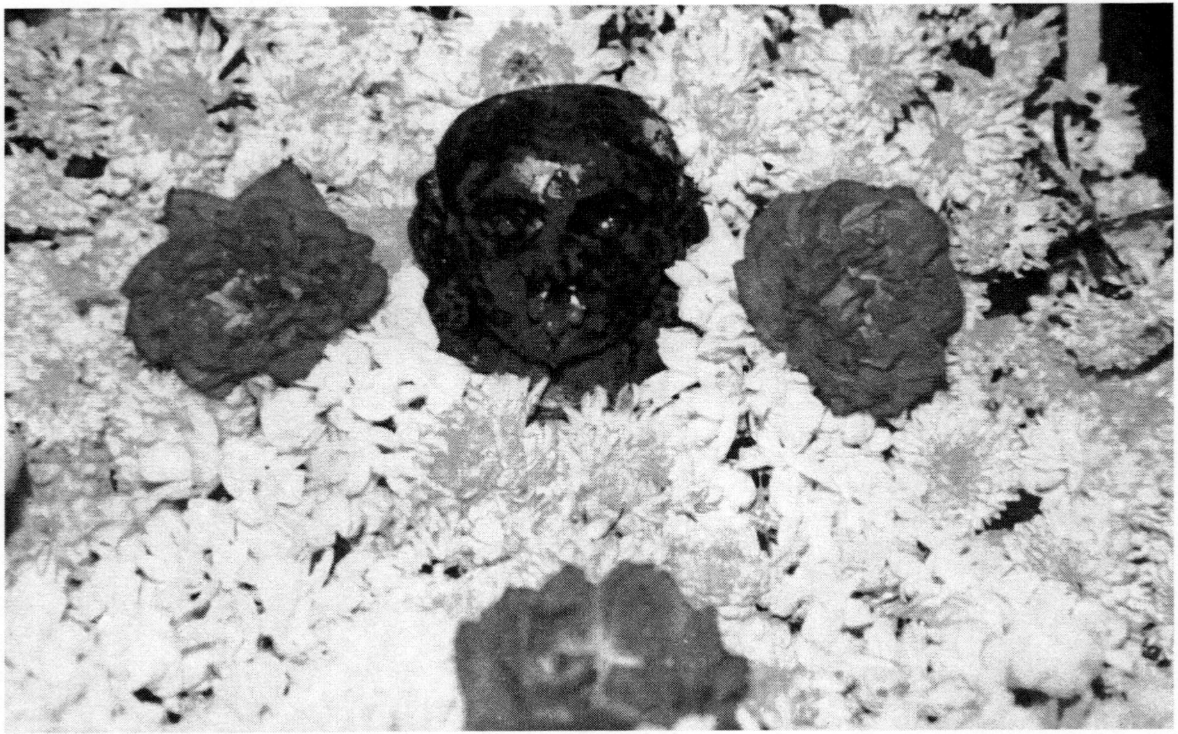

FIGURE 5.2 Close-Up View of the Image of Karumāriyamman̲ in Sunithi's Shrine, 1987. Photograph by R. Arjunan.

a large bucket of milk (8–10 liters) that was poured over the deity icons, splashing guests seated nearby. After finishing this and decorating the icons, Sunithi distributed limes to six of the women present. They were cut in half, *kuṅkumam* was smeared on the flat sides, and a chunks of camphor were placed on the *kuṅkumam.* These lamps were then lit, and *āratti* was done with them. Finally, a large bucket filled with flower petals was brought in, and audience members were asked to toss handfuls of the petals on the shrine. Once this was completed, sweets were distributed and Sunithi blessed everyone. Throughout the ritual, everyone present sang *bhajans*.

Her *pūja* had taken nearly two hours to complete. Sunithi then went to her bedroom to rest while Sunithi's mother and some of Sunithi's closest female disciples served coffee and snacks to the guests. Sunithi returned a bit later. Speaking as the *tēvi,* she responded to people's questions about work, health, and so on. Later, adopting the manner of small girl, she entertained guests with singing, pranks, and chatter.

* * *

In the months that followed, Minakshi and I often talked about Sunithi. Minakshi was convinced of the authenticity of Sunithi's mediumship, referring in English to Sunithi's "control," that is, the consistency of her behavior when the goddess came to her. Minakshi also thought that her behavior at those times when the goddess came was neither typically human nor like the ordinary Sunithi. She noted that Sunithi's voice took on a singsong quality when she spoke as the goddess and that she spoke in Tamil, whereas she usually spoke Telugu at home.[4] The performances were persuasive despite what Minakshi recognized as their unorthodox and unpredictable qualities. Minakshi (like Sunithi's other followers) found the performances aesthetically appealing and enjoyed attending them. She was quite awed and flattered when, soon after our first meeting with her, Sunithi asked Minakshi to assist with the rituals and to occasionally interpret the goddess's *uttaravu* for the audience.[5] They soon became very close.

The pleasure that Minakshi derived from attending Sunithi's performances told me something about why and how other Brahmans entered Sunithi's circle of clients and initiates. The ritual format, based on Sanskritic *pūja,* was familiar to the mostly Brahman, middle-class audience; even the improvisations played on gestures, images, and idioms that were part of this genre. The format also recalled the devotional styles favored by middle-class, urban devotees of Sathya Sai Baba, among whom Sunithi and her husband counted themselves. *Bhajan* singing has become, over the past fifty years, an established practice among urban elites, and groups dedicated to particular deities and saints are common.

Sunithi as *amma<u>n</u>* was soft-spoken and used the version of colloquial Tamil spoken by Smārta Brahmans. She accepted only vegetarian foods. This was notable because Karumāriyamma<u>n</u>, the goddess who came to her, was ordinarily classified as a village deity who, like the Sanskritic Kali, accepted animal sacrifice and meat offerings. Thus, just as Sunithi's body was inscribed with the markings of the goddess, Karumāriyamma<u>n</u> embodied as Sunithi was Brahmanized by being offered cooling foods, by being made into a Brahman *cumaṅkali*, and by having her volatility translated as playfulness. Also instructive in this regard were the elements that were absent from her performance. Most importantly, Sunithi's version lacked the kinetic signs of mediumship often associated with the practices of the rural and urban poor. Sunithi did not dance or move rhythmically, and her words were comprehensible and uttered in a singsong manner. In fact, when evaluating Sunithi's claims, her followers emphasized the subtlety of her shift from an ordinary person to a divine being.

Despite the familiarity of her ritual syntax, Sunithi did challenge bourgeois Brahman aesthetics. Shortly after the wedding of Sunithi's son, the goddess asked that her shrine be moved into the front room to avoid inconveniencing the newlyweds. This took the shrine out of a controlled, ritually pure space and into a far more accessible area. A more radical transgression of Brahmanic norms occurred when the goddess declared that devotees need not remove footwear in her shrine and that menstruating women and couples who had recently had sex could enter, provided they had bathed.

Valli

Standing in counterpoint to Sunithi's story, and further revealing the tacit dimensions of the caste and class boundaries of her practice and persona, is the story of the medium who helped initiate Sunithi. Valli's story shows the edges, occlusions, and refractions in the imagery of femininity that Sunithi drew on and reworked.

* * *

A couple of months after meeting Sunithi, Minakshi and I went to the Karumāriyamma<u>n</u> temple near Sunithi's house. The temple occupied the ground floor of a large house. Valli lived in the temple while her husband, children, and other relatives occupied the remainder. When we arrived, Valli was in the temple and was preparing to perform *apiṣēkam*. Her appearance was striking—she had piercing eyes and long, matted hair, which she had wound into a topknot. She invited us into the temple, saying, "I knew you were coming. I know who you are, also." She invited us to stay, though she pointed out that she did not ordinarily allow visitors to watch her performing *apiṣēkam,* commenting, "When you bathe, you do so alone. Shouldn't it be that way for the *tēvi*?"

We watched her perform *apiṣēkam.* After sluicing, anointing, and dressing the deities, she applied a thick layer of turmeric and large daubs of vermilion to the *tēvi*'s face. Her daughter, who was assisting her, applied similar decorations to a large silver *mukam.* Minakshi later described her style of decoration to me as "Sudra taste."

When Valli had completed the *apiṣēkam,* she told us that the *tēvi* had first come to her in 1972.

> At that time, there was no house here, only a hut. The *tēvi* came then [in 1972] as a snake, in that very spot [pointing to the platform on which the deity figures stood]. After that happened, people started coming for predictions. They donated money, jewels, saris—all that you see here—and with that, the *tēvi*'s reputation grew. Now the *tēvi* has provided us with all these conveniences—a car, electricity, television—and her shrine has been built up into a permanent structure. (Field notes, September 8, 1987)

Since 1972, the place in which the snake had appeared had changed as well. A mound developed on the site and continued to grow. Valli recognized it as a marker of the goddess's presence; she decorated it and honored the site by performing rituals of worship. The donations she received had allowed her to build the elaborate structure that now stood on that site. When she told me about this, she also observed that among those donors was an anthropologist, a woman who, like me, was devoted to the goddess.[6]

She asked how we had come to know of her, and we told her that Sunithi had described her to us. She then began to speak of Sunithi in very flattering terms and pointed out that Sunithi donated to the temple each month without fail:

> She [Sunithi] was not prepared for the *tēvi.* It was I who brought that *shakti* out and convinced her the *ammaṉ* would come to her house. When the *ammaṉ* first came to her house, she tested Sunithi and it was I who counseled her. I was the only one able to help her with her medical problems. (Field notes, September 8, 1987)

Valli told us more about her own past when we visited her the following week. She herself had had doubts initially, but they were dispelled by a dream in which the goddess had appeared to her with assurances that she would always remain with her. When she got up the next morning, her hair was matted. Her mother had been alarmed when she saw Valli's hair. The family was already so poor and ill treated, she had lamented, why invite further insults? Her husband too was skeptical about Valli's story. But, Valli pointed out, his doubts ended when the *amman* came and spoke to him through Valli, saying,

> I am going to ask you something. You can do it if you wish. If you do not wish to do it, I will leave this place. . . . From today, you should forget that she is your wife. Stop looking at her with those feelings of attachment and desire. She has had sixteen pregnancies and eight children remain. With that, now, it should stop. Give her to me; she will cease to be your wife hereafter. . . . If you accept this, I will stay. . . . otherwise, I will go from here. (Field notes, September 10, 1987)

Her husband did as he was asked, she said, and he had moved, eventually, to a separate section of the house. Valli lived, for the most part, in the temple she had built.

She told us about other miracles the *tēvi* had brought about—cures, wealth, sexual fulfillment. Just before we left, she revealed something that (like Sunithi's earlier pejorative remarks about her) injected complexity into these women's interactions. She alluded to an argument that she was having with the *tēvi.* Her daughter and grandson had recently died, and she was inconsolable. She had, she said, challenged the *tēvi,* wanting to know why Karumāriyamman had allowed these things to happen. Having said that, she then mentioned that when her daughter had been ill, she had called on Sunithi but had not been treated well by her.

* * *

Sunithi had never mentioned Valli's visit and had resisted my efforts to probe her on the subject when I brought it up a few days later. She did, however, reveal the following to Minakshi in my absence, and Minakshi relayed it to me:

> Valli had come one day while they were eating. . . . A cousin was visiting, and he opened the door. He brought her in, and once they had finished eating they came into the front room to meet her. Valli said that she herself had received the *tēvi*'s *uttaravu* telling her to seek Sunithi's advice about her daughter. Sunithi told her that she should return on one of the days that the *amman* comes. Valli was shocked—she expected the *amman* to come right then and there. "But when it is I who have come!" she exclaimed. . . . She continued to press Sunithi . . . saying that she should not have to join the throngs who come at those times. . . . Sunithi simply told her that she might do as she liked. During the next *apiṣēkam,* [Sunithi's] mother asked about Valli's daughter. The *amman* responded, saying that for those who are so ar-

rogant and full of ego, there is no answer. Again, [Sunithi's] mother asked, pleading that they had to send word to Valli about her daughter. The *amman̲* remained firm, saying that there is no need to reply to arrogance. . . . The daughter was dead within ten days. (Field notes, September 25, 1987)

Saraswati

After our brief meeting with Saraswati at Sunithi's house, Minakshi and I were eager to visit her, though I had by that point realized that Minakshi's desires in this regard were not contained by or comprehensible through her role as my research assistant. We both desired knowledge, though my desires stemmed from my intellectual and professional goals. Minakshi, on the other hand, saw these encounters as opportunities to honor the goddess and to seek her intervention.

July 22, 1987. When we arrived at Saraswati's house, we found her alone. She had specified that we visit at midday, she told us, so that we would not be interrupted. We sat in her living room, and she immediately began telling us about what she called, using the English word, her "experiences."

He [her husband] and I usually go to the Karumāriyamman̲ temple in Perambur [a neighborhood in the northern part of the city], even though it is far from our home. . . . We were visiting [my] younger sister in Besant Nagar and a neighbor named Shila was there. Now Prakash's mother [Sunithi] is Shila's guru, so Shila spoke about her and about how the *tēvi* came to her. I listened, but I did not immediately decide to go to see her. After all, we were going to the *tēvi* in one place [Perambur] so it did not seem necessary to see the *tēvi* in other places. . . . Sometime later, though, I accompanied my sister to see Prakash's mother. This was in May or June of 1986. It was a Thursday, so no *pūja* was being done, but in her presence there was lightness, peace, and contentment—no burdens. It was then that Prakash's mother told the story of her experiences with the *tēvi*. . . . I asked her about [my] sister's marriage, but no answer was given. (Field notes, July 22, 1987)

Saraswati then described two subsequent occasions when Sunithi had been asked about the marriage but had given no answer. This had put her into a deep depression, and on one Saturday, in the midst of it, she heard a voice, asking,

"Have you not bathed?" I answered that I had not bathed, nor had I given milk. I was in the habit of offering milk each day to the goddess in our *pūja* room. The voice then spoke again: "Oh, if you have not bathed today, don't

> give me any milk. I want rice and dal." After I bathed and put on *kuṅkumam*, I saw a small girl in a green skirt and red blouse. She pointed out the vessels in which I should keep the food; then she asked for a mirror. . . . Sometime later the vegetable vendor came to the door, but that girl told me that I should not buy any vegetables. She said, "Just fry seven *appaḷams*[7] and give me one, and you all eat the rest." . . . The girl gave me exact instructions for preparing the offering. . . . and then told me to clean the area and draw a *kōlam*.
>
> When I draw a *kōlam*, I usually write, in Tamil, *Om Śrī Cakti Tēvi Karumāriyammaṉ Tuṇai*. When I wrote *Om*, the girl said, "That is most important." When I wrote *cakti*, the girl said, "It is me." When I wrote the remaining words, she asked, "Is it me? Is it me?" To which I answered, "Yes." I then offered rice, dal, and *appaḷam*. I closed my eyes, and I saw the girl taking the food and eating. Then I myself went to eat, and the girl asked, "Should I serve?" I answered, "No." Then the girl told me that for the next nine days, I should offer food to her, but not *cāmpār*—just like that day. In the evening, I was to do *āratti* using *mañcaḷnīr* with coins in it. (Field notes, July 22, 1987)

Saraswati explained that she did as the girl instructed and that she sent word to Sunithi about what had happened. She also said that she had other unusual experiences at that time. When traveling on the bus or by foot, she sensed the girl's presence and sometimes saw her. She noted that the girl looked like a young version of Sunithi. Some months later, around December or January, she had another experience:

> It was a Thursday, around 4:00 in the morning. I felt something hitting me so I turned over and asked my husband if he had done it. He said he had not. Then I saw Shirdhi Sai Baba and Puttuparti Sai Baba. The elder one was sitting on top of the television set, on the left side, and the younger one was standing to the right of it. Puttuparti Sai Baba said, "I am the guru for Prakash's mother, and she is your guru." (Field notes, July 22,1987)

After she finished outlining those experiences, she told us more about the problems that had multiplied in her life since June 1987. Her elder sister's husband had had an accident, and her servant's husband had had a kidney operation. She said that she had prayed for both and had received the *uttaravu* to keep a lamp lit for nine days and to offer one banana each day. She then received another *uttaravu*, the words *maṅkalayam pattiram* [the marriage necklace is strong], and she interpreted this as meaning that both women's husbands would recover and that neither woman would be made a widow. "And that is what happened," she added. Now, she said, "to bring the girl, I need only close my eyes and meditate in the way that Prakash's mother instructed." To underscore the point about the *tēvi*'s presence, Saraswati explained that Sunithi, speaking as the *tēvi*, had said, "I've already come to her [Saraswati's] house. She no longer has to come her for *uttaravu;* she can meditate at home." Saraswati added that she sometimes had visions of the goddess in the form of Sunithi. She specified that once, while offering milk,

> I saw Prakash's mother in my mind, coming and drinking three times. The three times signified wealth, fame, and character. The fame and character are already here, but the wealth will come with *tēvi,* when Prakash's mother comes to this house wearing silk. (Field notes, July 22, 1987)

Though Saraswati stressed that she made efforts to advise family members based on what she understands to be the *tēvi*'s *uttaravu,* not all of them believed that she had such powers. Her brothers, she said, were skeptical. Saraswati followed this allusion to domestic fault lines with some background information about her family. Her only child was a son (14 years old), though she had a second son who died in 1981 at the age of sixteen months. She attributed his death to a smallpox-type disease. She was despondent over the baby's death and stopped going to all temples except the Karumāriyamma<u>n</u> temple in Perambur. She also returned to the fact that her younger sister was not married. This had been the original impetus for her going to Sunithi, but because it was still not resolved she suffered anxiety over that as well. Finally, she confided that although her husband believed in her "powers," her in-laws did not; that was a source of continuing friction with her in-laws and with her husband. As she continued, though, her husband's position was shown to be more ambiguous:

> We used to go to the Karumāriyamma<u>n</u> temple regularly, but I stopped going after having those visits from the little girl. He [her husband] continues to go. . . . Lately, he has been very tense and prone to anger. On the most recent Tuesday that he went, the goddess asked me why he went that distance when the *shakti* is right here, in his own house. (Field notes, July 22, 1987)

Saraswati's revelations about these familial conflicts seemed to strike a chord with Minakshi. We had listened sympathetically, and Minakshi responded by sharing some of her own difficulties—her efforts to arrange her daughter's marriage, her husband's difficulties in business, and her son's lack of employment. She also mentioned the earlier, still unresolved disagreements between her and her in-laws that had led to the breakup of their joint household. With this, Minakshi began to sob, and both Saraswati and I tried to comfort her. Minakshi then asked Saraswati why the goddess was putting her through these things.

It was at that point that the event, which had begun as an interview, shifted in form and content. Its tacitly understood organization—our elicitation of "data" from Saraswati the "informant"—changed as Minakshi and Saraswati discovered that they had shared painful experiences. Completing this turn, Saraswati asked Minakshi to accompany her into her kitchen. Her shrine was located there, and Saraswati intended to ask the goddess about Minakshi's problems. I felt uncomfortable intruding, so I did not accompany them. Later Minakshi told me what had happened. She said that Saraswati had lit two incense sticks and then closed her eyes, meditating; Minakshi closed her eyes also. They sat like that for some time, without speaking, though Minakshi said that she had no clear idea about the duration. Minakshi finally broke the silence and asked about her daughter's marriage. Saraswati responded that it would take place by *Tai* month if Minakshi made a strong effort. Minakshi then asked about her son, but there was no answer. After they left the kitchen and joined me in the living room, Saraswati offered to "light the lamp for forty-five days"[8] for Minakshi's son, and she advised Minakshi to do the same.

* * *

Shortly after we visited Saraswati, I left Chennai for a week. When I returned, Minakshi and I talked about events that had occurred in my absence. The wedding of Sunithi's son had taken place, and, as had been predicted, the goddess had come and blessed the couple and the guests. More interesting to me were the deepening connections among Minakshi, Sunithi, and Saraswati. In our conversation, Saraswati had spoken of the goddess's prediction that she would become prosperous after Sunithi, clad in silk, came to visit. Thereupon Saraswati had invited Sunithi and her husband to her home on July 31. No ritual was scheduled, but other guests had also been invited—Saraswati's sisters and mother, her mother-in-law, Minakshi and her daughter. Minakshi described the event to me. The women gathered in the kitchen and watched as Sunithi dressed and decorated the figure of Karumāriyammaṉ. Minakshi remarked on Sunithi's skill and described having a sensation of happiness and contentment upon seeing how beautiful the goddess looked after Sunithi's ministrations. Saraswati then meditated, and the goddess came to her; in that state, she responded to the other women's questions.

When Minakshi told me about this, she described Sunithi's questions to the goddess but not her own. In a reversal of the relations of authority that I had assumed to exist (i.e., Sunithi initiated Saraswati and was her "guru"), Sunithi sought the *tēvi*'s counsel through Saraswati. Most of the questions concerned family relations. Sunithi asked about her mother's health, about the upcoming wedding of her son, and about whether she and her husband would die together. Saraswati responded that her mother was only tired and overworked, the marriage would go off well, and that "she" (Karumāriyamman̲) would be there. Finally, it was "too sad to ask about last things, what will happen will happen." Minakshi then repeated a comment that Saraswati had made to her: "She [Minakshi] is devoted to me. She goes to my temples and provides me with nice things; I will take care of her."

* * *

These moments of apparent reciprocity and bonding among the women were soon ruptured, just as earlier Sunithi's deference to Valli had eroded. Domestic conflict and friction surrounding Saraswati's and Sunithi's competing claims of authority fractured relations among the women and within their respective families. Their dedication to and identification with the goddess made their negotiation of *cumaṅkali*hood more perilous. At the same time, any flaws in their wifely performances could tarnish their reputations as goddess *bhakta*s and, worse, dishonor the goddess herself. Into this mix, another complicating factor was added. Sunithi revealed to Minakshi that she [Minakshi] also had a "hidden power": The goddess would soon come to her. This moment came on Varalakshmi *nōn̲pu,* an annual observance undertaken by Smārta women to ensure their husbands' long lives and their own auspicious deaths as *cumaṅkali*s. This was the same occasion on which the goddess had chosen to come to Sunithi's household years earlier.

August 11, 1987. Minakshi, her daughter, and I visited both Sunithi and Saraswati the first day of Varalakshmi *nōn̲pu.* Minakshi wanted to present both with small bowls for holding *kuṅkumam,* and she decided that we ought to call on Sunithi first because she was the guru. When we got there, Sunithi, speaking as the *amman̲,* invited us to come in and sit down. Sunithi first addressed Minakshi's daughter and then praised Minakshi's goodness and devotion.

SUNITHI: If she sincerely wishes good for someone, then it will happen—that is her power. . . . I am inside you. You have a *shakti* of which you are not aware. Once it emerges, your power will increase and many things will happen as signs.

MINAKSHI: I'm not fit to have this power. I go to temples because it is part of my job.

SUNITHI: I know when to bring it out.

MINAKSHI: I don't want to become arrogant. I want to remain humble—I want to stay as I am.

SUNITHI: You don't have to worry; mistakes will be pardoned if they are not intentional. I am deep in your heart. (Field notes, August 11, 1987)

Sunithi then advised Minakshi to limit her visits to Saraswati:

> She is a good person, but her husband is not as kind as she is. He becomes impatient with her, and with her friends. He may insult you, and that would bring about the degradation of her power. . . . You need not go there often, for you have so much power yourself. (Field notes, August 11, 1987)

Minakshi had listened to all this with complete absorption. Later, after we had left, she continued to mull over what Sunithi had said. She seemed hesitant to accept Sunithi's words as true, yet she also seemed intrigued by the possibility of an emergent power. We went directly to Saraswati's after leaving Sunithi's. There we found Saraswati along with her sister. Minakshi told them about her visit to Sunithi and about Sunithi's revelation concerning her powers. Shortly after we arrived, Saraswati meditated and entered the goddess state, in which she praised Minakshi's goodness and power, and counseled patience with regard to her family problems. To Minakshi she said, "When I am in you, why should you worry?"

Later that day, as Minakshi and I sat together having coffee, we reviewed the day's events. She repeated some other things that Sunithi had told her about Saraswati. Later, in my notes, I wrote:

> Since her experiences with the *tēvi,* Saraswati's feelings have changed. Her mind is more occupied with matters of a religious nature than with family things. She is becoming less attached to her husband; she is less interested and there is sexual tension between them. Saraswati has been told by the *tēvi* that she will soon move to a large house with a separate room for the *tēvi,* and she will spend most of the time there. Saraswati feels that her husband is not like Sunithi's husband, who does not lose his temper and does not become irritated with the crowds that are often present at their house. Saraswati's husband tends to become angry often. (Field notes, August 11, 1987)

The network around Sunithi had shifted with this repositioning of relations of power and affect. Saraswati's domestic problems brought friction into her friendships with Sunithi and the other women in Sunithi's circle; Minakshi, on the other hand, was the rising star—the client/initiate for whom both Sunithi and Saraswati competed. It was possible that I was one of the prizes in this tourney, though as things continued to unfold, my own marginality became more apparent to me. It was not my attention that they sought; they were negotiating reputation and subjectivity in a moral and political landscape that was outside my experience and difficult for me to fully grasp. This became more apparent over the next few weeks.

August 20–September 27, 1987. After Sunithi's disclosures to Minakshi about Minkshi's *shakti,* Minakshi had what she called a "vision" (using the English word). She felt that she could detect the outline of the face of the goddess Kamakshi on her kitchen wall. Shortly after that, she thought she saw the outline of Shiva. She told me that she had asked Saraswati about these phenomena and Saraswati, speaking as the goddess, had confirmed that Kamakshi was present there. Minakshi quoted Saraswati's words:

> I am there because of all of the attention that you have paid me—going to temples and visiting other devotees with the American woman [Mary]—and because you speak of me so often. You have said my name and have praised me. For all these reasons, I have become happy and have come to your house. Nataraja is there also because of the joy and contentment that is in that house. That house is overflowing with the presence of God. (Field notes, August 22, 1987)

Minakshi had told me, a few months earlier, that she wanted to begin a new *pūja* cycle.[9] These experiences clinched things for her, and on the first new moon day, an auspicious time for starting new projects, she invited a friend's guru, an elderly man, to her house to initiate her. Later that same day, she and her husband had a fight. He criticized her, she said, observing that all of her devotions were of no good if they caused her to speak sharply to him or to ignore him. This made her indignant—she retorted that she was only human, not a saint, and that it was impossible not to make mistakes. But, she asserted, she was entitled to involve herself in devotional practice if she felt drawn to it.

The argument was not resolved and was replayed on several occasions thereafter. Minakshi's position, as she described it to me, was based on a general idea about family responsibilities. The husband should be the breadwinner and the wife, the cook. Together they were responsible for their children's well-being. She pointed out, however, that her particular situation required that she contribute to the household's income and that she seek other avenues of advice and assistance—consulting astrologers, mediums, and so forth. She admitted that she, counter to her feminine virtues, became impatient at times but maintained that she always regretted it and apologized.

Despite domestic conflicts (which had damaged Saraswati's reputation), Minakshi retained Sunithi's favor. In early September, at her next *apiṣēkam* (about a week after Minakshi's *pūja* initiation), Sunithi asked Minakshi to assist her. During the ritual, Minakshi sat facing Sunithi and poured the liquids as Sunithi held the figures. She also announced each step as Sunithi performed it. Saraswati was also at the *apiṣēkam,* and when she saw Minakshi, she chided her for not visiting. She said that she had done an *apiṣēkam* at her house on the preceding Friday and had wanted her there. She said that she had sent word through Sunithi. Minakshi, however, had not been told, though she quickly excused Sunithi's forgetfulness.

Later that same day, when Sunithi had assumed the *ammaṉ* form and was giving predictions, she told Minakshi that she was "testing" Saraswati to determine if she was strong enough to hold the *tēvi*'s power. A couple of weeks later, Sunithi (in ordinary form) elaborated about this to Minakshi. (Here I have relied on Minakshi's reporting, for I was not present.)

Minakshi paraphrased Sunithi, telling me (in English) that Sunithi thought Saraswati too emotional and unstable. When the goddess came to her, she lost strength and consequently confused her personal feelings with the goddess's intentions. Sunithi attributed Saraswati's weakness to both psychological and physical factors, describing how the strain on the body caused by the goddess's presence sapped Saraswati's ability to restrain her own intentions, desires, and feelings.

Sunithi explained to Minakshi that it was necessary to rest after the goddess had come—that the *shakti* of the goddess was so great that it drained the body of her human host. Sunithi invoked the same principle in response to Minakshi's question about why the goddess manifested herself differently in different persons. It was this differential ability to control the *tēvi*'s power that caused this. She pointed out that Valli had also lost control and attributed her requests for specific types of gifts and payments, as well as inaccurate predictions, to this decline. Similarly, another sign of Saraswati's weakness was the fact that she had made some serious errors in advising people. Sunithi said that Saraswati had recently told an expectant couple, with whom they were mutually acquainted, that the wife would give birth to a healthy boy. It turned out that the woman had to have an abortion, and when they returned to Saraswati to find out why things had turned out differently than expected, she (as *ammaṉ*) attributed it to "fate" *(viti)*. Sunithi dismissed that explanation as inadequate and irresponsible; a better response, and one more worthy of the *ammaṉ*, might have referred to *karma* and the sins of past lives. With that, Sunithi concluded that Saraswati had obviously overextended herself.

She added that these kinds of inaccuracies could endanger Saraswati, especially because she was issuing predictions for servants and *cēri* people. Sunithi added that "such people" tended to resort to violence when they felt that they had been cheated and that Saraswati was courting danger by involving herself too closely with their lives. Finally, she pointed out that if Saraswati continued in this vein, it would appear to devotees that the *tēvi* was contradicting herself, and this would degrade Sunithi's status as well as Saraswati's.

The conversations that Minakshi recounted to me marked the growing intimacy between her and Sunithi. Minakshi had moved from being an interested outsider to being a disciple and then an initiate. Their mutual dependence was cemented when Sunithi paired criticism of Saraswati with praise for Minakshi, and Sunithi repeated this strategy on several occasions thereafter. Following an *apiṣēkam* that took place a couple of weeks later, Sunithi (speaking as the goddess) assured Minakshi that she was much stronger than Saraswati and that because of her power, she need not consult Saraswati. Minakshi would not acquire the strength of Sunithi, however, but would remain just a "notch below."

As these debates escalated over the following months, Sunithi's claims of authority within her client circle also intensified. She, as *amma<u>n</u>*, became more demanding of her followers—asking for larger donations and greater loyalty from disciples of whom she approved. Correspondingly, she distanced herself more sharply from Saraswati, whom she had come to see as a blight on her own reputation. Minakshi continued to visit Saraswati and Sunithi, trying with great difficulty to remain friend and disciple to both.

The Letter

In October 1988, some months after I had returned to the United States, I received a letter from Minakshi telling me that Sunithi's daughter-in-law had left her husband and had returned to live with her own parents. She indicated that the daughter-in-law had become disenchanted with Sunithi's domination in household matters, and she reported (in English) that the daughter-in-law had begun to "speak ill of the *amma<u>n</u>*" (i.e., of Sunithi as *amma<u>n</u>*). Other devotees had become skeptical of Sunithi's powers as a result, and this, Minakshi wrote, had caused the size of Sunithi's following to diminish. She herself ceased visiting Sunithi not long thereafter.

Improvised Lives

The ascetic's matted hair. Beads of divine nectar. *Kuṅkumam* and turmeric. A wedding sari of maroon silk. These images, drawn from the repertoire of Hindu orthopraxy, were deployed in novel ways by Sunithi, Valli, Saraswati, and Minakshi. A deity's coming to a devotee, though not common, was part of a continuum that included a variety of types of bodily transformation, all of which were considered parts of Brahmanical orthopraxy.[10] These transformations (discussed in Chapter 3) included people's devotional "surrender" *(caraṇam)* to deities, the dangerous and beneficial effects associated with the physico-moral energy of sight (as *tiruṣṭi* or *darshan*), and the capacity of both deities and humans to absorb and to be transformed by the qualities of substances used in worship. The improvisations enacted by the women described in the present chapter are examples of such transformations, and they speak, as well, to the dilemmas of everyday life and the societal architecture of power and authority in which such dilemmas arise. They speak, as well, to the women's own creativity and thus to the importance of religious imagination as it appropriates and invents culture.

Reinventing the Body

Sunithi's and Valli's bodies and homes were transformed in ways that were intelligible to others as signs, albeit contestable ones, of divine power. The presence of the goddess was signaled by changes in their hair.[11] From the ninth *apiṣēkam,* around the time when she started to speak with the *tēvi*'s voice, Sunithi noted that "the *tēvi* told me to leave my hair loose. I should not do anything except comb it. My mother asked the *tēvi* to allow me to fix it for one day—for my son's wedding—but the *tēvi* said no even to that." Valli indicated that her hair had become matted spontaneously after the goddess appeared to her in a dream. She also was rebuked by her mother, who feared that it would put her completely outside the bounds of respectability. Notably, both women also felt themselves to be capable of resisting the goddess's requests and controlling her power. Each hesitated and argued. Even when they complied, they referred to the tension that existed in that relation and emphasized the strength needed to control the goddess.

When the goddess came to a woman, the contradictions that were implicit features of bodily experience were exhibited and dramatized. They were enacted through and on the body—by dissociating consciousness from the body and the world of objects of which the body is part, by fracturing intentionality, by displacing agency, by multiplying subject positions. Sunithi distinguished the "light" *(oḷi)* of the goddess's voice from the "body" *(uṭampu)*—her own—that uttered the words. The boundary between "light" and "body," however, was permeable. The relationship between the goddess's voice and Sunithi's body was dynamic, and it changed over time. During the first nine *apiṣēkam*s that Sunithi, as *ammaṉ,* had performed, her body was not her own. She could not speak; she lacked intentionality and conscious awareness of her actions. Yet with the tenth *apiṣēkam,* she began to speak; the goddess's light infused her body and she acquired the "strength" *(palam)* to control the goddess. Later this strength enabled her to remain conscious while possessed. By the time I knew her, she had reassembled a new subjectivity that fused the light of the goddess's voice with her own human body.

Equally dramatic were the changes in the other objects that had become imbued with the goddess's energy at her coming. The snake pit near Valli's hut and the Varalakshmi *mukam* in Sunithi's shrine changed as the women's relations with Karumāriyamma<u>n</u> changed. The ordinarily permeable boundaries among material substances to which notions of pollution attest were, in these instances, intensified. The snake pit and the *mukam* were indices and icons of the goddess that changed physically as the power of the goddess and her desire for Sunithi's and Valli's acquiescence grew. Miming the objects' transformations, the women changed bodily as they surrendered to the goddess. Finally, it was the goddess, in a multiplicity of forms, who acted and was acted upon. It was *as* Karumāriyamma<u>n</u> that the women ministered to that goddess by worshiping her as she was embodied in the objects.

The transformations were not smooth. For Sunithi and the others, they began in places and actions that were sites for the iterations of womanhood—in kitchens and in domestic ritual practices. The women acted in accordance with the cultural logic of *cumaṅkali*hood. They were angry, frightened, and anxious because of a child's death, sexual discord, reproductive problems, and dysmenorrhea. The goddess offered comfort and resolution, but even that brought uncertainty and domestic friction.

The intelligibility of the goddess's coming to them depended on shared understandings about the permeability of bodily boundaries and the transferability of substance that were part of the women's everyday experience. For all of them, femininity was negotiated aesthetically, on and through the body and other objects, like clothing or jewelry. Thus, the body and sexuality, far from being natural sources of experiences that defined womanhood, were themselves shaped by the women's performance of gender identity and difference. I explored this logic in Chapters 3 and 4. Women assumed and lost *cumaṅkali* identities through practices that included bathing and dressing, cooking and serving food, praying, fasting, and visiting temples. Their performance of femininity also depended on negative agency, such as the strategies of avoidance and silence derived from concepts of pollution, modesty, and familial honor. In each practical iteration of womanhood, however, women encountered abjection. Many, like Janaki and Anandaveli, strove to resolve these contradictions within the bounds of normativity. But others, like Sunithi, Valli, Minakshi, and Saraswati, experimented with and tested those boundaries, thereby formulating new meanings in the ritual repertoires of daily life.

Fracturing Womanhood

The stories and the ways that they were told to me suggest how discourses on femininity both militate against and mediate inequalities among women. Women's participation in goddess devotion was not restricted to any caste or class. This might have been the case because it was a way of dealing with issues that affected many women, such as problems with menstruation and childbearing, childrearing, sexuality, and marriage. After completing my fieldwork, I learned that another anthropologist, Margaret Trawick, had worked extensively with Valli (1982a, 1982b), whom she called Saraswati. Trawick's rich and nuanced analyses emphasized the importance of suffering in Valli's experiences of mediumship. Valli's suffering—due to poverty, marital tensions, and ill health—had defined the essence of *shakti* for her and had shaped her notions of womanhood (Trawick 1982b, 11–15). The association of some goddesses with particular diseases like measles, tuberculosis, or typhoid only strengthens this. Such principles may have informed the understanding of the goddess, held by Valli, Saraswati, Minakshi, and Sunithi, as a being who invited all women into her presence.[12] Their own interdependence, precarious as it was, suggests how ritual practice and universalizing images of femininity may foster connections among women. And the different forms of the goddess who came to women hinted at the existence of a variety of ways of performing Hindu womanhood.

The appeal that such practices held for women lay in their reliance on bodily modalities. Goddess devotion expressed and, in limited ways, resolved contradictory features of *cumaṅkali* identity. This was amplified in the case of mediumship. None of the women entirely relinquished her domestic identity as a *cumaṅkali.* It was *as* a *cumaṅkali* that each woman formulated a special relationship with the goddess, and it was through the household as a collectivity that this relationship was accorded social value. Though they advocated a release from worldly and sexual attachments, they represented this not as detachment but as weightlessness *(ilecu).* They used this term, as well as peace *(amaiti).* Although their comments referred to sensations that were physically perceptible, these expressions entailed implicit metaphors of release from duties and relationships that shaped *cumaṅkali* personhood. Instead of being a permanent removal from the house, release could involve an inversion of roles within the house. As *amma<u>n</u>,* for example, Sunithi temporarily relinquished her duties as wife, mother, and mother-in-law, while retaining the privileges and authority of her divine persona. These desires for release, however, were carefully hedged. Unlike the goddess Karumāriyamma<u>n</u>, whose power remained unrestrained and unchanneled (due to the absence of a husband), the women described here were not eager to be similarly independent, apart from during the liminal interludes of the goddess's coming. Indeed, Sunithi set about redressing the goddess's own independent status by displaying with the Varalakshmi *mukam* images of Shiva, Murukan, and Ganesha, which she described as the goddess's family. Autonomy, with its connotations of loneliness, pride, and boldness, was similarly troubling. Minakshi, for example, often stated that she did not wish to become arrogant with the emergence of her powers.

Their strategies point to the ambiguities and boundary transgressions that *cumaṅkali*hood entailed for Brahman women. In the first place, women embodied Otherness in that their own bodies were sites of regular, polluting states. There were also contacts between Brahman women and persons deemed, by Brahmans, to be categorically Other. This occurred on an everyday basis in their relations with non-Brahman servants; women's participation in *nōṉpu*s could also entail similar boundary transgressions. For example, the goddess temples that Brahman women visit on Fridays and Tuesdays, and during *Āṭi* month, were often maintained by non-Brahmans. Valli's abrupt and creative refusal of the *cumaṅkali* mantle with its implied "respectability" (i.e., accommodation to upper caste/class mores) may have inspired Sunithi's own reinterpretation of *cumaṅkali* identity.

Being a *cumaṅkali,* then, involved a regular negotiation of identity and difference among women. As such, these practices articulated with other forms of social inequality. For many in Tamil Nadu, the condition described as *āvēcam* (often glossed as "spirit possession") had low-caste, rural associations. Its conventional behaviors (dancing and self-mortification) were considered features of poor, low-caste identity by urban elites. It is worth noting that neither Sunithi nor her clients spoke of her condition using the term *āvēcam.* Her followers, in fact, supported Sunithi's claim that the goddess regularly came to her because her experiences were *not* conventional. Over time, Sunithi came to use Valli as a boundary marker, as the negative case that demonstrated her own authenticity as the goddess's oracle. Valli's "Sudra" tastes were seen as consistent with arrogance and commercialism; they were the codes that placed her style of *cumaṅkali*hood outside the ambit of femininity with which the Brahman women identified. Sunithi's criticisms of Saraswati (and her support for Minakshi) exemplified a comparable boundary. Saraswati's experiments with autonomy rendered her a dangerous Other and put her in the same category as the "*cēri* people" who were her clients. Saraswati, like Valli, was represented by Sunithi as a failed *cumaṅkali* and thus as a deceiver whose oracular pronouncements were unreliable.

The differences to which I have referred were related to both caste and class. Indeed, the ways that women talked about and enacted difference show the extent to which they operated within a socially situated common sense in which caste and class identities interpenetrated. Markers of respectability could refer simultaneously to class privilege and to caste superiority. In this regard, the presence of Sathya Sai Baba in their devotional practices deserves mention. Sathya Sai Baba has become extremely popular in urban south India in recent years, especially among elites (Babb 1987; Swallow 1982). Babb identified Sathya Sai Baba's appeal as a type of religious modernism having particular resonance with the experience of India's "bicultural elites" (1987, 200). He explained that Sathya Sai Baba's reconfigured Hinduism, with its miracles such as medical interventions and the spontaneous appearance of sacred ash and *shivalingams,*[13] did several things for his followers:

> Allegiance to Baba might serve to revive a sense of the efficacy of a tradition that otherwise seems to be rendered increasingly irrelevant by modern conditions of life. For those among his devotees whose religious lives were relatively unenergized before they entered his cult . . . devotion to Sathya Sai Baba may also represent a way of reclaiming the religious culture of childhood that makes less than onerous demands on spiritual sensibilities. . . . Sathya Sai Baba's cult makes a strong appeal to feelings of simple cultural nationalism in some devotees. . . . it also appeals to a sense of social altruism that has an honored place in India's modern culture of nationhood. . . . but Sathya Sai Baba's profound conservatism on fundamentals like caste and gender ensures that doing good is unlikely to challenge his devotees' more basic sense of propriety and order. (Babb 1987, 200–201).

It was both Sathya Sai Baba and the goddess Karumāriyammaṉ who mediated Sunithi's experiences and her interpretations of events in her disciples' lives. This occurred without any physical contact between her and Sathya Sai Baba. It was her interpretation of his visual image that guided her understanding of his interventions. The contention that Sathya Sai Baba provided idioms for an elite appropriation of tradition is further supported by contrasting Sunithi's devotion to him with Valli's disinterest. Sathya Sai Baba was an unproblematic feature in many middle-class families' domestic pantheons; his pictures were absent from Valli's temple, however, and (according to Sunithi) she viewed Sunithi's devotion to him with suspicion.

To understand the nature of the Brahman women's encounters with beings like Karumāriyammaṉ or Sathya Sai Baba, it is helpful to consider these phenomena in the context of Smārtas' intentional world. In some schools of Hindu thought, including that to which Smārtas subscribed, monism—the unity of body and mind, matter and spirit—is a central tenet. The multiple forms of alienation and recombination that the goddess's coming might involve rupture these dominant discourses. In the cases recounted, however, these ruptures did not yield a Euro-Western mind-body duality but instead produced shifting subjectivities that were grounded in but detachable from the object world. These subjectivities depended on, transformed, and were transformed by materialities. As she lived within Hindu orthopraxy, a woman *was* her body and existed within the terrain of its contradictions. Entered by a goddess who lived at the edges of orthopraxy, women became temporarily alienated from their bodies, though they did not relinquish that materiality but remade it. Sunithi remarked that when the goddess came to her, she felt as though she could fly *(paṟa)*. Such experiences enabled women to control, temporarily, the forms of binding and tying that metaphorically made *cumaṅkali*hood, to escape the abjection manifest in menstruation and childbirth, and to recirculate the energy of sexual desire in relations that fell outside heterosexual married life. This was all possible without compromising their marital fidelity *(kaṟpu)*.

Each woman's narrative revealed less about the institutional constraints on them than about how institutional forms and institutionalized representations emerged "as constructs . . . out of [the] experience[s] presented in her story" (Behar 1990, 229; see also Behar 1992; Sangari 1991). In everyday talk, discourses of taste, style, and aesthetic preference were constructed and circulated; conversational and narrative practices were produced and reproduced distinctions. These modes of discourse should be considered in making sense of the ways that privilege is understood and delimited in society (Bourdieu 1984). In India, caste exists bureaucratically in the institutionalized discourses and practices of state-authored reservation policies. It is present, also, in the visceral realities of torched squatter settlements and gang rapes. I contend that it exists, as well, in everyday discourses of aesthetic judgment, desire, and identity. The ways in which the women framed their narratives (and commented on those of others) were in no sense reducible to caste/class positioning, though they did reveal the extent to which caste identity was negotiated, intersubjectively, as part of an everyday politics of identity in which the stakes were the wealth, good name, and moral integrity of human persons and deities.

Notes

1. See Sarkar (1991) and Sarkar and Butalia (1995) on the ways that the current Hindutva movement foregrounds the militantly communal woman. Chakravarti (1990), Chatterjee (1989), and Mani (1990) discuss colonial deployments of woman and nation. Lakshmi (1990) and Ramaswamy (1997) focus on idioms of motherhood in Dravidian nationalism.

2. The term refers to divinely inspired predictions, advice, or directions issued by a superior.

3. A Sanskritic word referring to divine nectar.

4. She spoke Tamil in our interviews, as well as some English. She understood English and thus was able to check on my translations and sometimes gave her own glosses for Tamil expressions.

5. This, like assistance with ritual, was very common among adepts. It was not a literal translation but an interpretation of the significance of utterances for the clients.

6. I decided that the anthropologist of whom Valli spoke might have been Margaret Trawick, for the story that Valli told me and the one that Trawick had published in her article "On the Meaning of *Sakti* to Women in Tamil Nadu" (1982b) were very close. When I got back to United States, I wrote to Trawick to inquire about it. In her response, Trawick indicated that she felt quite sure that the woman I met and the woman named Saraswati whom she described in her article were one and the same.

7. *Appaḷam* is a type of wafer made from dal flour. It is fried and eaten as an accompaniment to a meal or snack. It is considered a Brahman-style food.

8. This was a reference to *tiruviḷakku pūja,* described in Chapters 3–4.

9. The cycle to which she referred was actually a graduated sequence of *pūja*s honoring the goddess, known as "Śrī Vidya" to which people were initiated by gurus, generally, male ritual adepts.

10. Anthropological studies of "spirit possession" reflect the diverse and contentious styles of interpretation that characterize the field as a whole (Bourguignon 1976). In a useful review, Janice Boddy (1994) has identified several major strands in the study of spirit possession: those that focus on biomedical and social functions (and/or etiology) of possession (Lewis 1989; more reductively, Ward 1989; Kehoe and Giletti 1981; Cardena 1992) and those that apply a religious focus (Bastide 1978)—frequently by seeing possession cults as the ecstatic fringe of orthodoxy (e.g., charismatic Christianity or products of syncretism of world religions with local, often animistic systems). Both of the latter aim for generalizable and thus decontextualized explanations; as such they offer useful, albeit limited insights. I argue with Boddy that it is better to explain acts glossed as possession as having multiple significances—as local idioms that can articulate a range of experiences (Crapanzano and Garrison 1977). Understood in this way, such behaviors can be interpreted as commentaries on morality or social order (often involving critique or resistance), as modalities for healing or expressing affliction, and/or as identity constituting practices (Boddy 1989; Lambek 1993; Comaroff 1985; Stoller 1989; Kapferer 1991; Obeyesekere 1981; Csordas 1993; Ong 1987).

I argue with Boddy that hermeneutic and practice-oriented approaches offer stronger, more context-sensitive explanations than functional or biomedical accounts. There are, however, additional issues warranting critical scrutiny, and these turn on the translatability of "spirit possession" as an analytic category. The entry for "possession" in the Oxford English Dictionary reveals that its usage derives from Euro-Western legal understandings of property ownership and alienability (1340 C.E.) and the notions of individual subjectivity derived therefrom, and from Judeo-Christian concepts of demonic possession (1590 C.E.). The behavioral repertoire that I discuss in this chapter certainly falls within what anthropologists have called "spirit possession," but I think that the term tends to misrepresent the phenomena that it purports to explain. The goddess's coming to a devotee is hardly a "demonic" visitation, nor does the deity "control" or "own" the devotee in any straightforward sense. Such events were described in Tamil using terms that were part of a larger semantic domain encompassing terms such as *eri, kaṭṭu,* and *paṟṟu,* which describe attachments among humans, between humans and inanimate objects, and between humans and deities; these terms also emphasize biomoral connectedness and/or exchanges of energies. I suspect that a careful study of early efforts to explain Hindu "spirit possession" would reveal that the discursive fields have been structured by Euro-Western, and particularly Judeo-Christian, assumptions about the intrinsically demonic quality of Hinduism (see Scott 1995, 111–169 for a well-documented and detailed critique of the influence of "demonism" in the interpretation of Sri Lankan Buddhism).

11. This loosening of her hair was significant in that it inverted normative feminine practice. The chastity that encircled married women's sexuality was registered in the imagery of tying and binding enacted in ritual, as well as in styles of grooming, dress, and behavior. Women's hair was particularly attended to in this regard; it was plaited, wound into a bun, or held by clips or cloth ties. It did not, in any event, fall loose around the face. Loose hair carried inauspicious connotations. Orthoprax women only loosened their hair at the time of a close relative's death, and that was done in association with the ritualized bathing that followed the announcement of the death. It could also connote the concentrated power of *shakti.* It was the latter association that was prominent in iconography of volatile forms of the goddess—she was usually represented with loosened hair. Similarly the matted hair *(jaṭai)* of ascetics, male and female, was a marker of the power that had accumulated as a result of their bodily disciplines (see Obeyesekere 1981).

12. This was sometimes conjoined with an explicit avoidance of male mediums, who were often perceived by women as sexual predators.

13. An aniconic form of Shiva in the form of a phallus.

PART FOUR

The Home in the World

6

Hinduism and the Spaces of Modernity

The Indian Census, 1961 . . . [has] undertaken a number of special studies to highlight the social and cultural heritage of India. In keeping with this tradition, a scheme for preparing a compendium volume on the temples of Madras state was mooted. South Indian temples, marvelous in architectural engineering and having a cultural greatness of their own, have attracted a large number of tourists from all parts of the country and even from abroad. South India has been least affected by the series of invasions which India witnessed because of its geographic isolation and the Hindu culture has been preserved in its most pristine form in Madras State. As Hindu culture is largely associated with temples, it is likely that a study of the temples of Madras State will give a background of what Hindu culture stands for.

—P. Nambiar and N. Krishnamurthy, *Census of India, 1961*, vol. 9, pt. 11-D, p. xv

Until about four years ago, this temple [Tiruvalluvar] was in the hands of godless people.. It was in terrible shape—overgrown and dirty—Sudras had overtaken it and spent their time within these walls drinking and gambling. Brahmans who lived nearby were loath to enter—they were ridiculed and even beaten by those who occupied the temple grounds. . . . A Brahman woman, living on the next street, had a dream in which Kamakshi appeared to her and chided her for allowing her shrine to fall into such a state. This woman decided to enter the temple grounds and to inspect Kamakshi's shrine. . . . She made up her mind to make the shrine more habitable for the tēvi and began that project about four years ago. Others joined her . . . and now the maṇṭali comes daily to recite Lalitha Sahasranaṉmam, continuing with bhajans as the mood strikes them. . . . On Tuesdays, [they] come to the Durga shrine during the rākukālam. . . . Also, on the Pradosham day of each month . . . they come for pūja.

—Lalitha, speaking to the author at the Tiruvalluvar temple, August 14, 1987

The first epigraph, taken from the 1961 Indian census report, is a state-sanctioned expression of the Indian government's interest in Hindu temples, and it alludes to two kinds of maps. One, a body count, is the sort of map ordinarily implied in the notion of the census; the other, an enumeration of temples, represents the cultural space of the nation. The second epigraph is an oral endorsement of one woman's efforts to redress what she viewed as the government's mismanagement of a temple. Like the cases discussed in earlier chapters, her actions were underwritten by the desires and quotidian practices of *cumaṅkali*hood. Lalitha's comments also refer to mappable spaces, though her map is positional and describes her own and other women's pedestrian traversing of physical space (see Figure 6.1) instead of recording a view from nowhere.

Although these excerpts come from divergent kinds of sources and appear to have contradictory implications, they typify two genres of narrative that often converge in discourses of collective memory and identity authored by urban Brahmans in Tamil Nadu. One tells of the past glories of the south, as under royal patronage Hindu culture flourished through the ministrations of Brahman priests and literati. It also asserts the modern state's continuing role as protector. The other laments the present dystopia—the denigration of Hindu culture by "godless people" and a neglectful government. These discourses appropriate "the state" as a trope, either enabling or oppositional, in their narration of collective identity.

The deployment of these discourses in creating new sites for public worship and thereby reconfiguring public culture within and against state institutions in urban south India is the subject of Part 3. In Chapter 6, I review the shifting relations between the state and the Hindu religious institutions and how this has shaped public culture in India. In Chapter 7, I focus on the efforts that two women made to fashion new forms of public worship that simultaneously relied on and resisted the appropriation of Hinduism by the state. In Chapter 8, I deal with a socioreligious movement headed by a Smārta religious leader. The movement, Ja<u>n</u> Kalyāṇ, promoted Hindu nationalism, or Hindutva, and had ties to nationalist political parties and voluntary associations. The different reinscriptions of Hindu practice and identity that Chapters 7 and 8 describe were enabled by the feminization of worship that has gathered momentum in many parts of India, though especially in the south, over the past half century. The cases, located at the intersection of a range of debates about India's "public sphere," about national ideology and its gendered subjects, and about the cultural politics of caste identity, present opportunities for a close look at these historical and social processes and their contested infrastructures.

Hindu Temples and the "Public Sphere"

The census passage extracted at the beginning of the chapter indicates that Hindu temples have served as sites for competitive constructions of a public sphere in modern India. Temples, as loci for collective ritual activity and sumptuary display, are certainly public places insofar as they are open and accessible to large sections of the populace. What has turned out to be persistently problematic since the colonial introduc-

FIGURE 6.1 A Woman Pauses At a Sidewalk Shrine in Mylapore, 1996. Photograph By Author.

tion of a modern state apparatus has been the relation between vernacular notions of collective life and the theoretical conception of the public sphere on which the existence of the modern nation-state is predicated.

Perhaps the most cogent expression of the meaning of the public sphere is found in the work of Jurgen Habermas:

> The public sphere is a sphere which mediates between society and state, in which the public organizes itself as the bearer of public opinion . . . grew out of a specific phase of bourgeois society and could enter into the order of the bourgeois constitutional state only as a result of a particular constellation of interests. (Habermas 1989a, 137)

He argued, further, that this socially and historically specific phenomenon accords with an analytic principle, or model, "the principle of public information which . . . made possible the democratic control of states" (Habermas 1989a, 137). This model was predicated on "communicative rationality," that is, the system of norms and behavior that promoted open, public deliberation among social equals, each of whom functioned as an autonomous, ratiocinating individual (see Habermas 1984). The legitimacy of a democratic state rested on consensual public opinion reached through these kinds of discursive practices; the state, moreover, acted as the executor of the public sphere by ensuring that institutional mechanisms for the production and dissemination of public opinion were operative (see also Habermas 1989b).

Internal critiques of Habermas's theoretical construction of the public sphere have focused on both its historical credibility and its utility as an analytic model. Nancy Fraser, for example, pointing to revisionist histories of modern public spheres in the United States and Europe, argued that the norms of rational deliberation that were hallmarks of the Habermasian public sphere often functioned as exclusionary devices (1996, 69–98). She suggested that the utility of the public sphere as an analytic model was limited by its failure to take into account the fact that its own boundaries could be subjected to critique, often by the very groups that had been systematically excluded. Her analysis concluded with a proposal that alternative models be used to theorize the public sphere, among them a notion of multiple, contesting publics.

Fraser's argument has strong affinities with other critiques that question the cross-cultural transportability of what Habermas designated the model of the public sphere. The critical historiography of colonialism, in India and elsewhere, has addressed the exclusion of colonized subjects from the civic public and the delineation of metropolitan public spheres against what were deemed negative cases, exemplified by the colonies (e.g. Chatterjee 1986, 1993; Chakrabarty 1992). A recurrent and vexing issue has been the emergence of nationalism in colonial societies. It countered European domination but retained the existing conceptual framework, with categories such as "nation," "citizen," "public opinion," founded in post-Enlightenment rationalist discourse.

Subaltern historians and ethnohistorians have treated nationalist discourses and the public opinion on which they were founded as matters of contestation; they have documented indigenous debates surrounding nationalism and have exposed the conceptual disjunctions that were present in South Asian appropriations of European categories (Chakrabarty 1992; Chatterjee 1986, 1993; Guha 1988a, 1988b, 1989; Pandey 1991). Of special concern has been the analysis of vernacular logics that were at work in creating discourses of and about the "public" but were part of different social and semantic fields (Haynes 1991). The location of Hindu temples in both the bureaucratic structures of the colonial state and in local discourses illustrates one set of circumstances in which such disjunctions have persisted.

Hindu temples are ubiquitous features in the built environment of southern India. As sites dedicated to individual and collective worship of Hindu deities, they are rendered sacred by the presence of embodied forms of the deities, usually as stone figures known as *mūrtti*s or *mūlavar*s. As institutions, they are constituted through ritually mediated relations between humans and deities, and among human temple servants, administrators, and worshipers. Most temples hold land, valuables, and money in the form of endowments that fund physical maintenance, ritual performance, and social welfare. Among the temples in Tamil Nadu (numbered around 75,000), there are vast differences in wealth and popularity, as well as in physical attributes such as size, layout, and iconography. There are, however, commonalities in the kinds of sensory engagement that temples afford their users.

Temples are built as spaces through and around which bodies of deities and humans move. In overview, they are contained wholes, the conflated landscapes of the body and the cosmos. Diana Eck explained that "in building a temple, the universe in microcosm is reconstructed. The divine ground-plan is called a *mandala,* a geometric map of the cosmos. At its center is the sanctum [the *garbhagrha* "womb chamber"], where the image will be installed. Its eight directions are guarded by the cosmic regents. . . . Various planetary deities, world guardians, and gods are set in their appropriate quadrant" (Eck 1985, 59).

The shrines, images, meeting spaces, and stages that together make up larger temple complexes are built in order to be experienced serially as spaces of pedestrian traversal. One of the most common worship genres, for example, is circumambulation. Worshipers walk, crawl, or roll around temple complexes, shrines, or deity images. These actions recapitulate a pilgrimage that "symbolically attend[s] to the entire visible world of name and form" (Eck 1985, 63). The visit is concluded by entering the temple's interior shrines, "the very center of the world" (Eck 1985, 63), and receiving the deity's *darshan.*

Visitors experience temples as successions of images, smells, tastes, sounds, and tactile sensations. For example, as you approach either the east or west entry of the Śrī Kapalēswarar Karpakampal temple, the large Shiva temple in Mylapore, you encounter beggars, barbers, and vendors of flowers and fruit; touts accost you and insist on guiding you through the temple (see Figure 6.2). Before passing through the temple gate located under its massive *kōpuram,* you hand your sandals to an attendant. Then you proceed across the cool, dusty stone floor of the entry. Once in-

FIGURE 6.2 A Small Shop Located Near the Entrance to the Śrī Kapalēswarar Karpakampal Temple, Mylapore, 1988. Photograph By Author.

side the courtyard of the temple complex, you are confronted by Ganesha, the elephant-headed god. A man facing the god is engaged in a stylized form of prayer composed of small, controlled movements. He raises one leg, he taps the top of his head with his palm, he crosses his arms in front of his chest. He is not distracted by a group of Danish sailors who surge past you, led by a government tour guide. At the base of the stone figure of Nandi, the bull who is Shiva's guard, some children are playing. Near them a man and a woman are arguing loudly. On the floor, to your right, a woman is moving clockwise around the sanctum; she bends and gently rolls a ripe coconut forward. When the coconut stops moving, she approaches it, kneels, and touches her forehead to the floor in the gesture of deference called *namaskāram.* Then she rises and begins the procedure again.

Continuing, you reach the main shrines of the temple—a cluster of rooms known as the *garbhagrha,* "womb." Images of the temple's most important deities are located in those dimly lit rooms. The air, heavy with burning ghee, camphor, and incense, seems viscous. Inside, worshipers move slowly around the periphery of the rooms, gathering near the *mūrtti* as the priest performs camphor *āratti.* In another room, a priest collects chits from the assembled worshipers. The threshold of each room was cleaned earlier in the day by an elderly woman using a twig broom, the wife of one of the temple's cooks. Later in the day she will wash the entryway of each shrine and draw a fresh *kōlam* before it.

As you reenter the temple courtyard, you notice that flanking the exterior walls are cooking areas, offices of temple administrators, storage rooms for the vehicles used in temple processions, and a ticket booth. Below a prominently displayed price list, people purchase the chits that you saw being collected in the shrine. When you inquire, one of the attendants explains that the chits entitle people to sponsor rituals or to receive shares of *prasadam.* Using a chit, a woman and her son make an offering to the planetary deity who rules Saturn, a celestial body associated with misfortune and ill luck (Figure 6.3).

This walk, obviously the path of a tourist rather than a worshiper, is an extension of other walks, especially those taken along the busy commercial streets adjacent to large urban temples. The individual is part of a stream of moving bodies traveling on foot, on bikes, in rickshaws, buses, and cars. The streets of Indian cities are inundated by human activity—people traveling to and from shops, schools, workplaces; sadhus begging; women selling vegetables or preparing meals for their street peddler husbands; men performing magic tricks or repairing sandals; children defecating or napping; squatters reclining on mats, clutching the cloth bags that hold their meager possessions.

FIGURE 6.3 An Offering Being Made to Appease the Deity-Ruler of the Planet Saturn, 1987. Photograph By Author.

City dwellers such as Lalitha (quoted in the epigraph) experience urban space through what De Certeau described as pedestrian speech acts, the rhetoric of use that appropriated urban landscapes (1984, 97–98). For the woman fulfilling a vow by rolling the coconut around the temple sanctum and for the man absorbed in prayer to Ganesha, the temple was a familiar space—perceived through sensory recollections and saturated by the routines of each traversal. Their practices inverted the encounters with space as it was mapped, that is, as presented diagramatically, in overview. Maps flatten and recreate space systems in miniature; the viewer's eye is a panopticon gazing across a synchronic landscape. By contrast, the spaces invented by walking encompass and surround the walker; what is seen is sequentially encountered and always constricted by the positionality of the viewer. Spaces as experienced, according to De Certeau (1984, 116–117), were singular, discrete, and invisible on the map's surface.[1] Space, he wrote, was "a practiced place" (De Certeau 1984, 117). Temples, when conscripted into the public sphere by the state, become visible as mappable places of a particular kind while remaining tangled webs of singular paths and hidden spaces. This is the conundrum on which this chapter turns. In the sections that follow, I review the conscription of temples into a modern public sphere. In Chapter 7, I turn to the practical, pedestrian logics of use that tactically reappropriated and reinvented those sites by transforming them into spaces delineated by memory and desire.

Temples As Contested Public Spaces

Implied in what I have presented so far is the fact that south Indian temples, like the cityscapes to which they belong, are public in several senses. In colloquial terms, they are public in that they are open, accessible spaces for collective and individual activity. They are also public in ways peculiar to the modern nation-state. Like government buildings or national monuments in which the nation's populace is deemed to have material, psychological, and social interests, they are officially designated as public trusts by the Tamil Nadu government and are administered as such. In the case of temples, this means that their accounts and organization are subject to state scrutiny and management. It also means that the state can collect and reallocate their surplus funds in the same way that it disburses other types of revenues. These arrangements stem from the state's constitutionally mandated obligation to protect temples and to ensure that they remain accountable to their users. There are, however, different and competing conceptions of those whom temples can be presumed to serve and represent and those to whom they should be held accountable.

The official, state-sanctioned discourse that constituted Hindu temples as public sites and the debates around the meanings of their public-ness were products of a history in which not only the form but the very possibility of a civic public in South Asia were contested. Precolonial Hindu temples were important nodes in regional political economies, as well as in the cultural politics of reputation and influence on which political economic systems depended. Larger temples were sites for public ritual directed to the deity conceived as a sovereign. They were often supported by wealthy and/or royal patrons through donations of land, jewels, money, and other valuables. Donors accrued prestige through their support of Brahman priests and scholars, and temple servants. In addition, kings were understood to be the protectors of temples, as well as courts of last resort in the event of disputes among temple servants and donors. As social institutions, therefore, temples controlled a matrix of material and symbolic resources and thus mediated both the production and exercise of political authority (Appadurai 1981; Appadurai and Breckenridge 1976; Dirks 1993; Mines 1994, 84–107; Stein 1980).

For European colonizers, however, temples marked the edges of the civic public (Dirks 1992; Inden 1990, 85–130). As sites of "idol-worship," bodily mutilation, and eroticism, temples were compact references to what colonizers and their missionary adjuncts viewed as the fundamental irrationality of Hinduism, its demonic tendencies, and its obsessive hold over a guileless and passive populace. Temples symbolized the excrescence of caste society and were thus the antitheses of civil society.

British policy with respect to temples was not crystallized until after the 1857 Mutiny, though there was subsequent vacillation between policies supporting direct involvement and those mandating nonintervention, due to political and ideological rifts within the colonial state.[2] Prior to the Mutiny, British authorities (many of them East India Company officials) had reckoned that their direct involvement in temples as ritual spectators, and even as donors or sponsors, might help them penetrate local political and commercial networks (Appadurai 1981; Baker 1975; Davis 1997, 51–87). The Mutiny, however, was taken as a sign of the depth and volatility of sectarian loyalties within the population; thereafter, the colonial state, with Religious Endowments Act 20 of 1863, adopted an official policy of nonintervention in religious matters. The only form of intervention that was sanctioned was judicial—courts could adjudicate conflict in cases in which the issues were addressed in the still evolving codes of civil and penal law.[3] Dispute adjudication, however, easily spilled over into reform efforts. For example, in appellate decisions on temple disputes during the 1860s, judges referred to the "immorality" of the temple services rendered by *devadasis* (temple dancers whose way of life included sexual liaisons with temple patrons/donors); it was only after the beginning of the twentieth century, when indigenous efforts to reform *devadasis*' lives expanded, that expressions of reformist sentiment from judges became bolder.[4]

The consolidation of the British colonial state during the nineteenth century was accompanied by the development of countercolonial discourses among South Asian elites. These discourses posed critiques of colonial domination that relied on premises associated with contemporaneous political philosophies (especially utilitarianism) and on Orientalist constructions of Indic culture. Accordingly, these discourses included both the rewriting of the past in ways that posited Indian nationhood as an incipient phenomenon, and the revising of the present through social reform measures, especially those directed toward women (Mani 1990; Nair 1996).

In many cases, the sentiments of colonial authorities and reform-minded critics of colonialism were identical (see, for example, Mani 1990). Both identified religious practices such as idolatry and self-mutilation, child marriage, and the immolation of widows as fundamental impediments to the progress associated with European sociopolitical orders; both identified women as embodiments of Indic tradition and focused on them as barometers of, but at the same time impediments to, progress. It was within this milieu that a succession of local religious associations emerged. The most prominent were outfitted with reformist agendas predicated on universalistic interpretations of Hinduism and derived from what they understood as its original teachings.

The Brahmo Samaj, founded by Raja Rammohun Roy in 1828–1830, sought to promote Hindu monotheism as a counterweight to idolatry, arguing that the latter was a degradation of original Vedic doctrine (Ghose 1982). This also provided Rammohun with a platform for condemning the tactics of Christian missionaries. Later, in 1875, Dayananda Saraswati founded the Arya Samaj in order to "revive" the Vedic religion of early Aryan populations—a system, he asserted, that lacked caste divisions and "idol-worship" (De Bary 1958, 76–84). In these and other reworkings of Hinduism, early nationalists found ideological grist to use in countercolonial discourse. In subsequent decades, Hindu idioms became the cornerstones in the militant nationalist ideologies that served as bases for Gandhi's conception of *swaraj* (self-rule) as well as for the violent Hindu nationalism of V. Savarkar (Gandhi 1982; Savarkar 1969).

In peninsular South Asia, these revisions of Hindu belief and practice, and the nationalist interest that underwrote them, were colored by emerging caste politics. Besides being sites of reformist discourse, temples possessed wealth and prestige that made them important tools of political patronage. With the changes in civil procedure codes that broadened the scope of government intervention in temple affairs around the turn of the twentieth century, temples were drawn into the emerging networks of local and provincial politics. Baker (1975, 84) noted that the elite South Asians who collaborated with the British as advisers and administrators attempted to use temples to create "supra-local networks of influence and control." A circle of lawyers and administrators known as the Mylapore group drafted numerous bills between 1878 and 1915 intended to reimpose government control on temple administration. They also sought administrative intervention through the courts. Baker observed that many of the interests disturbed in these suits quickly allied with a Mylapore group rival, the Justice party, after its formation in 1916 (1975, 84–85).

The Justice party represented the political wing of the new Non-Brahman movement. Inspired by the "Tamil Rennaissance" and controlled by wealthy and prestigious non-Brahman males, the movement emerged shortly after the turn of the century. The Non-Brahman movement rapidly gained ground in Madras presidency, in part because of the demographic preponderance of non-Brahmans in the population and in part because of the colonial government's willingness to support their cause by instituting positive discrimination measures—first in institutions of higher education and then in administrative and legislative bodies.[5] Under the system of dyarchy mandated by the Montague-Chelmsford constitution (in effect between 1919 and 1935), the Justice party received a majority of seats in the provincial Legislative Council in the 1921 elections and formed a ministry. Once the party was in power, temple patronage came under its control. Despite its opposition to temple legislation prior to 1920, the party subsequently imposed a centralized system of temple administration in the presidency (Baker 1975, 85–89). Under the Justice ministry (which remained in power during most of the period that Montague-Chelmsford was in effect), additional measures for communal representation were enacted, as was the Hindu Religious Endowments Act (1926). The latter was promoted as a progressive, anti-Brahmanical measure that would hold temples accountable to the Hindu populace by placing temples under the nominal management of the state. The act authorized the formation of a board whose members were empowered to monitor temple finances and organization (Appadurai 1981; Mudaliar 1974; Presler 1987).

The act has remained in force since, though it has not always been perceived as serving the ideological agenda of its non-Brahman framers. For example, under the Congress ministry of C. Rajagopalachari (a Brahman and a Gandhian nationalist) (1937–1939), the Hindu Religious Endowments Board was encouraged to accelerate its "notification," or takeover, of temples from local boards, a policy that encountered resistance (Irschick 1986, 228–231).[6] The centralization of temple management was further facilitated following independence. In 1952, under the Congress party's ministry, the Hindu Religious Endowments Board became the Hindu Religious and Charitable Endowments Department (HRCE) under the authority of the executive branch of the Tamil Nadu (then Madras) state government.[7] In 1959, the act was amended to ensure that temples' material resources, such as land, jewels, and money, would be dedicated both to their own support and, more controversially, to the promotion of government-mandated social welfare programs. These measures, coupled with the redistribution of agricultural land (much of which was owned by temples) and the introduction of rent concessions for tenants of temple land, resulted in a loss of land and income for temples.

The legislation just described received the endorsement of the central government and illustrated the constellation of nationalist concerns following independence. Writing about the first decade after independence, Tharu and Lalita (1993) observed that

> if the early decades of the century had authorized the idea of a nation-people and their many struggles for freedom, the approaching climate of power demanded the setting up of a nation-state and a relationship between the state and "its" people that was designed for governance. The nation had to be restructured, rewritten. *Its story was no longer to be told as it had been during the freedom struggle, from its many contested frontiers, but from its new center.* (1993, 56; emphasis original)

To an important degree, the Indian state—despite its commitment to secularism—relied on Sanskritic Hinduism as an ideology of national integration. Following independence, it was incumbent on the state to reorient nationalisms of the colonial era into a homogeneous and legitimizing discourse for the Indian state. The efforts to accomplish this included the state's reappropriation of the Hindu idioms that had suffused anticolonial nationalisms.

The enumeration of temples in the 1961 census, to which the first epigraph to this chapter alludes, was just one of many efforts by the postcolonial state to reinvent the nation through, rather than against, the state's governing apparatus. Temples, homes, and schools were deemed critical sites for the inculcation of nationalism, and a series of committees and commissions were convened by the central government to survey these sites and make recommendations about how they might be better organized or administered to fulfill their role in nation building.[8]

Whereas schools and homes were refurbished in accord with the dictates of modernity, temples seemed to hold residues of tradition. In the new map of the nation, they were remade into artifacts of an *Indian* past but were shorn of unprogressive attributes. In this move, illustrated in both the census report (1961) and the *Report of the Hindu Religious Endowments Commission* (1962), tradition and modernity were self-consciously named and sutured by positing Hinduism as a form of incipient nationalism. Pluralism and tolerance were foregrounded as Hinduism's defining qualities; it was no longer merely the expression of sectarian identity but an ensemble of territorially bounded cultural traits. Hinduism was thus rendered serviceable as a postcolonial ideology of nationalism. Hindu temples, represented as expressions of the inherent religiosity and assimilative character of Indian civilization, were described by the Hindu Religious Endowments Commission (HREC) as the foundation of the nation (1962, 6). By promoting their charitable as well as didactic and ritualistic functions, the authors of the report argued that it would be possible to "effect that integration of Indian endeavour and that sublimation of ideals which are of special significance to resurgent India" (1962, 194).

Temples, therefore, became available as impersonal maps of the cultural space of the nation. In addition to being enumerated in the census, temples of "All-India" importance were identified by the HREC on the grounds of their artistic merits (1962, 162–168). The location of a national ethos in temples underwrote the interpretation of their public dimensions (see also Derrett 1968, 500). Temples and other religious institutions were described as "public trusts in the sense that the public or a section thereof are [materially, psychologically, and spiritually] interested in and have the right to enforce their proper administration and management" (*Report of the Hindu Religious Endowments Commission* 1962, 146). Along with this nationalization of the public sphere, new practices of national identity were proposed. Though an officially secular state could not promote conversion, under the broader rubric of consumption it could encourage other practices by which the population might be exposed to a Hindu national culture. The HREC report urged that the government, besides facilitating religious pilgrimage among Hindus, promote Hindu temples as tourist destinations (1962, 171).[9]

The task of protecting Hindu temples, already in the hands of the state, was thus rendered more urgent with the commission's report. Not only was it necessary to manage them financially and legally, but their material infrastructure also had to be preserved. To this end, the HREC recommended a larger role for the Archaeological Department (1962, 170–172).

In justifying the central government's ideological claim on Hindu temples and the increased bureaucratization that it implied, the authors of the HREC report pointed to the Hindu Religious and Charitable Endowments Department in Tamil Nadu (then Madras state) as a model.[10] By appropriating the Madras model in the service of a nationalized public, the contestation out of which the Hindu Religious and Charitable Endowments Department developed was elided. What was preserved was the conception that the temples should be managed in ways that made them accountable to their respective "worshiping publics." The irony in this became evident in 1967, when the Congress party was voted out in Tamil Nadu and a new ministry, headed by a regional opposition party, the Dravida Munnetra Kazhagaham (DMK), was formed.

With the ascendence of Dravidianist parties in the state government, temples became more enmeshed in the bureaucratic structures of governance, and their autonomy in Tamil Nadu was further reduced. In 1971, the DMK government issued a moratorium (subsequently renewed annually) suspending the payment of accumulated unpaid rent by tenants of temple lands and prohibiting their eviction.[11] In late 1970, the Hindu Religious and Charitable Endowments Department instructed temple priests to use Tamil rather than Sanskrit in performing *arccaṉai,* a popular form of worship. Shortly thereafter, the Tamil Nadu legislature passed a law that made temple priesthood (the office of *archaka*) open to qualified persons, regardless of caste. Both measures were appealed by temple priests, and the matter was eventually brought before by the Supreme Court. The Court's findings were not wholly in favor of the priests, but they effectively limited the types of intervention that the two measures had been designed to promote.[12] By the time of the rulings, however, the DMK party had split. In 1976, a year into the Emergency, Prime Minister Indira Gandhi dissolved the state's government. The next election, in 1977, saw the victory of the DMK's rival offshoot, the All-India Annadurai-Dravida Munnetra Kazhagam (AIA-DMK).

Though the period of AIA-DMK rule was not marked by any significant changes in the state's temple management policies, increased attention was given to the legal and financial problems of temples, and nationalist claims on Hindu temples were intensified. Much of this interest (described in detail in Chapter 8) was fanned by Hindu nationalist organizations, namely, the Rashtriya Swayamsevak Sangh (RSS) and its affiliates, the Vishwa Hindu Parishad (VHP), the Hindu Munnani, and the Hindu Temple Protection Committee. Their actions were part of a nationwide mobilization of the Hindu right that included the incitement of communal violence, besides rallies and the use of mass media (Basu et al. 1993). As part of their strategy to cultivate Hindu resentment toward minorities, these groups focused on a succession of mass conversions of low-caste and Harijan Hindus to Islam (beginning in 1981 in rural areas of southern Tamil Nadu) as evidence of the government's neglect of the country's Hindu majority. They charged the government with mismanaging temples as well, and they wove these two phenomena together as proof of the government's complicity in a broad-based "Muslim conspiracy" against India's Hindu majority.

A number of Hindu leaders, among them the Shankaracharya of Kanchipuram, collaborated with the nationalists and used the conversion issue as a device to revisit old conflicts over temple management and to propose new measures allowing them greater autonomy in controlling Hindu temples. By the late 1980s, what nationalists characterized as problems in the south had been woven into a narrative of all-India proportions. In 1985, the VHP demanded that the gates to a mosque located on the supposed birthplace of the god Ram be reopened (after having been closed since 1949) as part of the "liberation" of the site of Ram's birth. The site became the center of right-wing agitation that culminated in a VHP-orchestrated attempt to stage a mass demolition of the mosque in December 1992 and the central government's subsequent takeover of the site.

As this brief review has indicated, many of the debates during the past 150 years about the public dimensions of the Hindu temple were occasioned by competing nationalist discourses among South Asians and contributed to them. Partha Chatterjee, writing about those debates and their entanglement with colonial modes of power, noted that "nationalism . . . produced a discourse in which, even as it challenged the colonial claim to political domination, it also accepted the very intellectual premises of 'modernity' on which colonial domination was based" (Chatterjee 1986, 30). Efforts to constitute temples as public spaces and to formalize the state's protection of them exemplify how one cluster of "intellectual premises of modernity" was transposed and institutionally inscribed.

The series of interventions in public religious activity that were initiated with the passage of the Madras Hindu Religious Endowments Act placed Hindu temples within the legal-rational-bureaucratic structure of the modern political order, while at the same time preserving the temple as a locus of Hindu tradition (Appadurai and Breckenridge 1976, 207). Importantly, however, these changes were framed within a conception of the relationship between the state and the temple in which the government's management of temples was perceived to be consistent with "the mandate of pre-colonial Hindu kings to protect such institutions" (Appadurai and Breckenridge 1976, 208). Consequently, the assertions of modernity offered in these measures were capable of sustaining an ensemble of disparate designs for the nation.

Religion and Urban Life

For agents of the state, Hindu temples have served as sites for enacting competing visions of nation, including its culture and its citizens. These related efforts to locate temples in a postcolonial public sphere carried with them implicit notions about the forms of sociality and subjectivity on which the public sphere was predicated. In administering temples, the state has sought to maintain their accessibility (see Madras Temple Entry Authorization Act 5 of 1947) and to ensure that they remain accountable to their users, through, for example, the monitoring of accounts and standardization of usage fees. Embedded in these policies are notions of the instrumentality of temple functions and, relatedly, of an instrumental rationality on the part of worshipers. An oft cited passage from the HREC report describes temples as

> occult laboratories where certain physical acts of adoration coupled with certain systematized prayers, psalms, *mantras* and musical invocations, can yield certain physical and psychological results as a matter of course, and if these physical processes are properly conducted, the results will accrue provided the persons who perform them are adequately equipped. . . . These ideas lead us to the irresistible conclusion that the *pūja*s, the rituals, the ceremonies and festivals in a temple must necessarily be conducted by persons fully qualified. (1962, 42)

The authors' language placed a culturally specific, ratiocinating individual at the heart of Hindu practice, as spectator, beneficiary, and/or performer of temple ritual. When a priest, worshiper, or tourist entered an urban temple (for example, the Śrī Kapalēswarar Karpakampal temple in Mylapore), she was met by the state—reified as appointed officers, government tour guides, or the signboard posting rates for various rituals.[13] She was also met by a subject position, that of Indian citizen. Do these dimensions of public worship inform, undermine, or normalize vernacular logics of practice? Or do local practices seek out the hollows and crevices in modernity's veneer? This dilemma is framed cogently by Dipesh Chakrabarty:

> But, if one result of European imperialism in India was to introduce the modern state and the idea of the nation with their attendant discourse of "citizenship" which, by the very idea of "the citizen's rights" . . . splits the figure of the modern individual into "public" and "private" parts of the self, these themes have existed—in contestation, alliance and miscegenation—with other narratives of the self and community that do not look to the state/citizen bind as the ultimate construction of sociality. (Chakrabarty 1992, 10)

The tension between "management" and "protection" in the state's relation with temples illustrates this juxtaposition between themes of modernity and "other narratives." Other sites for this juxtaposition lie in the practices of worshipers; the disjunctions to which Chakrabarty alluded are reenacted in myriad subtle ways whenever persons visit Hindu temples. For the authors of the HREC report (chief of whom was C. P. Ramaswamy Aiyer, an eminent Smārta Brahman lawyer and senior government official), the dual narratives were locked together in a rationalized discourse whose unifying theme was instrumentality—it was a discourse, moreover, that was thoroughly compatible with the logic of compartmentalization and its ideal (elite male) subject, bifurcated by interior "tradition" and exterior "modernity." The ways that this discourse might be read by the anonymous members of the "worshiping public," for whom the authors of the HREC report spoke, however, remained opaque. It is to some of these local constructions of public culture that I turn in the next chapter.

Notes

1. Though not directly in response to De Certeau, Casey (1996, 16–17) suggested that the space-place dichotomy was misleading as often used in anthropological writing because it implied that "space" was empty, absolute, and objective, whereas "place" was culturally constituted. He argued that such a conception of "space" was socially and historically derived from lived experiences of place, and he proposed that a phenomenological account of those lived experiences should be the main subjects of inquiry. De Certeau's approach (although inverting what Casey considers the anthropological definitions of the terms) is consistent with those goals, for in employing the dichotomous categories of "space" and "place," he did not assume "place" to be natural or experientially anterior to "space." Indeed, he recognized that the privileging of "place" as an absolute and objective category was part of a modernist project.

2. Instabilities in policy were also related to the gradual and contentious shift, during the first half of the nineteenth century, in the locus of British power on the subcontinent from the East India Company to the Crown.

3. See Religious Endowments Act 20 of 1877 and Charitable and Religious Trusts Act 14 of 1920 (Mukherjea 1962).

4. See *Chalakonda Alasani v. Chalakonda Ratnachalam, Madras High Court Reports, 1863–1874* (Madras: Government Press), 2:56; *Guddati Reddi Obala v. Ganapati Kandanna, Indian Law Reports, 1875–present,* Madras Series (Madras: Government Press), 32:493.

5. British support for the Non-Brahman Movement has been interpreted as a calculated "divide and rule" strategy engaged in order to undermine the Brahman-dominated nationalist movement in Madras presidency (Washbrook 1989).

6. Act 12 of 1935 empowered the provincial government, through the Hindu Religious Endowments Board, to suspend the managers or trustees of temples and to replace them with its own appointees. See discussion by Presler (1987, 51).

7. Officials of the department were to be paid out of a fund made up of moneys extracted by the state from temples (Presler 1987, 51).

8. See, for example, the *Report of the Secondary Education Commission* (1952–1953), especially parts 3 and 8; the *Report of the Committee on Religious and Moral Hygiene* (1959); the *Report of the Committee on Emotional Integration* (1962).

9. The Ministry of Information and Broadcasting and the Ministry of Education have continued the promotion of domestic tourism.

10. "Certain states like Madras, Andhra Pradesh and Bombay have been the pioneers in the matter of legislation governing the administration of religious institutions, and some of the institutions like . . . Palni in Madras [state] are examples of fairly well managed institutions. It would be very useful for representatives from other States to visit such institutions and study their working on the spot" (*Report of the Hindu Religious Endowments Commission* 1962, 170).

11. Contrary to its stated intent, this measure benefited wealthy rural landlords rather than small tenant farmers. Although landlords were exempted from paying rent to the temples that owned the land, they were still able to collect rents from their sublessees (Washbrook 1989).

12. In 1972, "the Court upheld the constitutionality of the *archaka* act, but did so in such a way as to render the act ineffective . . . [by] affirm[ing] that the government could abolish heredity as a principle of priestly appointment, but it also affirmed that the state was bound not to violate the regulations laid down by the religious *agamas*" (Presler 1987, 152). (The agamas stipulated that the *archaka*'s competence rested on his descent from a priestly family.)

The court in 1974 stayed the operation of the Hindu Religious and Charitable Endowment's orders on the use of Tamil, pending its review; a short time later, the Tamil government rescinded that order (Presler 1987, 114–118).

13. See Gupta's (1998) development of these themes in his ambitious analysis of the Indian state as it is inflected in the lives and experiences of rural agriculturalists.

7

Urban Places and Female Spaces

Michel De Certeau's (1984, 93) differentiation between the *concept* of the city and urban *practices* illuminates disjunctions within modernity. The concept of the city inheres in the totalizing view from above—the city as cosmological landscape, the city as seen from a skyscraper or envisioned by planners and bureaucrats. Practices, especially walking, are, on the other hand, the modes by which the city may be experienced.

De Certeau's distinction suggests how one might think about the disjunctions that are played out in temple visitation. De Certeau began by comparing the concept-practice dichotomy with language; he glossed walking, the core of urban practice, as a "space of enunciation" (1984, 98) and distinguished the pedestrian "speech act" *(parole)* from the totalized spatial "system" *(langue)*. Walking was thus seen as a rhetorical gesture: "The art of 'turning' phrases finds an equivalent in an art of composing a path" (1984, 100). Working on this parallel, De Certeau then stated that pedestrian practices "organize the topoi of a discourse on/of the city . . . in a way that eludes urbanistic systematicity" (1984, 100). They rendered the cityscape meaningful and habitable by transforming mapped places into enveloping spaces imbued with the accumulated practices, memories, and desires of their creators. Such spaces, negotiated on a depersonalized map of places, contained the alterities, the "other conceptions of self and community" to which Chakrabarty (1992) referred.

The method that De Certeau proposed was to "analyze the microbe-like, singular, and plural practices which an urbanistic system was supposed to administer or suppress" (1984, 96). In these practices might be found a body of procedures constitutive of "the everyday regulations and surreptitious creativities that are merely concealed by the frantic mechanisms and discourses of the observational organization" (1984, 96). It is to the heterogeneous logics of religion in public, as practiced by two Brahman women, that I wish to turn in this chapter.

The locales in which the women operated were socially distinct in terms of caste and class, and each woman drew on different kinds of material and symbolic resources ("capital" in Bourdieu's terms). Their homes and immediate neighborhoods were indicators of these differences. Rajalakshmi lived with her husband, son, and daughter-in-law in a spacious house built in 1964. As was typical for bungalow-style residences such as theirs, the house and yard were surrounded by a wall. The other houses on that street and in the immediate area were of comparable age and size, and many of the compounds contained well-tended gardens. All of the houses had their own wells and electrical connections. The streets themselves were paved and were wider than streets in older parts of the city. There was very little commercial activity on her street—no shops and few street vendors. It seemed to be an exclusive, upper-class neighborhood bearing the imprint of bourgeois domesticity—single family residences furnished with consumer goods (e.g., refrigerators, air conditioners, water heaters, Euro-Western furnishings) purchased by the salaries of (mostly male) white-collar professionals and presided over by housewives. My visual impression of the exclusivity of the neighborhood was borne out in the limited census data from which socioeconomic status can be inferred. The area in which Rajalakshmi lived was located in the administrative division known as Alwarpet (North). According to the 1981 census figures, 2.2 percent of the division's total population of 25,085 people were members of scheduled castes or tribes, whereas the SC/ST population in the city as a whole made up 14.45 percent. Out of the forty-five enumeration blocks[1] that made up the division, only seven had more than ten persons designated as SC/ST, and these blocks were grouped into four spatial clusters.

By contrast, Tiruvalluvar Nagar, Parvati's residence, was far more heterogeneous in regard to class and far less affluent on average than was Rajalakshmi's neighborhood in Alwarpet. The 1981 SC/ST population there—19 percent out of 18,769 residents—was greater than the citywide average. There also appeared to be less spatial segregation: Persons identified as members of scheduled castes or tribes resided in twenty-three out of the thirty-two enumeration blocks that made up the division. Visually, Parvati's neighborhood was quite different from Rajalakshmi's as well. In the first place, Tiruvalluvar Nagar was located in an older and more commercial section of the city. The courtyard houses that lined the narrow lanes and streets abutted each other, and most had been subdivided into a number of separate residential portions. Many lacked wells, and persons living in those residences obtained water from municipal taps. Foot traffic was heavy due to the presence of the temple and a variety of shops, and consequently street activity was varied and lively. The streets were crowded with kiosks selling snacks, newspapers, and coffee; flower and fruit vendors competed with beggars for space near the temple entrance; tailors, video merchants, grocers, and small appliance dealers worked out of small storefronts located on the ground floor of courtyard houses.

As will be seen, the audience and patrons that each woman attracted and the sorts of transactions in which they engaged were markedly different, reflecting the very different social and economic boundaries of their local worlds.

Parvati

Lalitha's statements about Parvati, which I quoted at the beginning of Chapter 6, were made during my first visit to the Tiruvalluvar temple. It was a Friday near the end of *Āṭi* month, and devotion to the goddess was in full swing. I had heard about the *maṇṭali* from a friend, and when I told Minakshi about it, she insisted that we go the very next Friday. She had been excited about visiting the shrine: "I've been in Madras for twenty-five years, but until now I had not heard of this place. I hadn't known that Kamakshi [the deity's shrine] was here." Her long-standing personal devotion to Kamakshi was one reason for her enthusiasm about visiting that temple. Recently, however (as discussed in Chapter 5), Minakshi's devotion had intensified due to Sunithi's influence and to her expectation that the goddess would soon come to her. As it turned out, the visit was auspicious in other ways: Parvati, the *maṇṭali*'s founder, invited all of us who were present to a *maṭimancaḷ* (turmeric distribution) ceremony (described in Chapter 4).

For Lalitha, speaking in 1987, the observations made in the 1961 census report merely stated the obvious. Like some other Brahmans I knew, she might have accepted their statements as descriptions of conditions that prevailed at an earlier time, before Dravidianist parties controlled the Tamil government. Moreover, she saw in the actions undertaken by Parvati the possibility of reclaiming those spaces, domesticating them, and restoring the good name of the resident deity. Minakshi, responding to Lalitha, opined that Parvati's efforts were consistent with popular dissatisfaction with the DMK government's interventions in temple organization during the 1970s. She had told me on previous occasions that the population of Tamil Nadu, regardless of caste, was deeply religious, and the DMK's disregard for those sentiments had caused it to be thrown out. Since then, she assured me, popular devotion had steadily increased, with *bhajan* groups and *maṇṭali*s appearing in many neighborhoods.

Minakshi and I returned to the Tiruvalluvar temple a week after our first visit, again on a Friday. At Kamakshi's shrine, about eight older women, including Parvati, were assembled, watching the priest perform *apiṣēkam* and singing *bhajan*s. Parvati recognized us from our previous visit and greeted us warmly. When the ritual was finished, we asked Parvati if we could speak with her about the *maṇṭali.* She agreed and invited us to return to her house, located on one of the narrow streets near the temple.

For about twenty years, Parvati and her husband had lived in the same apartment in a two-story courtyard building. The building was owned by one of her nephews, who had divided it into several residential units (of one and three rooms each). We climbed a small stone staircase to reach the three-room unit, consisting of a central room flanked by a kitchen and a sleeping room, in which Parvati lived with her husband. A boy was studying in the central room, and Parvati introduced him. "This is my grandson; my daughter and her family live in this building also."

I asked her about the origins of the *maṇṭali,* and she recalled her initial visits to the nearby temple, which had commenced shortly after she had moved into her current home:

> You remember that young priest who did the *apiṣēkam* today? His father, Kumaraswamy, was an astrologer who stayed on the grounds of that temple, and I went to him for his predictions. At that time, the temple was surrounded by forest; it was completely overgrown and untended, even though the E.O. [government-appointed executive officer] at the Muṇṭakakaṉṉiyammaṉ temple[2] was in charge. Some clearing had been done about sixteen or seventeen years ago, when the government had taken the decision to install a monument to Tiruvalluvar on this site. That project was not completed, though, so the temple was again left. (Field notes, August 20, 1987)

Besides her occasional visits to the astrologer, she also had made a point, soon after moving to that area, of going to the temple on Fridays to offer milk to Kamakshi at the small shrine within the temple precincts that housed her image. Her involvement had intensified only four years ago.

> I was in business, selling saris with a friend who lived in this same house. We got the saris from a merchant in Kanchipuram and sold them here, in our houses. She also accompanied me to the temple on Fridays. One day, we saw a dead bandicoot there! We became thoroughly disgusted by the conditions there and decided that the [Kamakshi] shrine, at least, should be cleaned. . . . Sometime thereafter, another friend, Jaya, was there with me. Just then, we thought it would be good to recite "Lalita Sahasranāmam." We made a practice of this, and gradually other ladies in this neighborhood came and joined in. Soon a large number became involved—it was some fifty or sixty—so we decided to form a *maṇṭali* and asked for five rupees for membership. Once having done that, we approached the E.O. at the Muṇṭakakaṉṉiyammaṉ temple. . . . We asked that he authorize improve-

> ments for this temple, especially the Kamakshi shrine. After all, 25 percent of the *hundi* collection at the Tiruvalluvar temple must be given over to the Muṇṭakakaṉṉiyammaṉ temple. The E.O., however, would not give money directly to us, nor would he undertake the repairs himself. But he did agree that nothing would be extracted from the collections that our *maṇṭali* made. . . . We then set about raising money for the shrine. One of my friends, Sashi, owns a printing press, and he made pamphlets and collection vouchers for us. I myself went around to houses—from door to door—to obtain donations. . . . It cost 7,000 rupees to renovate Kamakshi's shrine. When it was completed, the E.O. told us that we should also improve the other shrines in the temple. That, we told him, was impossible—the expense would be too great. So he okayed work on some of the other shrines and together we financed the *kumpāpiṣēkam* for the temple. (Field notes, August 20, 1987)

Parvati had told me that she was seventy-six years old. She had started the *maṇṭali,* had begun negotiations with the temple's administrator, and had taken up door-to-door collections four years ago, at the age of seventy-two. I wondered whether her children and grandchildren had helped her and whether her husband had protested her absences and her lack of attention to him. Questions like those, asked directly, might have embarrassed her, so I queried her in more general terms. "Were there hardships for you in doing this work?" She smiled and assured me that Kamakshi had paved the way:

> After the *kumpāpiṣēkam* had been done, I thought that it would be good to install [a figure of] Durga, in order to bring more people in for the Tuesday *rākukālam pūja* and to build up the reputation of this temple. In Villivakkam there was one sculptor, a Muslim, who was recommended. So I went there by bus; I had no address, but I got down near the Ammaṉ temple there and asked for directions. When I reached his workplace, we bargained for the cost. He asked for six hundred [rupees], but I could pay only four hundred. It was settled at four hundred, and he agreed to deliver it after fifteen days. . . . It was not ready [then], but we went back ten days later and it was finished. You see how smoothly it went. . . . that is because I had Kamakshi's blessing. (Field notes, August 20, 1987)

She offered a few more anecdotes that were intended to illustrate her point. The stories also were evidence of the ways that persons from caste and class backgrounds other than her own were persuaded to take an interest in the temple. For example, Parvati mentioned that when she was trying to raise money to purchase and install the figure of Durga, she approached a "miserly advocate." "He gave us 601 rupees without the slightest hesitation." She asserted that "it was Durga who compelled him, not I." Another such story surrounded the installation of

Daksinamūrtti (Shiva in the form of the guru). It was financed, she noted, by a businessman, one Ramajaya Nadar. Later, when the group decided that a vehicle (with an estimated cost of Rs. 4,000) was needed for processions, she sought the advice of an auditor about how to raise that money. "He directed me to a Mudaliar living opposite him. That man agreed to donate the money but said that he did not know the formalities and asked me to make all of the arrangements."

At this point I should note that I had learned about Parvati from others before I actually encountered her. Besides attesting to her own good name, this fact demonstrates the practical logic involved in the negotiation of reputation *(pukaḻ).* Like many local notables whose renown rested on religious virtuosity, Parvati was the subject of stories, such as the one that I used as an epigraph for this chapter. That is, reputation was as much a matter of people's words as one's own achievements. The laudatory content of people's words and the frequency of utterances together confirm a dense net of intersubjective relations. Parvati's friends were anxious that her experiences and accomplishments receive public exposure. Besides telling me that Parvati had been visited by Kamakshi in a dream, they also told me that she had received the goddess's *darshan* at other times. When I asked Parvati about this, she disclaimed her friends' assertions, though her revised version of the story had similar rhetorical potency:

> I had no dream like that; I had only felt strongly that the temple was neglected. It was a person named Sampath . . . who had a dream that a woman was worried about a certain temple and that that her name started with an S. He came to the temple with Sashi, the one who had the printing press, and he told me that his dream had been about my worry but that in the dream Kamakshi had come and reassured him that everything would be all right. He advised me to keep Śrī *cakkaram* in that temple. So I obtained one made of copper through him, and I installed it in the temple myself, in Kamakshi's shrine. [For the installation] I performed a milk *apiṣēkam* and recited Lakshmi *stōttiram.* (Field notes, August 20, 1987)

The latter story, which reported her achievements indirectly, made the intersubjective creation of Parvati's good name apparent. It also revealed another important dimension of renown—the inextricability of one's own good name from that of others, underscoring the point that the accomplishments that are celebrated are not the products of individual intentionality but are negotiated through more oblique channels. Parvati's desires and the interventions of those who mediated those desires stemmed from sources that were inside their own persons, as well as outside. Kamakshi stood as the other locus of intentionality. And for

Parvati, it was Kamakshi's good name on which her own reputation depended.

These stories, of her own interventions in temple spaces and ritual rhythms and of people's acclamation of those efforts, revealed how tightly her daily domestic life was interwoven with temple activity. The boundaries between domestic and public space were being reimagined in the course of these actions. As Parvati explained it, she acted on desires that were expressed through her but originated elsewhere, and it was the social and material backing of others that enabled her to domesticate a public site. When she reported Sampath's dream, she also described her own labor and expenditures—a third feature of renown. Her purchase and installation of the *cakkaram* skirted the edges of orthopraxy but were crucial transactions that enabled her to stake a claim on the shrine. The goddess's wishes, mediated by men, legitimated Parvati's claim, but her material interventions secured it.

Parvati's domestication of the shrine was effected by the accumulated weight of small gestures. Once her cooking for the day was completed (usually by midmorning), she normally went to the temple with a food offering. On Tuesdays and Fridays, she joined other members of the *maṇṭali* there to worship Durga and Kamakshi. She also initiated and participated in several monthly observances, such as Pradosham and Ēkātaci, in honor of Shiva and Vishnu. Finally, she had initiated a number of annual festivals at the temple, including Āṭi Pūram, Navarāttiri, Vināyakar Caturtti, and Mahācivarāttiri. For those performances, she prepared food offerings and engaged priests to officiate.

These public events, although conducted in accordance with textual prescriptions, were invested with Parvati's desires for and images of *cumaṅkali*hood. The priests and other specialists whom she engaged were the official intermediaries between those desires and ritual practices; however, Parvati self-consciously shaped the temple's repertoire around practices that evoked the domestic world. Āṭi Pūram, she pointed out, was a very important day for the goddess because it commemorated her pregnancy. On that day, members of the *maṇṭali* conducted a ceremony for her called *vaḷaikkāppu.* (This is a ceremony ordinarily conducted for women during the fifth or seventh month of pregnancy. It involves the presentation of bangles and other adornments intended to please and protect the pregnant woman and to protect her fetus.) The women engaged a temple priest to officiate, and they made several different rice dishes as offerings. Women seeking to conceive often participated, and both Parvati and Minakshi assured me that it was efficacious—polite hints, perhaps, about how I might remedy my own childless state.

Parvati spoke with greatest animation, however, about the ways that the temple observed Navarāttiri—*both* Navarāttiris, she specified.

> Dasara marks the nine days of penance that Parvati [the goddess] had to do in order to return to Shiva, from whom she had been separated. But, after the new moon of Paṅkuni month, there is another nine-night festival, Vacanta Navarāttiri. This is the time when Ampāḷ is happiest because she is reunited with her husband. This one is the more important festival because Ampāḷ is fully a *cumaṅkali.* . . . During both of these festivals, I recite Lalita Sahasranāmam at home each morning and evening, and then I go to the temple. I make all of the *naivēttiyam* that is offered at home and at the temple, and I serve people in both places. I pay for all of the food myself—I make *vaṭai*[3] and at least five kilos of rice for *carkkaraipoṅkal* on each day of the festival. (Field notes, August 20, 1987)

In effect, Parvati labored as an unpaid temple servant, producing renown for Kamakshi and the other deities housed in the temple, thereby negotiating a good name for herself and her friends. Her "capital" included the symbolic and material dimensions of *cumaṅkali*hood, which were located in her body and in the material resources of her own household, including her husband's labor. Because the HRCE Department audited temple accounts, she and her husband kept records of all of the *maṇṭali*'s financial transactions. (Her husband was retired and tutored students to augment their small income.) The temple's dependence on domestic resources was also apparent in Parvati's financing of improvements:

> A year and a half ago, I decided that Pradosham should be celebrated each month. I had to get a figure made of *pañcalōkam* for that. A friend who is a *stapati*[4] told me to collect old kitchen vessels for the figure, and then he would make it. Now the most common type of metal among those vessels that we collected was brass. So we sold some of those pots and bought the necessary amount of copper. . . . Recently, a processional image for Kamakshi was made, and we had to beg once again for old vessels. (Field notes, August 20, 1987)

Thus it was domestic durables, largely women's wealth *(cīr)*, that through material transformation and spiritual transvaluation became constituent features of the temple as objects of worship.

Parvati's energy was remarkable and the particulars of her story were marked by uniqueness of her life history. But the kinds of interventions that she made represented a genre of action that had emerged over the past half century, according to many people's memories. It initially gained momentum in the latter period of anticolonial nationalism, as caste politics became increasingly entwined with the contentious politics of cultural nationalism in south India. As Anandaveli pointed out (Chapter 4), in the late 1930s the Shankaracharya had toured areas of the south, urging women among his following to take up public worship of the goddess. Since then, that Shankaracharya and his successor have issued regular requests of this nature and have extended patronage to organizing groups dedicated to such activities, and have taken active roles in them.

The Shankaracharyas' interest in activities such as those organized by Parvati, however, pointed to a notable absence in her narrative. Her efforts to improve the temple, inspired, she felt, by Kamakshi, were not directly guided by either the current Shankaracharya or his predecessor. Even though their pictures were in her *pūja* room and she mentioned having gone to Kanchipuram for their *darshan* in the past, they were not among any of the advisers she mentioned. Rather than seek support from the top down, she sought patronage through local networks of kin, friendship, business, and shared devotion. And though she never repudiated or disparaged her own Brahman identity, her friends and supporters came from varied caste and class backgrounds. This contrasted with narratives recounted by some of the other older Brahman women who had carved out identities as ritual adepts under the patronage of the Shankaracharya.

Her maintenance of unsullied *cumaṅkali*hood was critical in these arenas because her actions, though products of her own energy and resolve, were critically dependent on her other *maṇṭali* members' reputations as devout *cumaṅkali*s and as trustworthy, albeit informal, temple servants. Furthermore, Parvati's reputation as a *cumaṅkali* and the goddess's reputation as a *cumaṅkali* were mutually dependent. Kamakshi was an idiom that mediated Parvati's understanding of womanhood. The aspect of the goddess's *cumaṅkali*hood that was most celebrated in Parvati's ritual program was wifely identity (as opposed to motherhood), this expressed by the *tēvi*'s sexual availability for her husband, her happiness in being united with him, and the resultant fulfillment of her desires evidenced by her pregnancy. In bolstering the goddess's renown, Parvati endorsed a reading of woman as *cumaṅkali* and invited others to frame her and their own actions with it.

Rajalakshmi

The goddess Kamakshi played a similarly crucial role in the ways that Rajalakshmi negotiated reputation, though in her case it was Kamakshi as mediated by the Kanchipuram *maṭam,* that is, in accordance with the Shankaracharyas's interpretations.

Near the end of June 1987, my friend Anita suggested that I join her at a public discourse on *advaitavēdanta* sponsored at the Chennai home of one of the patrons of the large Kamakshi temple that is located in Kanchipuram and controlled by the *maṭam.* We took a rickshaw to an affluent neighborhood in Alwarpet and got down at the gate of a high wall that surrounded a large house and yard. Several cars and scooters were parked in the compound's yard. As we approached the meeting hall that abutted the house, we could see that a sizeable crowd had already assembled. To reach the meeting hall, we had to pass through a room that housed a small shrine containing a decorated stone figure of Ganesha. In the hall itself, there was a canopied platform on which pictures of Kamakshi were displayed.

I counted thirty people seated in the hall, twenty-two men (including the speaker) and eight women (including the speaker's wife, Anita, and I). The men were all employed (or retired) white-collar professionals, and the women were relatives of the men present. The speaker was a Sanskrit scholar and Śrī Vidya adept; like many of the other men present, he worked for the Reserve Bank of India. The discourse focused on the benefits associated with the performance of *shakti pūja.* Although instrumental ends, such as prosperity and relief from illness or infertility, could be achieved, the primary value of that *pūja* cycle was the inculcation of yogic self-control, with its mastery of the body and of bodily desires. The lecture was followed by a class in spoken Sanskrit in which younger women, married and unmarried, constituted the majority of students. That class, Rajalakshmi later told us, was part of a ten-session "crash course."

Rajalakshmi was one of the few women disciples of the male gurus affiliated with the Kanchipuram *maṭam,* and she enjoyed the patronage of the elder Shankaracharya. She, like others among his following, referred to him as Paramacharya. She was not his formal disciple, however, because of restrictions on cross-sexual discipleship. In the early 1940s, after petitioning the then Shankaracharya (Chandrasekharenda Saraswati), she had become a disciple of one Swami Chidananda (a sadhu affiliated with the *maṭam*), who initiated her into Śrī Vidya. This tantric-influenced system was thought to be derived from Adishankara's original teachings, which had revised and attempted to systematize Hinduism in response to Buddhist and Jain critiques. It was thus consistent with the principles of *advaitavēdanta;* the current Shankaracharyas were Śrī Vidya adepts and were described as having "surrendered" to the goddess Kamakshi.

The principles of Śrī Vidya were normally transmitted from a guru to selected students, and the disciples' mastery of texts, ritual forms, and yogic bodily discipline was stressed. Persons became adepts by learning from their gurus a sequence of *pūja*s honoring *shakti,* meaning both the cosmological principle of feminized, creative energy and the female consorts of the major Sanskritic deities. As might be inferred from its tantric influences, the esoteric knowledge and practice of Śrī Vidya was saturated with idioms of sexuality. Devotion, for example, is likened to heterosexual intercourse, and other key concepts are represented through metaphoric and metonymic references to sexuality (see translations and commentaries by Avalon 1921, 1927; Leadbeater 1952; Woodruffe and Pandit 1965; and recent work by White 1996).

Rajalakshmi submitted to her guru's training for about fifteen years before acquiring a following of her own, and it was another ten years before she began to sponsor large-scale ritual activities (such as *hōmam*s in honor of her guru) and to publicize those events in the local press. By 1987, she estimated that she had about two hundred disciples, nearly all of whom were affluent Smārta men.

The discourse had taken place at the end of June 1987, though I did not have another chance to meet with Rajalakshmi until November of that year. (She had left Chennai on a lengthy pilgrimage to important *shakti* temples in northern India.) By then, I had come to realize that private temples, some like Rajalakshmi's and others more modest, were ubiquitous features of the urban landscape in Chennai (e.g., Figure 7.1). It was also clear that they were sites for contestations about the boundaries and meanings of the public sphere. Rajalakshmi's description of the temple's construction was revealing in this regard:

> I was among a group of pilgrims traveling in Trichinopoly district. . . . When we were emerging from one of the temples, a *stapati* approached me and told me that he had had a dream that a Vināyakar[5] *mūrtti* was to be donated to me so that I might build a temple and install it there. I did not wish to take it without paying anything, so I collected three or four hundred rupees from the group with whom I was traveling, and with that paid for it. I returned to Chennai with that *mūrtti* and kept it in our house's well for one year; after that I covered it with paddy *(nel)* for six months. Following that, I had a platform made in the house yard and kept the *mūrtti* there. My friends and family encouraged me to build a temple to house the *mūrtti*, but I was hesitant because having a temple would expose the *mūrtti* and our home to public visitation and damage, like spitting, littering, graffiti, and things like that. We would also have to allow the government to have access to our financial records. I decided, therefore, to keep the *mūrtti* within our house. . . . [It] was installed on the full moon day during the month of Cittirai in 1982. Forty days thereafter, the Durga *mūrtti* was installed. Things were done in that way on the Paramacharya's order. (Field notes, November 27, 1987)

Rajalakshmi's distinction between the domestic site for the figure's installation and a "temple" (*kōvil* or *kōyil* is normally used) was a revealing

FIGURE 7.1 A Private Temple Located Within a Domestic Compound in Mylapore, 1988. Photograph By Author.

detail. By "temple" she meant a separate building containing consecrated images that was architecturally and organizationally patterned on temples found in public places to which any Hindu (and in many cases, non-Hindus) was guaranteed access in principle. By housing the *mūrtti*s in a space that was physically attached to her home, not in a "temple," Rajalakshmi eluded the state's control of that space and with it the requirement that it be open to public visitation.

In creating this alternative space for worship and assembly, however, she delineated an interstitial zone, one placed ambiguously between the bounded world of domesticity (centered jointly on the connected activities and spaces of worship and cooking) and the more permeable and inclusive "exteriors," such as temples, schools, work sites, streets, performance venues, and so forth. This enabled her to stipulate the criteria for entry—disciples, patrons, and other interested parties came on her invitation. The explicit restriction was sectarian, but there were also implied restrictions of caste and class. She appealed, finally, to tacit aesthetic criteria in identifying legitimate entrants. The "littering and spitting" that she found distasteful were reminiscent of "Sudras," a catch-all term used to conflate poverty, low-caste status, and aesthetic crudity, from which the upper-caste bourgeoisie distanced itself.

The household shrine and meeting hall, I learned, had been built only after Rajalakshmi had established herself as a guru and had initiated a large number of men as disciples. Her creation of this alternative space for a specified worshiping public rested on a critique of governmental policies, though it was a relatively late step in the expansion of her following:

> All throughout my married life, I had followed devotions at home as directed by my guru. . . . From 1957, devotional groups began gathering at my home or in public halls that had been rented out for the occasion. In 1957, I organized three hundred *suhasthinis*[6] for *pūja*, in which they chanted the three hundred names of the *tēvi*. . . . Ten years later, in 1967, there was a much larger event, during which 1,000 *cumaṅkali*s were gathered for recitation of *sahasranāmam*, 1,000 names of the *tēvi*. When the *pūja* was finished, the ladies were fed and given blouse pieces and *tāmpūlam*. . . . Prior to 1967, the events that I sponsored were not publicized; however, during those ten years [1957–1967], through word of mouth increasing numbers of people became involved in doing these *pūja*s with me and in learning from me. Once, a college principal, wanting initiation into Śrī Vidya, met with the Paramacharya, who advised him to come to me for this. (Field notes, November 27, 1987)

As was the case with Parvati, Rajalakshmi's daily life and the household's domestic space and time were all organized around her devotional life and her teaching. The household was enmeshed in an institutional nexus of her authorship that extended outside the spaces and relationships of the household. With her own money and contributions from others, she had organized two trusts and was on the managing committees of both. One was organized for conducting her guru's annual death anniversary. The other was dedicated to social service. Its members administer private and governmental funds to aid Brahmans and non-Brahmans in contracting marriages, in education, and in assisting disabled persons.

Her reputation and the revision of public space that it entailed were secured by several sets of relations. These included the patronage of Paramacharya and her guru, her links to her own growing body of followers and formal disciples, her familial network, and, lastly, her relationship to "womanhood," by which I mean other women and the notions of femininity encapsulated in the goddess Kamakshi. These relations were in turn inscribed spatially. Although the building of the shrine/meeting hall area was a culminating expression of these relations, in the household's *pūja* room, Rajalakshmi's own biography was congealed. At its core were her dependencies on her male patrons (her guru, the Paramacharya, and her father).

Her domestic *pūja* space consisted of an entire room; the materials it housed were related to her transactions with her various patrons. The walls were covered with pictures of deities and saints, among which were her own guru (and his guru). There were also numerous *cakkaram*s, several smooth river-washed stones (considered aniconic images of Vishnu), *trisula*s (three-pronged weapons wielded by Shiva and the goddess in her fierce manifestations), conch shells (used for an elaborate type of *apiṣēkam*), and assorted vessels and trays. The *cakkaram*s were essential items within the Śrī Vidya system that were considered extraordinarily powerful representations of particular deities and their abodes. Someone who was progressing in the system gradually gained access to successively deeper levels of meanings attached to the designs.

The main icons were kept in a closed cabinet; central among them was a gold figure of Kamakshi. The figure was seated atop a silver figure of a coiled cobra; placed in front of the cobra was a pyramid-shaped *cakkaram*, which Rajalakshmi referred to as Meru, the abode of *shakti*. That arrangement was a condensed reference to the relations of patronage that had enabled her to become a Śrī Vidya adept. Like many of the objects in the *pūja* room, the cobra and the *cakkaram* had belonged originally to her father's paternal grandfather. They were in Rajalakshmi's hands because her father had provided her earliest initiation into Śrī Vidya, teaching her how to perform a very simple form of worship when she was six years old. Those things revealed her initial encounter with Śrī Vidya, though it was the Kamakshi image that represented the critical moment—in her retelling of her life history, the arrival of the Kamakshi figure was the birth of her saintly life:

> This figure of Kamakshi was given to the Paramacharya forty years ago [1947]. I was present when it was given to him, and he handed it over to me—telling me to bring it home. At the time, I did not want it. Gold figures make great demands on devotees—they require special care and complete purity. I also felt that I needed to obtain [my] husband's permission before bringing it into the house. He [her husband] said that there were enough icons and pictures in our *pūja* room, that no more should be added to the collection. In the meantime, the Paramacharya had instructed that it be delivered to our house. Once it was there, what could he [her husband] say? He could not send it back! So, he agreed that it would remain in the house for one month only, saying that if anything bad happened during that time he would take it as the deity's displeasure and would send it back. During the month nothing especially bad or good happened, so we brought the figure to the Paramacharya and asked him to keep it. The Paramacharya still declined to accept it and told us to keep it along with everything else because it was so beautiful. All that has happened since—all of my devotion to *shakti*—is because of Kamakshi coming into our house. (Field notes, December 11, 1987)

With that set of transactions, the Shankaracharya usurped the authority of Rajalakshmi's husband, as well as the power of her deceased father and her guru in the household. Kamakshi was the medium for these transactions in the object form of the icon and in bodied manifestation as the Paramacharya and as Parvati's guru, both of whom, as Śrī Vidya adepts, had "surrendered" to the goddess. As *cumaṅkali* and Śrī Vidya initiate, Rajalakshmi was also an incipient body site for Kamakshi and was thus connected by substance to the Paramacharya and her guru. The sexual idioms of Śrī Vidya disciplinary practice and discourse—including the metonymic expressions of sexuality, male and female, that are parts of its object world—create relations among practitioners that are articulated through a logic paralleling that of kinship (i.e., of bodily substances, especially sexual fluids, mixing and bringing about regeneration of life) but fostering ties having the capacity to supplant those generated by kinship.

Rajalakshmi's authority as a Śrī Vidya adept (and thus her legitimacy as arbiter of the public space of her temple) rested ultimately on the patronage of Shankaracharya and her father's and guru's roles as her initiators. It also depended on her disciples. Because most of them were elite men, ranging in age from their twenties to their seventies, her reputation was further enhanced. Many had heard about her through class-based social networks linked to occupation and education. One man said he had heard about Rajalakshmi through the Lions Club of which he was a member, and many were employees of the Reserve Bank of India (RBI), who said that they had learned of her through work associates. The sexual idioms of Śrī Vidya made it possible to cast their relations with her in the kinship idiom described above. One man, who held a supervisory post in the RBI, told me (in English) that at the center of Śrī Vidya was the figure of the mother,

> the figure to whom humans are most attached and of which they are physically a part. The mother is also the figure that does not inspire fear but is nonetheless the most powerful, because it is the form to which people will be most willing to surrender. (Field notes, December 20, 1987)

When speaking of Rajalakshmi, he was visibly affected and near tears:

> She is guru to me, she is *amma<u>n</u>* [mother/goddess] to me. To take up Śrī Vidya, one must be found by one's guru—it is not a matter of one's own wish. None of this happened by chance. . . . Why, out of four hundred other employees [who knew of Rajalakshmi], should I be drawn to these beliefs? (Field notes, December 20, 1987)

What I have described as parallel worlds of kin relations and of relations mediated through Śrī Vidya were not in any sense separate compartments of Rajalakshmi's life. As the story of the Kamakshi acquisition revealed, these relations were densely interthreaded and sometimes conflictual, for each rested on different patterns of power and authority. And Rajalakshmi's subjectivity, emergent at the point at which they intersected, was constituted through these relations, their material foundations and precipitates, and the conflicts that they engendered.

One way to appreciate the complex and open-ended qualities of her subjectivity is by considering her daily routine. After arising at around 4:00 A.M., she mediated for a half hour and then recited *japams*[7] for an hour. While she prayed, one of the young men she had educated and found employment for came in to help set up things for the *pūja* and to assist with cleaning and cooking. When she finished reciting the *japams*, she bathed and then performed *pūja* for the deities in her *pūja* room and hall. On Sundays, she did a more elaborate *apiṣēkam* for the deities kept in the shrine area, and her disciples and other interested persons were invited to attend that. Following *pūja,* there were more prayers, after which she ate. During weekday and Saturday afternoons, she made herself available for consultations with disciples, and it was at that time that she always scheduled our appointments. On Sunday afternoons, she sponsored scriptural discourses in the meeting hall; those were publicized in the local press.

There were several annual and monthly observances that Rajalakshmi, assisted by her family and disciples, celebrated elaborately. These took place in the meeting hall or the temple, and most were in honor of the goddess. The other category of rites were those in honor of her guru—these included the annual ceremonies commemorating his death anniversary as well as a monthly ritual honoring his birth.

Most of the rituals mentioned were funded by her, either directly or through trusts that she had endowed. The costs of doing these *pūja*s covered expendable supplies (like flowers, sandal paste, milk, and ghee) and the snacks that attendees were served. The expenses for weekly and monthly *pūja*s averaged about Rs.500 each. The annual events cost two or three times that amount because meals were prepared and served to all of those who attended. She specifically mentioned using the interest that had accrued on her marriage settlement, though she also acknowledged that she had occasionally sold jewelry to pay for rituals. Some of her disciples, however, contributed by providing materials or money for the *pūja*s—among them, she noted, persons whom she had helped with education and marriage arrangements. The only ceremony that she did not finance herself was one sponsored annually at her house by her disciples to commemorate her birth.

Rajalakshmi's authority as a ritual adept and guru was underwritten by her father's wealth. It was her father's money and property that secured her husband's dependence on her family and that enabled her to negotiate greater independence within the household. (She barely mentioned her husband's kin in the life history she gave me.) It was that material wealth that ensured her a physical base of operations—a place, secured by ownership, from which to enact the strategic negotiations essential to her reputation. Her life history and the spatio-temporal architecture of her domestic life revealed these strategies:

> I was the eldest of four children, all girls. My father received the deity's *uttaravu* . . . that I should be married into a particular family. . . . Father's parents were not pleased with this arrangement because that family was not wealthy, whereas our family was. However, [my] father remained firm. . . . He decided that I should be married into that family, and in order to ensure that I would live comfortably, he spent money to educate the boy and set him up in business. . . . I was married at the age of eleven [in 1937], after completing my education up to the fourth form. [My] father supervised my informal education, however. . . . When he taught me how to perform *pāla pūja,* he taught me to read rudimentary Sanskrit and to converse in that language. . . . Two or three years after the marriage, [my] father died. . . . His death was a great blow because I worshiped him. I was sick for an entire

> year after he died, and our grandparents brought me home to the village so that I could regain my health. During that time, I went through my father's books and tried to learn about the formalities and rituals of the Hindu religion. I wanted to have a guru in order to get the proper explanations of the things in the books, and [my] mother advised me to seek out the family's priest for guidance. But he was very mercenary, and that put me off. On my own, I sought out the Paramacharya. He told me to return after two weeks, explaining to me that as a renunciant, he could not teach a married woman but that he would find a proper guru. When I returned, he directed me to Abhinava Bhaskera Chidhananda. This guru formally initiated me to *pāla* and Ganapathi *pūja*s at the Kamakshi temple in Kanchipuram. (Field notes, November 13, 1987)

Her father, her guru, and the Shankaracharya were the focal figures in her life—the ones who defined for her the horizon of the possible. Though she fulfilled her duties to her husband and son and was always deferential to them, her husband was a cipher in this story—a surrogate caretaker put in place and outfitted for the job by her father. By implication, *cumaṅkali*hood, though it could not be refused, clearly had a limited hold on her attention and was hardly the focus of her desires. She made these points explicit when telling me about her son:

> I had one son when I was sixteen years old, but I have never had a strong attachment to the family, except for [my] father. Our son's birth was "accidental" [English]—I had no intention to bear children. . . . Now our son and daughter-in-law live here, though she is childless. . . . I was disappointed by the lack of grandchildren . . . and I sought the advice of the Paramacharya. He told me that as a teacher to others I was like a mother and grandmother to many children and that I had more grandchildren that way that would be possible otherwise. (Field notes, November 13, 1987)

At the center of this complicated world was Rajalakshmi's extremely complex relationship to womanhood. She was, as she put it, not strongly attached to her husband or son, though she fulfilled all of the obligations that Brahman convention and Tamil society assigned to wives and mothers. This detachment carried with it a revision of maternity—her motherhood encompassed all of her disciples and was derived from her surrendering to Kamakshi.

She spoke of these matters during one of our visits in response to a question posed by Minakshi regarding Minakshi's concerns about installing a *cakkaram* in her own *pūja* cabinet. A couple of months earlier, Minakshi had been initiated to the first phase of Śrī Vidya, *pāla pūja*. Minakshi was uneasy because the *cakkaram*'s power demanded of the devotee greater attention to ritual formalities. Like independent forms of the goddess, the *cakkaram*'s power was capricious and unpredictable, as well as intense. Minakshi feared that despite her best intentions, she, a novice, might make mistakes that would displease the goddess and invite her wrath. Rajalakshmi replied as an experienced teacher:

> Are you afraid of your mother? Are you afraid of having your mother in your home? [Minakshi smiled and said no.] It's like that; Śrī *cakkaram* is our mother and there is no need to be afraid. The power of the *cakkaram* is *shakti; shakti* is the source of all energy and life. It is the mother to whom a child is naturally attached, and it is the mother who makes the father known to her child. This is not someone to be feared. Śrī *cakkaram* is the center from which all other *cakkarams* emanate; it is the first one and the most important one. . . . The birth of anything is through the female aspect. That is so for all living things—animals, plants, and humans. All of the earth has its source in the female, though all things are completed in the joining of female aspect, which is blood, and the male aspect, which is semen. . . . Śrī Vidya puts greater weight on the qualities associated with the female aspect as the source of all life. (Field notes, November 27, 1987)

The "female aspect" that is central to the system of Śrī Vidya has its origins in tantrism and retains within its conceptual framework references to some of the symbolic inversions associated with tantric practices, for example, animal sacrifice and sexual interaction. None of the adepts whom I knew acknowledged incorporating such activities into their ritual forms, though all invoked idioms of sexuality in describing the intentional world framed by Śrī Vidya. Rajalakshmi's description of one of the *shakti* temples she had visited on her just completed pilgrimage relied on those idioms:

> In Gauhati [Assam] there is a temple dedicated to the goddess. . . . Women go there for relief of problems associated with childbirth and menstruation. The form of the goddess in that place is a stone shaped like a vagina. . . . From this stone, water oozes continually. The stone is a self-generated form of *shakti*—it was not made by a *stapati*—and this place is one of the fifty-one *shakti pīṭams*.[8] Every two or three months, the water flow is interrupted and blood seeps from the stone for a few days. At these times, the doors to the temple are closed—the goddess is isolated in the same way that women are isolated during their menstrual periods. After about four days, a *kumpāpiṣēkam* is performed and the deity is once again available for visitation. During the days of isolation, a yellow cloth is kept on the stone until it becomes saturated with the blood. It is then removed and auctioned off by the temple. It brings prosperity to the household in which it is kept. (Field notes, December 11, 1987)

Those idioms, referring to the sexuality and maternity of married women, were important as legitimators of Rajalakshmi's autonomy and her status as guru (recall her disciple's description of her as a mother and as a mother goddess). Certainly Rajalakshmi would have been a less persuasive, and probably less wealthy, figure had she remained unmarried. She seemed mindful of this when she advised other women about religious matters, though as she pointed out there were few women among her disciples. During another of our visits Minakshi sought her advice about how to resolve an argument she had had with her husband about how to balance her devotional interests and her domestic duties. Rajalakshmi replied that she should fulfill her obligations as a mother first and that once that was completed she might immerse herself fully in devotion. She glossed householders' duties as *karmayoga* (as had Janaki; see Chapter 4) and asserted that they had to be completed properly; but one could cultivate *bhakti* in one's mind or heart *(maṉam)* alongside those duties.

Another aspect of Rajalakshmi's complicated relation to womanhood was evident in her interactions with her daughter-in-law. That woman (whose name I was never told) had no formal employment, though I rarely saw her when I visited Rajalakshmi at home. She supervised the family's servants, cooked, and cleaned. She also assisted Rajalakshmi by preparing ritual offerings, cleaning the *pūja* space, and helping her perform some of the large-scale rituals. Those duties, however, were shared by others among Rajalakshmi's disciples, and it was to those other disciples that Rajalakshmi referred when discussing how her public performances were orchestrated. I often wondered about Rajalakshsmi's daughter-in-law. Did she share Rajalakshmi's interests in Śrī Vidya? Rajalakshmi had been able to negotiate maternity on her own terms, but had this been so for her daughter-in-law? Rajalakshmi had said nothing about having initiated her to Śrī Vidya, and I saw no evidence of her own autonomous ritual life. What were her feelings about being childless in a world that judged her harshly for it—a world that presumed women's desire for marriage and motherhood and a world in which women rarely voiced any dissatisfaction with maternity? Because of my relationship with Rajalakshmi, whose authority in the household was never openly questioned, that terrain remained inaccessible to me. I was left with the sense that Rajalakshmi's autonomy, predicated on her detachment from the entanglements of *cumaṅkali*hood and on the creative energy of femininity, depended as well on her daughter-in-law's subordination.

Conclusion

In earlier chapters, I argued that distinct and competing configurations of the home/world dichotomy were encoded in ritual practices. The actions of both Parvaṭi and Rajalakshmi reconfigured this dichotomy in yet other ways, by blurring the boundaries of the home and the world. Each created interstices, Parvati by domesticating a public site and Rajalakshmi by opening the domestic interior to a select worshiping public. Their pathways moved under and around the mapped city—at times eluding and at other times attracting the panoptic gaze of the state.

Rajalakshmi's path led from her *pūja* room into her meeting hall—from a zone that was visually, acoustically, and socially sequestered into one of greater permeability. Her traversals of that route echoed and incorporated other paths—her own life history and her pilgrimages to other temples were evoked by the memorabilia kept in the *pūja* room and by the condensed cosmic maps of the *cakkarams* that consumed her attention. It was, in fact, the presence of the *cakkarams*—each a *mandala* conflating the body, the cosmos, and India's sacred geography—that signaled the particular style of Rajalakshmi's invention of space. In De Certeau's terminology, her home was a mappable site located in the *place* administered by the modern state. Within that home, however, other mapped *spaces*, whose coordinates were invisible to the state, were embedded.

The practices by which she constituted her invisibility were simultaneously tactical and strategic. Vis-à-vis the state, her moves were tactical. She eluded the state on its own terms in that her home and meeting hall were deemed "private" by the state and thus not subject to the surveillance ordinarily exercised over temples. The space invented within her home's boundaries, however, comprised nothing less than the Hindu macrocosm. It was "circumscribed as *proper*" [emphasis original] and served as the material and ideological base for strategic action "for generating relations with an exterior" (De Certeau 1984, xix).

Parvati, on the other hand, carved a path that led from her kitchen to the neighborhood temple. There, in a succession of tactical gestures, she seized Kamakshi's shrine, a place left unattended by the state. She negotiated with the state's agents to assume the state's duty of protection and maintenance. The role she sought was not modeled on the pre-British pattern of donation and receipt of honors, but was one that involved direct and innovative action on the state's own territory. Her social imaginary was grounded by domesticity, and her techniques were derived from the its everyday repertoires. Consequently, her space making implied an exclusionary etiquette—the substantialization of an "us" *(the maṇṭali)* in contradistinction to a "them" (the "godless people" previously settled there).

Her boundary practices, however, resulted in different, more inclusive networks of caste and class than did Rajalakshmi's. Parvati and the women who formed the *maṇṭali* were bound by mutual sympathies stemming from the precariousness of *cumaṅkali* identity. Those sympathies, at least on occasions when they gathered together as a group, bound together women of different castes, classes, or ethnicities, replicating the diversity of the neighborhood.

*Cumaṅkali*hood was at the heart of Rajalakshmi's practice as well, but for her, womanhood (as expressed in Śrī Vidya) was mediated by male authority, patronage, and power. For Rajalakshmi, womanhood neither began nor ended with women's bodily experiences, and she admitted that her own religiosity was not derived principally from her wish to perpetuate her *cumaṅkali* status. On the contrary, the womanhood that was at the core of Śrī Vidya was entered by detaching herself from the desires and experiences of a sexed female body and *ritually* appropriating the power *(shakti)* manifest in sexuality. Accordingly, Rajalakshmi's predominantly male circle was bound by the secrecy that shrouded these semiotic technologies. Those boundaries conformed to the boundaries of other social networks—of education and occupation, of leisure and consumption, and of caste—in which she and her family moved.

Parvati's and Rajalakshmi's covert movements, under and around the state, created sites that were barely visible on the city's surface and remained outside the state's bureaucratic control. These practices depended on a complicated matrix of values and interactional styles coming under the rubric of reputation or renown. This rubric encompassed "other narratives of the self and community that do not look to the state/citizen bind as the ultimate construction of sociality" (Chakrabarty 1992, 10). I close this chapter with some comments about how those other narratives might be read in the women's stories recounted here.

Parvati's and Rajalakshmi's ritual practices and their narratives about them were characterized by intersubjectivity. The "renown" *(pukaḻ)* and "good name" *(nallapeyar)* that they enjoyed implied that selfhood, instead of being defined in terms of autonomous intentionality, was experienced through and for others, among whom the goddess should be numbered. The sphere of those actions was not the "public" of official state discourse but the "public" celebrated in Tamil poetics, *puṟam*—a relational exterior. A. K. Ramanujan (1985) explained *puṟam* as a category of poetry associated with "a real place, a time, an event of history" (1985, 233). *Puṟam* poetry was the "'public' poetry of the ancient Tamils" (Ramanujan 1985, 235). Such poems contrast with the *akam* genre, which stems from an archetypal interior—the thoughts and feelings of a moment of experience. *Puṟam* poetry is structured around the movement from interiority to exteriority. These passages and their recurrent images (e.g., cities, open spaces, streets, battles, and praise) are suggestive of Parvati's and Rajalakshmi's work in creating reputations and creating "public" spaces.

In re-presenting their stories, I indicated that their negotiation of renown had two modalities: being spoken of favorably and frequently and being able to establish themselves as nodal points in expanding relational networks. Renown and the good name that accompanied it only came about through deeply etched patterns of interdependence and the talk that sustained these relations. I participated in conversations in which others acclaimed both women's religiosity and recounted formulaic stories about their experiences. In still other conversations, Rajalakshmi and Parvati reported what others said about them and recounted their own actions, framing them in terms of displacements of agency and intent. That is, neither Rajalakshmi nor Parvati represented herself as the author of the desires that propelled action; instead, they described themselves as being subject to desires of uncertain provenance. Recall Parvati's explanation of how the goddess's wishes, transmitted through another's dream, compelled her to act. If Parvati or Rajalakshmi were to be categorized as autonomous, ratiocinating individuals, weighing costs and benefits as they translated self-promoting impulses into action, these other logics of sensory engagement and sociality would remain ancillary or epiphenomenal, just as their productions of space were not fully seen on the city's surface.

The visibility or invisibility of "other narratives" is, therefore, positional and political. The hyphenated connection between nation and state has been predicated, since independence, on the state's effort to appropriate Hindu idioms of nationhood. Consequently, the state has issued ideological liens on temples and other spaces deemed as sites of incipient nationhood, and both women's paths were carved into its terrain. On that terrain, the women could be seen as "citizens" exercising rights stemming from property ownership or rights, and/or as members of the worshiping public, seeking to put their "occult laboratories" in good working order. On the other hand, their practices might also be read as traces of other narratives, born of Hinduism's heterogeneities, contradictions, and aesthetic sensibilities.

There are dangers in conceding the multivocality of Hindu belief and practice to the normalizing imperatives of modernity and nationalist ideologies (see, for example, Bharucha 1994; Chaitanya 1993; Misra 1993). The religious practices described in this chapter are co-optable by both the state and the Hindu right, but those are not inevitable scenarios. This chapter documents some of the ways in which Brahman women—simultaneously dominant and dominated—have resisted the state's appropriation of Hindu practice. Their interventions suggest other social imaginaries, albeit with unclear and not necessarily progressive political implications. To identify their habits and sensibilities solely with the version of Hinduism promulgated by the VHP and its affiliates effaces the heterogeneity of their practice; their hesitation and their resistance are occluded.

Even critiques of the Hindu right may be unwittingly complicit with the logic of Hindutva. Although the strength of the right's grip on Hindu audiences demands critical scrutiny, to focus solely on their own assertions about the extensiveness of popular support is a backhanded endorsement of the right's authorial claims on Hinduism. It is the polyglossia of Hinduism that continues to slip out of the grasp of both the state and the Hindu right, despite their unrelenting efforts to conscript it as a national culture. The residues that remain, and over which the Indian state and its nationalist critics continue to squabble, are orthogenetic caricatures of Hinduism. In the next chapter, I examine these slippages by addressing the ways in which some Tamil Brahmans, using the paired discourses of reform and Hindu nationalism, have entered this contest.

Notes

1. Enumeration blocks vary in area and population size. It is common to find two or more streets included within a single one, and the population can range from about two hundred to a thousand. Typically, each division contains between thirty and forty enumeration blocks.

2. The Muṇṭakakaṉṉiyammaṉ temple is a large, well-maintained, very popular goddess temple located less than half a kilometer from the Tiruvalluvar temple.

3. *Vaṭai* are savory fritters made of ground rice and lentils and seasoned with chilies and other spices. They are eaten by themselves as light meals or snacks, and are requisite as food offerings for a number of festivals.

4. A *stapati* is a person who is responsible for designing and building temples and the sacred deity figures therein in accordance with shastric precepts.

5. A name for the god Ganesha.

6. A Sanskritic expression for a chaste married woman.

7. Sanskrit phrases, often praise names of a deity, which are repeated multiple times as a meditative exercise.

8. *Pīṭam* refers to a seat or abode of the goddess; it is thought to be established by the emergence or emplacement of the goddess in a particular location.

8

Hindu Culture for an Indian Nation

Sri Jayendra Saraswati, Shankaracharya of Kanchi, after a three-day worship of Lord Venkateswara at Tirumala, has come out with a solution to "redeem the nation from the present turmoils and restore peace and tranquility among its various citizens." . . . In the course of the dhyanam [meditation], three things occurred to him as the factors responsible for the present disquiet. These were a steep fall in the spirit of nationalism and the quality of polity and the existence of constitutional lacunae. The Acharya said despite the handicaps the people's spiritual fervour had not died out completely. He felt that a "movement for spiritual, national and economic development" was the only answer to stem the rot.

—*The Hindu*, July 7, 1987

Hindutva Goes South

During the 1980s, right-wing Hindu nationalist organizations grew in size and strength in India and among Hindu Indian populations abroad (Basu et al. 1993). Most of the groups are part of a nexus comprising the Rashtriya Swayamsevak Sangh (RSS) and its "family" of affiliated groups: a religious association, the Vishwa Hindu Parishad (VHP); a trade union, the Bharatiya Mazdoor Sangh (BMS); a student association, Akhil Bharatiya Vidyarthi Parishad (ABVP); and a political party, the Bharatiya Janata Party (BJP). In national elections held in February 1998, the BJP gained the parliamentary majority needed to form a government and did so under the leadership of A. Vajpayee. Hindu nationalism, or Hindutva, is promoted in a variety of English and vernacular publications produced by these organizations.

One major offensive by Hindu nationalists was the December 1992 orchestration of the destruction of a mosque that allegedly had been constructed on the birth site of the Hindu deity Ram at Ayodhya in the northern state of Uttar Pradesh. Thousands of volunteers organized by the RSS and VHP descended on the mosque and were met by Muslim opponents; several days of violence resulted in death tolls reaching into the thousands (Basu et al. 1993). In the weeks that followed, riots occurred in other major Indian cities. For several months prior to the destruction of the mosque, the RSS and its affiliates had fueled communal antagonisms, systematically inciting smaller-scale confrontations throughout India and using the media to promote the idea that Hindus were a majority at risk. The gains of Hindu nationalism have also been evident in the growth of the BJP electoral base in the northern states that make up the Hindi belt.

Because much of the current wave of Hindu nationalism has emanated from centers in the north, peninsular India has sometimes been thought to be immune to its spread. Its northern, "Aryan" associations supposedly ensured that it would not play in the south. This view carried special weight with regard to Tamil Nadu. Since the early twentieth century, a cultural nationalism framed in terms of the Dravidian linguistic and ethnic identity of southern populations has been a dominant element of political and social life. Proponents of Dravidianism defined their identity in opposition to that of northern Indo-Aryan populations and also to that of Tamil Brahmans, who were regarded as descendants of the early Aryan conquerors of southern populations.

The confrontational tactics of nationalists in Kerala and the related successes of the BJP in Andhra Pradesh and Karnataka, however, indicate that Hindu nationalism does have bases in the south.[1] In Tamil Nadu, although the BJP has yet to claim either legislative assembly or Lok Sabha seats, the VHP and affiliated organizations have found receptive audiences for ritually mediated forms of Hindu nationalism, such as the Ramshila *pūja*s, in which bricks for the construction of a Ram temple at Ayodhya were blessed. The movement heralded by the passage cited in the epigraph also exemplifies the receptivity to Hindutva that has developed in the south in recent years.

This growth owes much to the work of Hindu nationalists. In their attempt to stoke up anti-Muslim sentiment, they have framed a series of large-scale conversions to Islam by Harijans as part of a Muslim conspiracy to dominate the sociopolitical and economic life of India (Seshadri n.d.). This commenced in 1981, following one such conversion in Meenakshipuram, a village in southern Tamil Nadu. It gained momentum with the publicizing of subsequent conversions and reconversions and through communal violence thought by many to have been orchestrated by the RSS and its affiliates.[2] The nationalist campaign included articles in the mainstream and RSS-controlled press that purported to document this conspiracy. Both the Arya Samaj and the VHP called for government inquiries into mass conversions, claiming that they were prompted by an influx of "foreign money" (i.e., funds from Muslims in other countries).

The same groups sponsored public rituals and other performances as part of an effort to proselytize among low-caste and Harijan populations considered susceptible to Islamic influence. In April 1982, the Arya Samaj held a reconversion ceremony for Christians in several southern districts (*Data India* 1982, 226). In June 1982, the VHP organized a *gnana ratham* (chariot of knowledge), which toured rural areas to campaign against "social evils" and bore VHP promotional material, films, a public address system, and deity images (*Data India* 1982, 419–420; *The Organiser*, June 27, 1982). In 1984, as a sequel, the VHP launched a *shakti ratham* (chariot of the goddess), a bus outfitted as a Māriyammaṉ temple, the aim of which was to promote *bhakti* and aid in the state's "Hindu renaissance" (*The Organiser*, August 16, 1984). Local protests directed at these events were unreported in *The Organiser* (*Data India* 1982, 419–420).

Among the religious leaders who contributed to these projects was Jayendra Saraswati, the Shankaracharya of Kanchipuram, to whom this chapter's epigraph refers. In 1981, he requested a government inquiry into allegations made by the Arya Samaj's that foreign funds were being used to encourage conversions. He called for the formation of a pan-Hindu association to combat the problem (*Data India* 1981, 407). He subsequently made shows of support for the RSS. The *Organiser* reported that the *gnana ratham* had been launched by Jayendra Saraswati, who anticipated that it would teach rural masses "disciplined devotion." During that same month, Saraswati also blessed an RSS youth camp meeting in Salem, a city in western Tamil Nadu (*The Organiser*, June 27, 1982). Shortly thereafter, in 1983, he convened the three-day Hindu Arts Festival in Chennai, intended to "revive [the] nationalist spirit" (*The Hindu*, March 31, 1983).

The March 31, 1983, edition of *The Hindu* described Saraswati's opening benediction for the festival. He stated that it was aimed at "children, women and weaker sections [poor and low-caste groups]" and should "remind people of the spiritual and cultural heritage" of Hindu civilization. He stressed the present need for unity among all Hindus, urging "Harijan youth" to follow Hindu religious practice. The resolutions announced at the festival included statements that the property and administration of temples should be directed toward propagating "Indian cultural traditions" and "spiritual values" and that the central government should extend rights enjoyed by religious minorities to "weaker sections."

The coalition of religious leaders and nationalist groups brokered by the VHP was successful, as well, in securing the patronage of Tamil Nadu politicians. Shortly after the Meenakshipuram incident, R. Veerappan, then the state Hindu religious and charitable endowments minister, indicated that the government was considering legislation to ban mass conversions and announced that a special campaign to "reassure Harijans of equality" would be inaugurated (*The Hindu,* August 11, 1981). Following Saraswati's Hindu Arts Festival, which had been attended by elected officials (including the state's chief minister, M. G. Ramachandran), Veerappan asserted that the government "respected Hindus" and that the festival had strengthened Hinduism by showing the "scientific basis of [its] customs" (*The Hindu,* April 5 1983).

As the 1980s progressed, the conversion issue was incorporated into the accelerating discourse authored by the Hindu right that focused jointly on Muslim and Dravidianist threats to Hindu religious institutions.[3] Hindutva, when filtered through religious practice, could be made attractive and even familiar to Tamils in ways that the Aryan imagery of the RSS could not.

In 1987 and 1988, my middle-class Brahman acquaintances in Chennai seemed, for the most part, uninterested and not particularly well informed about the formal programs of Hindu nationalist organizations as reported in the national press.[4] They did, however, disparage the politicization and "corruption" of religious practices and institutions that they encountered on a day-to-day basis, something that they associated with the state government's administration of temples. They were deeply disturbed, as well, by the "preferential" treatment accorded by the government to religious minorities and to members of "scheduled" and "backward" groups. Accordingly, many among the urban bourgeoisie were eager consumers of proposals such as Jayendra Saraswati's, and they were active in voluntary associations that were geared to the rather ambiguous but nonetheless nationalist ends that the Shankaracharya identified. Women in particular seemed receptive to such programs, something that can be attributed jointly to the government's solicitation of female voluntarism in the delivery of social services (consistent with bourgeois nationalisms of the colonial and postcolonial eras), as well as to the spaces for autonomous action that such practices offered women.

In this chapter, I want to explore this willingness to "consume" Hindutva by considering Jayendra Saraswati's mediation of Hindu nationalism through the Ja<u>n</u> Kalyāṇ movement.

Consenting to What?

While living in Chennai, I had seen press releases about the Shankaracharya's movement for several months before I encountered it directly. It was dubbed Ja<u>n</u> Kalyāṇ (a Sanskritized expression ordinarily translated as "people's welfare"), and its founder was the important Hindu preceptor Sri Jayendra Saraswati, who headed the Kanchipuram *maṭam.* That monastery was estimated to be the wealthiest of the *maṭam*s that trace their genealogy to Adishankara, and Saraswati was the sixty-ninth in the line of preceptors initiated by Adishankara (Cenkner 1983; Mines and Gourishankar 1990). As head of the *maṭam*, Saraswati controlled several voluntary associations, of which Jan̲ Kalyāṇ was one. It was through these organizations and others (including RSS affiliates) that he staged the events described above and pursued what he referred to as "social activism" through the brokerage of cross-caste alliances. With this agenda he has distinguished his style of leadership from that of previous Shankaracharyas.

I was introduced to Jan̲ Kalyāṇ in December 1987, when I attended a performance of devotional songs sponsored by one of the voluntary associations affiliated with the monastery. Its president, Uma Radhakrishnan, a Smārta Brahman in her late fifties, had organized the event, which took place in what people referred to in English as a "private temple." The performance was introduced by a short dedication to the goddess Kamakshi. Following that, Uma delivered a short speech about Jan̲ Kalyāṇ and distributed copies of its slogan and members' pledge to the audience. She then asked the audience to join her in a prayer consisting of sixteen repetitions of the Sanskrit phrase that served as the movement's slogan. Devotional songs in honor of Kamakshi were performed by the musicians whom Radhakrishnan had hired for the evening. The audience of nearly a hundred men and women consisted largely of Smārtas and other Brahmans who resided in Mylapore and adjacent sections of the city.

Though Jan̲ Kalyāṇ was represented by its founder as a grassroots movement of national scope, its operations and effectiveness suggested otherwise. In the first place, it remained locally centered in Tamil Nadu's municipalities, and in Chennai especially. Second, the bulk of its membership was drawn from the urban Smārta bourgeoisie, the *maṭam*'s original core constituency. Despite its ostensible commitment to social welfare, Jan̲ Kalyāṇ functioned both as a node for brokering cross-caste alliances among middle- and upper-class populations and as a vehicle for Smārtas to assert a group identity derived from efforts to create ties with, and to speak for, other caste and class groups.

In typical urban bourgeoisie fashion, Smārta internal organization was mediated by diverse voluntary associations, from neighborhood clubs to international groups such as the Rotary Club. Although such associations mediated cross-caste networks among middle- and upper-class urbanites, there were also caste-specific nexes, in particular, the Tamil Brahman Association (TAMBRAS), a statewide caste association that operated through a series of local units.

A prominent feature of Jan̲ Kalyāṇ was its attention to what Saraswati defined as "cultural" phenomena. In its promotional literature, the term *kalāccāram* was glossed as "culture." This Tamilized Sanskrit word refers to textually mediated artistic and scientific knowledge. Culture was also circumscribed in the forms of belief and practice promoted through Ja<u>n</u> Kalyāṇ, which derive from the theological principles of *advaitavēdanta,* to which Smārtas adhere.

The discourse of culture provided opportunities for its Smārta membership to assert an identity that had continuities with their previous role as cultural intermediaries. Saraswati's representation of Smārtas as culture brokers depended on prior authorization by colonial administrators and judges. In chapters 1–2, I described how they, as educated elites, were inducted into the colonial state as lawyers, judges, and administrators but at the same time drew on the lexicon of modernity to fashion languages of nationhood and resistance to colonial rule. In those chapters I also discussed the Smārtas' roles as anthropological interlocutors, showing how Milton Singer's collaboration with Indologist V. Raghavan produced the contours of an Indic "Great Tradition" in which Smārtas were both protagonists and authors.

Ja<u>n</u> Kalyāṇ was a vehicle through which its Smārta members articulated a group identity through the deployment of key symbols that embodied what Saraswati defined as Indian culture, thereby creating opportunities for Smārtas to identify their particular, caste-based community with the more extensive community of the nation. This amounted to a rhetorical claim that Smārtas, as a community, were brokers for, as well as legitimate representatives of, the Indian nation by virtue of their ownership of the key elements of the cultural traditions that allegedly defined India as a nation.

The discourse on *Indian* culture was part of the discourse of the nation and modernity. The boundaries of Indian culture, however, were ambiguous. A factor keeping this debate active is the constitution's recognition of distinct religious and cultural groups, and its assertion that state and central governments are obligated to protect the interests and autonomy of these groups (see the constitution of India, part 3, articles 25–30). Because the nation is also identified as a community and is imagined as a mosaic of constituent but bounded communities, "culture" is brought into play at another level—as an ideological glue whose key idioms are pluralism, tolerance, and integration (see, for example, the report of the Committee on Emotional Integration 1962).

The efforts by Ja<u>n</u> Kalyāṇ and other cultural nationalist movements to contest the government's reading of secularism were grounded in the ambiguity, and hence the instability, of these uses of culture.[5] Rhetorically, Ja<u>n</u> Kalyāṇ used culture against politics, that is, against central and state institutions. With this argument, Saraswati emphasized the gulf between the authenticity of (Hindu) "culture" and the expediency of (secular) "politics." His nationalist rhetoric was linked, as well, to a critique of the anti-Brahmanism associated with the policies of the current government in Tamil Nadu. Ja<u>n</u> Kalyāṇ recoded Brahmanism as Hindu tradition, arguing that Hindu tradition, as interpreted by Saraswati, was the most effective regulator of social life and political action.

Smārta claims of culture brokerage were lodged performatively through Ja<u>n</u> Kalyāṇ—with ritual and devotional music conducted by and for a mostly Smārta membership. These claims were reiterated in Ja<u>n</u> Kalyāṇ's member's pledge, which stipulated that members apply moral discipline to the poor.

Though Ja<u>n</u> Kalyāṇ was not a women's movement, like many other modern discourses of national culture, it deployed women in public as metaphors for the representation of the traditions that supposedly generated the Hindu nation and as actors engaged in the cultural production of that imagined community (Anderson 1991). In so doing, it adopted the rhetoric of womanhood found in colonial and postcolonial constructs of the nation, such as the metonymic connection between oppressive institutions like *satī* with India's civilizational deficits (Mani 1990), the early nationalist feminization of Indian tradition (Chatterjee 1993, 117–134), the Dravidianist gendering of language as Mother Tamil (Lakshmi 1990; Ramaswamy 1997), and M. K. Gandhi's feminization of the nation (Kishwar 1985; Nandy 1983, 48–55; Patel 1988). These varied representations came together in one part of the Gandhian construct of the nation that continues to be celebrated in bourgeois nationalism: its "separate spheres" ideology (see Minault and Papânek 1982), in which a "private sphere" of naturalized, feminine virtue is considered different from, but strategically connected to, a "public sphere" of political action.

Despite the appropriation of femininity as a sign under which the Indian nation might be written, there have been ambiguities with regard to the space for female action accommodated by various nationalisms. Women, marked as spiritual and tradition bound, have been cast both as reformers and as beings in need of the reforms promised by modernity. In Gandhian nationalism this tension was partially resolved by conceiving of woman's nature as essentially domestic and a resource for the nation—if it is freed from the strictures of child marriage, *satī,* and dowry. Viewed as patient, pure, courageous, and self-sacrificing, women were models for nonviolent civil disobedience; similarly, the home was envisioned as the site of feminine action for the nation (e.g., spinning thread for *khadi*).[6] The focus on woman as mother cohered as well with the urban, upper-caste, middle-class Hindu male's perception of what a woman should be (Patel 1988, 378). This image stood in counterpoint, however, to the equally important figure of woman as renouncer of family life—working selflessly for the nation and represented in the paradigmatic form of the ascetic Brahman widow.

As Patel (1988) observed, the tension between these two images, both anchored in separate spheres ideology, was never resolved, though Gandhi's fashioning of ideal womanhood shifted from its early focus on the mother to a later focus on the widow. In both cases, however, women were defined in and through a patriarchally ordered domestic life, conceived as both source and homology of the nation. In practice, this gave way to further contradictions, for women who wished to participate in the mass disobedience actions orchestrated by Gandhi had to renegotiate the boundaries between the home and the world, thereby risking the damage to their reputation (and to their family's reputation) that followed from transgressions of patriarchal norms (see Visweswaran 1996; Hancock forthcoming).

This conflation of femininity and domesticity was frequently invoked as common sense by urban elites in India. Jayendra Saraswati's solicitation of women and his usage of feminine ritual idioms reiterated this while connecting it to the feminized idioms of the monistic and tantric-influenced teachings of the *maṭam* that he heads. One of the ritual genres associated throughout Hindu South Asia with femininity and domesticity, *tiruviḷakku pūja,* was annexed by the Shankaracharya to publicize Jan̲ Kalyāṇ and to recruit members. This use of women and femininity was a critical feature in Jan̲ Kalyāṇ's claim to represent the cultural domain that grounded the "Hindu nation" and in its conscription of culture to contest the legitimacy of a realm that it defined as political (the secular state). Moreover, by entwining its nationalist message with everyday domestic practice, it inserted nationalism into the home. Urged on by their wives, mothers, and sisters, men might be persuaded to take up the cause of Hindu nationalism in other venues.

On the basis of both its short life (the movement was defunct for all practical purposes by 1990[7]) and its use of "social service" for Smārta Brahman self-representation, Jan̲ Kalyāṇ arguably represented just a reactionary social twitch—a "public transcript" of underclass acquiescence (to paraphrase Scott 1990, 85–90) unworthy of further scrutiny. Critics have called it a Brahmanical version of Hindutva camouflaged by a thin veil of social reform, something that probably accounts for its failure in Tamil Nadu (Pandian 1990). It is precisely this aspect of Jan̲ Kalyāṇ, however, that invites attention. Clearly, Saraswati was making claims through Jan̲ Kalyāṇ about the continuities between Smārta interests and the interests of the nation. It is evident also that these types of elite appropriations of nationalist discourse have not actually abated, for they continue to be articulated by the Shankaracharya and by upper-caste associations such as TAMBRAS in prosaic and ostensibly benign terms. The need to specify local appropriations of Hindutva only increases as Hindu nationalism makes inroads within India's diverse population. To whom were Saraswati's claims addressed and in what ways did they make sense to audiences? In what cultural debates were these discourses of identity situated? What continuities and discontinities existed between Ja<u>n</u> Kalyāṇ's discursive construction and its enactment, especially with regard to its deployment of feminine idioms and its solicitation of women workers?

Using feminine idioms and women's bodies was one of the modalities with which Ja<u>n</u> Kalyāṇ sought to both penetrate and reshape what Gramsci described as "common sense": a sedimentation of "conceptions of life and of man . . . popular knowledge [that is] . . . not something rigid or immobile, but is continually transforming itself, enriching itself with scientific ideas and with philosophical opinions which have entered ordinary life" (Gramsci 1971, 326). Through Ja<u>n</u> Kalyāṇ's imagery of a gendered, Hindu national culture, Saraswati sought a hegemonic principle consistent with caste and class privilege but at the same time capable of articulating different (and antagonistic) interests and idioms associated with different classes and castes (Gramsci [1929–1936] 1971, 349–350; see also Mouffe 1979).

Ja<u>n</u> Kalyāṇ, however, had less salience as a form of class domination than it did as an ensemble of hegemonic practices designed to secure the compliance of elites in the constitution of their own nationalized identities. My analysis focuses on the practices entailed by the education of consent. I am interested specifically in the production of hegemonic power through the "hailing" or interpellation of subjects, as well as in the ways that hegemony is implicated in the very constitution of subjects.

In Ja<u>n</u> Kalyāṇ, it was the woman, the Brahman, and the nation that were mutually configured as subject positions, and women were doubly caught in its solicitation of consent. They were positioned as agents whose function was to seek the consent of others—Brahmans, as well as poor and low-caste persons—in implementing Saraswati's project. They were also asked to embody an imagined nation.

The horizon of desire and imagination signaled by that intersection of positions, however, was not wholly contained by Saraswati's project. Even those most loyal to him acted on understandings and wishes that ran counter to or were unanticipated by Ja<u>n</u> Kalyāṇ's tenets. These observations suggest neither a resisting nor a complying subject but rather a complex and to some extent underdetermined subjectivity whereby both consent and resistance are concatenated in indirect and "negative" forms of agency, as well as in voluntary, conscious action. This in turn undermines the closure or totalization ascribed to interpellation by Althusser, but it retains Althusser's attention to subject constitution as a mode of domination. Following Williams (1977), I emphasize the unevenness of hegemonic power and the practices that produce it.

In order to understand Jan̲ Kalyāṇ as hegemonic practice, I will examine Jan̲ Kalyāṇ's charter and its operations as conveyed by its author and as interpreted by one of its members, the already mentioned Smārta woman who headed the devotional society. Analytically, Jan̲ Kalyāṇ offers a window on the gendered politics of culture in Tamil Nadu, particularly as these discourses are emergent in debates surrounding Brahmanism and Hindutva. It also offers an opportunity for addressing broader issues related to women's consent and agency within the entwined structural inequalities of caste and class.

Jan̲ Kalyāṇ as a Discourse of Hindu Nationalism

In remarks that accompanied the formal inauguration of Jan̲ Kalyāṇ in October 1987, Saraswati stressed the *national* scope of the program—it was for all Indians, not just for Hindus (*The Hindu,* October 3, 1987). At the same time, he asserted that Indianness was derived, ultimately, from the worldview and practices of Hinduism, which contained the essence of the "country's traditions." In terms even more starkly substantive, he has located Hinduism in the blood of India's people (*The Illustrated Weekly of India,* September 13, 1987) and in the land. "Bharat being a 'karma, jnana and dharma' bhumi, the term Dharmo Rakshati Rakshata should be expressly declared side by side with . . . the country's motto. . . . [and] India should be called Hindustan" (*The Hindu,* October 3, 1987).[8]

If the nation is an "imagined community," as Anderson (1991) has suggested, how did Jan̲ Kalyāṇ propose to fashion persons capable of such imaginings? How were Hindu "citizens" to be created? Prior to launching the movement, Jayendra Saraswati had already established English medium schools and had produced audiocassettes and pamphlets detailing the lives of the Shankaracharyas, the history of the *maṭam,* and the formats of important rituals.[9] The members' pledge of Jan̲ Kalyāṇ continued in this vein, specifying the creation of "book banks" and "exhibits" (articles 20–21), assistance at private schools and hospitals (article 17), the conduct of public ritual (article 5), dress and commensal codes (articles 3, 8, 10), and the performance of certain domestic and neighborhood duties (articles 1–2, 4, 7, 15–16) as obligations of membership.

The official tenets and practices described in the pledge suggested, on the one hand, that India already *was* a Hindu nation, culturally speaking: "Any man or woman who proclaims the nation of India as their mother country and as their cultural homeland may become a member" (article 11). On the other hand, the pledge implied that India's cultural identity was imcomplete and had to be brought to fruition by the work of Ja<u>n</u> Kalyāṇ. Article 20 advocated that members build libraries of religion, culture, and nation for the poor. The same themes resounded in the styles of collective ritual that were the authorized modes of self-presentation and recruitment. Saraswati mapped the social distinctions between cultural leaders and followers in an interview in which he discussed his plans for Ja<u>n</u> Kalyāṇ, differentiating "intelligent" and "unintelligent" citizens and specifying the latter—rural, "common people"—as his "true parish" (Sunil 1987). It was these people, glossed in the same interview as lower castes, who in his observation were enticed by the monetary inducements of "other religions." The caste system, however, was not in itself a problem: "It should exist just the way it has" because "they [castes] are all equal . . . but they have specialist functions" (Sunil 1987, 11–12). The practices advocated in Ja<u>n</u> Kalyāṇ were meant, therefore, to circumscribe moral self-improvement and social service, including attention to public space and activity, with the values of Hindu "culture," the subjects of which define themselves and others in light of caste and class distinctions.

In stipulating the practices of cultural citizenship, the members' pledge provided a blueprint for the ways in which class and caste distinctions were consolidated and represented as integrative rather than conflictual categories. Membership duties implied the existence of both autonomy and moral agency among Ja<u>n</u> Kalyāṇ's volunteers. Members, as implied in articles 1–3 (which stipulated daily rituals), were capable of self-discipline; they were to be abstemious in consumption (article 8) and capable of material sacrifice—giving food, money, clothing to the poor (articles 12, 14, 17, 18). Those who were served by Ja<u>n</u> Kalyāṇ, on the other hand, were inferior in their passivity (they *received* assistance) and in their propensity to succumb to violence and to moral depravity. It was the poor—especially "backward" and Harijan groups—who engaged in communal violence, suffered familial disputes, and were unable either to redress these problems or recognize their causes, thus necessitating the intervention of Ja<u>n</u> Kalyāṇ (articles 6, 17, 20–21).

Members' affluence was acknowledged in the references to their employment, to the yearly dues calculated on the basis of salary (articles 10–12), and to the private homes and cars that they were expected to decorate with the movement's logos (articles 15–16). This material affluence accompanied their superior cultural capital; as article 11 suggested, those who sought membership were already capable of imagining India as a Hindu nation. They also had to be willing (as stipulated in articles 4, 20, 21) to teach those who were culturally impoverished. Finally, in order to have transformative effects, these cultural endowments had to be used to refashion public life—to clean up public spaces (article 4), to initiate new types of Hindu public ceremony (article 5), and to expand the Hindu colonization of public space with new temples, *maṭams,* and "cow protection homes" (articles 7, 21). The members' pledge thus yielded a vision of the Hindu nation—enumerating the criteria for good citizenship, indicating what categories of persons were and were not predisposed to it, and prescribing correctives for the latter.

The Ritual Remaking of Society

The outline of Hindu society in the members' pledge privileged the role of ritual practice, though it told very little about the specifics of those activities apart from the references to daily water offerings and mantra recitations. As noted earlier, I encountered Ja<u>n</u> Kalyāṇ in December 1987, having been invited to attend one of the ritual performances staged by members to recruit volunteers. My analysis of Ja<u>n</u> Kalyāṇ's ritual infrastructure is based on my discussions with Uma Radhakrishnan about her participation in the movement. I use this material to explore Ja<u>n</u> Kalyāṇ's annexation of womanhood and the possible readings that middle-class Brahman women might give to these processes.

A few days after the Kamakshi *bhajan*s, Minakshi (my research assistant) and I visited Uma at her home in an affluent neighborhood on the city's south side. Her life was one of marked material privilege. She lived with her husband in a spacious, well-furnished house. Her husband, then retired, had been highly placed in the Indian civil service, and her father had been similarly employed in her youth. In our subsequent conversations (which were conducted in English), she detailed the history of her involvement in Ja<u>n</u> Kalyāṇ but presented it within a life history narrative that focused on her religious interests. She began by describing the founding of the Samajam (the group that sponsored the *bhajan*s) in April 1985. She had sought an audience with Saraswati, and on that occasion he had told her,

> "There is a supreme *shakti,* above all *mahā*s [saints], and by praying to that, one is worshiping all." . . . He then advised me to sponsor a *shakti pūja* on every full moon day in some public place so that people would come to understand the principle of the supreme *shakti* power. I told him, though, that to do that on such a big scale would be difficult, and I asked that he assign me some other activity. He then said that I should sponsor *bhajan*s on the full moon day [of each month]. I agreed to this and began immediately on the next full moon day, May 4, 1985. . . . I organize everything having to do with these performances—I place advertisements, engage performers, reserve the hall and equipment, and send invitations to special guests. . . . I try to get everything by donation though I pay some of the costs myself. (Field notes, December 17, 1987)

In September 1987, Saraswati had asked her to assist him with his new campaign, Ja<u>n</u> Kalyāṇ. He gave her a copy of the movement's flag and asked her to teach people a Sanskrit prayer, which they were to repeat three times each day.[10] She explained, "In the morning, it should be said for the sake of ancestors, at noon for the gods, and in the evening for the family. The meaning of the prayer is 'surrender to the one who saves you from all danger.'"

I asked her about her willingness to take on the sort of responsibility that the Shankaracharya had stipulated. She replied that her inclination had stemmed from her own background in music—she had studied singing with several Carnatic musicians, and in 1972 she had founded the Madras Music Circle. She quickly pointed out, however, that the Shankaracharya had not known of that when he asked her to sponsor *bhajans*; she attributed that to his special insight into people's character. She went on,

> In 1979, I had to abandon it [the Music Circle] because I had other obligations. Many were connected to my husband's job; he was in the IAS [Indian Administrative Service] and was a chief secretary at that time. . . . However, most of my time now is free for doing the work connected with the *bhajans*. My husband is a noninterfering type. He doesn't help out a great deal but neither does he hinder me. He does assist by taking phone messages and keeping a diary for me; he also types letters when I need that done. (Field notes, December 17, 1987)

She also pointed out that the Shankaracharya's request and her acquiescence were both ascribable to the goddess's intention. It was her conviction that she had been drawn by the goddess Kamakshi to receive the Shankaracharya's instructions about her participation in both the Samajam and Ja<u>n</u> Kalyāṇ. Her notion of the goddess's intervention was paired, however, with the displacement of her own intentionality. She said that she had not been particularly religious before receiving the Shankaracharya's directives, despite growing up in a wealthy and devout Brahman household. "When I got married, my husband was the district collector. I was very busy with our household, and I did not have a great deal of religious interest. After my daughter got married [about 25 years earlier], my interest started to build." (Field notes, December 17, 1987).

Since founding the Samajam, however, she explained, "My mind has no longer been on the family. . . . Now I think mostly about organizing the *bhajans*, and my work for Ja<u>n</u> Kalyāṇ."

She said that the purpose of the Ja<u>n</u> Kalyāṇ movement was to establish uniform standards for Hindu practice and that there were to be no caste barriers. The Shankaracharya, she pointed out, was going to put out books and cassettes with the correct formats for daily devotions and festivals. One prescribed activity was the public performance of *tiruviḷakku pūja,* an act ordinarily performed by women in their homes.

> I am organizing a *tiruviḷakku pūja* myself to take place in . . . February. This will be the first I have done. In Kanyakumari, 1,008 ladies gathered to do this *pūja* in accordance with the Acharya's directions. . . . To do this *pūja,* the lamp should be decorated with vermilion powder and flowers, and a water pot placed in front of it. For the food offering, puffed rice, beaten rice, and crystal sugar should be given. It's not a complicated *pūja*—one lights the lamp, [recites] the 108 names of Lakshmi. One then circles the lamp. (Field notes, December 17, 1987)

Uma had already begun to plan the *tiruviḷakku pūja* that she had scheduled for February. A hall had been engaged and she was having invitations printed.

Although she had said that Jan̲ Kalyāṇ was caste blind and suggested that bonds of femininity could cut across caste boundaries, she made other comments that undermined those apparently egalitarian sentiments. When I asked her about the other domestic rituals that she performed, she spoke about a *pūja* honoring the goddess Santoshima that had recently become popular in Chennai. She said that she had completed that *pūja* cycle four times, each for some specific aim, and that all had been successful. Two of the cycles, she noted, had been for her grandson's benefit—once for his exams and once because

> he had been denied a seat in engineering college because he was a Brahman, a member of a forward community. Merit carries no weight because of the anti-Brahman sentiment—those with lower marks gained admission, yet he was rejected for no good reason. We tried to use influence to gain his admission, but nothing came of that either. Then, I did Santoshima *pūja,* and one Friday—just when I was completing it—I got a call from my daughter to say that the boy had gotten a seat in another engineering college. Santoshima had gotten him a seat in the best college and in the best course—electrical engineering. (Field notes, December 17, 1987)

The caste inequalities that invited the goddess's intervention were those that she, like many other Brahmans, ascribed to governmental policies of positive discrimination. It seemed that what she sought in everyday ritual and in her work for Jan̲ Kalyāṇ was a form of personal autonomy, albeit one located in a naturalized system of privilege that stemmed from "merit" and, in Saraswati's words, "intelligence."

*Women, Womanhood, and the Politics of Inclusion in Ja*ẹṇ̄ *Kaly*āy

Uma's experiences and perceptions, although not necessarily shared by others in the movement, are illuminating because they reiterated what other Brahman women found appealing in Ja<u>n</u> Kalyāṇ and they located the movement within broader categories of caste, class, and nation. These categories were emergent in her narratives. They were described in neither objective nor disinterested terms but were positionally appropriated. Her words communicated the complexity of her consent to Hindutva—she incorporated little of the obvious rhetoric of Hindu nationalism, focusing instead on the engendering rituals of *cumaṅkali*hood, the personal autonomy that she derived from her work for Ja<u>n</u> Kalyāṇ and the reverse discrimination toward Brahmans that she associated with governmental policies on education.

Let me consider her articulation of Brahman identity first. I have described already the political distinction that is made in Tamil Nadu between Brahmans and non-Brahmans, explaining that it originated when the colonial administration recognized and officialized caste as a politically salient category. Under the Dravidianist parties that have controlled the state government since 1967, Tamil Nadu has retained and expanded the policies of positive discrimination authored under colonialism and, in an atmosphere of interclass and intercaste conflict, has enlarged the state list of "backward classes" that complements the central "schedule" of groups that have been discriminated against historically. Tamil Brahmans, like Uma, see their own status as a "forward caste" as a mark of reverse discrimination. Adding fuel to Brahman discontents was the DMK government's increasing intervention in Hindu religious institutions during the 1970s (discussed in Chapter 6). What Saraswati derided as "political" uses of religion resonated with what I heard from Smārtas and other middle- and upper-class persons in Chennai, who similarly disparaged what they saw as the state's intrusion into religious life and the waste of temple resources. They criticized the policies and institutions developed and implemented under the rubric of the government's protection of religious institutions. The Hindu Religious and Charitable Endowments (HRCE) department, the scope of which was broadened after the DMK took control of the Tamil Nadu state government, was one of the main culprits as far as they were concerned.

Such dissatisfactions contributed to Brahmans' receptivity to Hindutva, for its critique of secularism resonated with their own sense of relative deprivation. In promoting Hindu culture as a corrective for secularism, it invited Brahmans (and others having a historical stake in the brokerage of culture) to assume authority in that arena. The Shankaracharya and his predecessor made similar use of culture in contesting the state in the past (see Chapter 6). The *tiruviḷakku pūja* that Jayendra Saraswati recommended to Uma typified the modes of goddess devotion that he and his predecessor have appropriated and publicized over the past few decades.

Saraswati's interest in women's ritual was consistent with the centrality of feminine idioms in the past and present teachings and ritual practices of the Kanchipuram *maṭam* (see Chapter 4). Saraswati and his predecessor have urged their followers to adopt these elements in their personal practice and in collective ritual activities. Urban women have become more familiar with these styles of ritual over the past three to four decades. The relocation of domestic practice into extra-domestic venues results in more diverse audiences and beneficiaries, and it offers opportunities for framing these practices as nationalistic. This feminization of public worship was underscored by the Shankaracharya's endorsement of the values associated with *cumaṅkali*hood as embodied in the paradigmatic wife and mother who is devoted, docile, and modest. It was the matrix of meanings embedded in this construction of womanhood to which Uma herself consented and to which she sought other women's consent.

As explained in Chapter 4, *tiruviḷakku pūja* was a signifying practice of *cumaṅkali*hood and was often performed as a component of a *nōṉpu* cycle by women in domestic settings. The relocation of this observance to other arenas was facilitated by the limited demands it made on women's time and material resources and by its lack of caste and class specificity. *Tiruviḷakku pūja* and rituals like it are predicated on a universalistic and patriarchally encompassed womanhood characterized by patience, auspiciousness, and chastity; it is defined by and within the domestic sphere. Paradoxically, such rituals also offered certain kinds of autonomy to women. Recall the stories told by Sunithi, Saraswati, and Minakshi. Even women whose devotion was less intense were admired by others because of their skills in decorating *pūja* spaces or in singing, or for their piety. Many women noted that the rituals offered a respite from other household duties.

The broad social distribution of *tiruviḷakku pūja* coupled with its universalizing images of womanhood were keys to its use in Jaṉ Kalyāṇ. These attributes suggest why upper-caste efforts to exert hegemonic power have sometimes been characterized by the appropriation of women's ritual and by the annexation of women as brokers of alliances among caste and class clusters. Because of their popularity and universalizing rhetoric, these practices can be translated across caste and class lines and used in the effort to co-opt subordinated groups. In connection with Jaṉ Kalyāṇ, Saraswati reiterated an earlier directive that Brahman women locate and patronize "neglected" goddess shrines, especially those found in slums. The incorporation of the poor was to be achieved by a process of domestication enacted by bourgeois women.

The Shankaracharya's exhibition of the *cumaṅkali* as metaphor and metonym for the nation and the annexation of women as missionaries in his program of cultural proselytization and social service were explicable in this light. Many who were directly involved in Jan̲ Kalyāṇ or at least were sympathetic to its aims saw their involvement in it as consistent with their involvement in activities that they glossed, collectively, as *bhakti* or *karmayoga* (worship through service), both of which were among the patterns of modern Hindu religiosity linked to class privilege (Babb 1987; Subramanian 1988).[11]

The history of Indian nationalism has seen similar deployments of womanhood, and this has not abated. Indeed, the common sense that Saraswati tapped into has been inflected by this. Tamil Nadu's former chief minister, M. G. Ramachandran (1977–1987), sought mass support by popularizing mother goddess devotion (Lakshmi 1990) and contributed (ironically, along with the Shankaracharyas) to the publicization of goddess shrines and ritual. Neither has the Hindu right been idle in this area. Its rhetoric incites Hindu (male) citizens to protect their women and their "motherland" against "foreigners" (Basu et al. 1993, 84). The right has also targeted women as an electoral block and as workers by appealing both to the idioms of motherhood and to desires for female empowerment using a language close to that of bourgeois feminism (Basu et al. 1993, 79–87; Sarkar and Butalia 1995).

Through women workers, feminine idioms, and moral discipline, Jan̲ Kalyāṇ sought to incorporate the poor as clients and beneficiaries of its moral and material largess. With this, the Shankaracharya continued efforts, begun earlier, to establish alliances among his core constituency of urban Smārtas, wealthy non-Brahmans, and the poor. Uma's consent to the Shankaracharya's directives and his vision of a Hindu nation, was, for her, consent to the engendering practices of *cumaṅkali*hood, consent to the entwined ideologies of class and gender perpetuated through status production work, and consent to the conceptualization of caste identity implied in her assumption of the role of culture broker. Saraswati's version of Hindutva kept class, caste, and gender distinctions intact by naturalizing them through Hindu practice. Religious idioms thus helped frame a nationalism that cohered with bourgeois class ideology even as they provided an ideological cement for dependency relations that perpetuated social inequalities.

So why did the movement fail? The semiotic density of *tiruviḷakku pūja* attracted women, but that same density also meant that their desires and understandings were heterogeneous and not necessarily commensurable with the Shankaracharya's intentions. Some Brahman women, like

Sunithi and Sankari, relied on these same idioms to resist or rework the ideologies from which the idioms emerged. Quite a few women were happy to perform the *pūja* in public settings, like that organized by Uma. They found the ritual appealing for reasons I have already mentioned, but they lacked any commitment to, or interest in, the movement. Others were guardedly critical of the Shankaracharya. Some told me that he was too "political" and was tainted by his prior association with the RSS. A few unabashed critics ascribed his "social activism" to an overdeveloped ego. Perhaps more important, the popular association of the Shankaracharya's movement with Brahmanism limited its effectiveness right from the start. The groups that he identified as potential recipients of his brand of social welfare were among his sharpest critics. Saraswati's version of Hindutva should be seen, therefore, as one among a range of competing imaginaries.

Bringing the Nation Home

Uma Radhakrishnan's role in Jan̲ Kalyāṇ illustrates the institutional structures in which the movement originated. Of greater significance, however, is its revelation of how Jan̲ Kalyāṇ linked the education of consent to the constitution of identity. It brings the politics of Hindu nationalism home or, alternatively, it reveals the degree to which this politics of identity revolves around questions of home and self.

In juxtaposing the interior world of the home and the exterior world of the street and public buildings, the lamp *pūja* offers a compelling image of some of the ways in which public culture is being imagined and contested in urban India. Do such places and performances "domesticate" the exterior world for participants and observers? Do they "publicize" the domestic interior? What happens when everyday ritual is extricated from its domestic trappings? Does it make the world (the nation) a "home"? Femininity provided the bridge between the domestic interior and the exterior world in Jan̲ Kalyāṇ's appropriation of the lamp *pūja*. Thus femininity was constituted in ways consistent with what Chakravarti (1986) has described as "purdah culture" with its normative ideal of the good wife. In conscripting womanhood for the nation, it linked the "home" and the "world," metaphorically and metonymically, through women's bodies. The mechanism for this was the displacement of ritual practice from its domestic site to public venues, as well as the enlargement of its pool of beneficiaries and spectators from husband and family to the nation's citizenry.

The *pūja*'s valorization of bourgeois domesticity was central to Jan̲ Kalyāṇ's representation of the Hindu nation. It construed the Hindu nation as a domestic interior—a protected space flooded by the auspiciousness of the *cumaṅkali,* centered by the authentic self, a stable ground of identity. It suggested to audiences that just as the *cumaṅkali* warded off widowhood with the lamp *pūja,* the aesthetic instruments of the *pūja* defined the nation against an oppositional exterior, be it the state, the street, or "foreign invaders."

As enacted by the members of Ja<u>n</u> Kalyāṇ, the ritual syntax and imagery of the *pūja* represent an interiority comprising womanhood, the nation, and Hindu tradition. This appeal to Brahmanical common sense was glossed by Saraswati as "culture" and placed in opposition to "politics." The nation, naturalized with the idioms of femininity and Hinduism, could thus be pitted against the state. These constructs played on an existing dichotomy. India's colonial history entailed the depoliticization of culture (as embodied in Hindu ritual practices) and the reclamation of those cultural forms in anticolonial nationalisms (Dirks 1992). Following this, postcolonial India saw the bifurcated repatriation of culture, with culture glossed by the state as both the "integrative" (state-authored) ideology of nationhood and the "fissiparous" ideologies of contestatory nationalisms such as Dravidianism. Saraswati tried to reconnect these disparate usages by arguing that Hindu culture *was* Indian national culture and that the Brahman middle class was capable of mediating divergent interests, using culture as currency.

In Saraswati's script, culture was a substantialized phenomenon that could be read through women's bodies. It was a system that generated and naturalized identity, difference, and inequality among persons. It was defined against, and in light of, that which was regarded as the disembodied world of the political. With this discourse of culture, Ja<u>n</u> Kalyāṇ sought to claim the nation rhetorically by setting the terms by which its community might be imagined and by etching its spaces and bodies with the stylus of Hinduism. Its claims, though, were belied by its failure as a mass movement and by the uncertainties attached to its solicitation of consent. Ja<u>n</u> Kalyāṇ's failure revealed the political limits of hegemonic discourses, and, more broadly, the political boundaries of culture.

Notes

1. See Andersen and Damle (1987, 209–246). *Aside* magazine estimated RSS strength (full- and part-time volunteers) in Tamil Nadu to be between 120,000 and 350,000 ("After the Ban," January 15, 1993).

2. See, for example, Geetha and Rajadurai (1990) and Narayan (1982).

3. The RSS English weekly *The Organiser* carried regular columns by H. V. Seshadri, one of the organization's southern zone officers, that repeatedly pressed these points (see also Seshadri, n.d.). The July 15, 1984, edition carried a typical example entitled "Tanjore Seething Under Muslim Offensive." In it Seshadri ac-

cused Muslims of the "systematic usurpation of Hindu lands and grabbing of government . . . lands . . . with the connivance of political parties, especially under the patronage of the DMK and the ruling AIADMK." The scenario, recounted in lurid prose, was presented without substantiation and was designed to appeal to Hindu chauvinism and to upper-caste resentments of Dravidian populism. It began with the impoverishment of priests and temple servants under the Dravidian government, followed by Muslims' purchase of houses that priests could no longer maintain. The putative source of the Muslims' money was "illgotten wealth" derived from smuggling and "Gulf [oil] money." Once ensconced in the priests' homes, the "Muslim fanatics" commenced slaughtering cows in order to drive any remaining Hindus out. The Muslim neighborhood was then able to obstruct Hindus' entry to temples and to present festivals. In this, Seshadri charged, they were abetted by the DMK.

4. I expect that by 1992 the organized Hindu right had entered their immediate concerns because of the conflict surrounding Ayodhya, which was linked to local caste and sectarian violence incited by the RSS and affiliated groups. *Aside* magazine, reporting on local responses to the carnage at Ayodhya, noted that "publicly, most Hindus expressed their horror over 'this act of brutality,' but this was frequently qualified by an off the record aside that usually began, 'But if you were to ask for my personal opinion'. . . and went on, 'I am glad it's been pulled down. It's been simmering too long. The minorities need to be shown their place'" ("The Ayodhya Outrage," December 31, 1992).

5. For further exploration of the link between bourgeois appropriations of culture and the discourse of "modernity," see Niranjana (1993) and Niranjana, Sudhir, and Dhareshwar (1993).

6. *Khadi* is cotton cloth that is unbleached and otherwise unrefined. In Gandhian noncooperation, it was both symbol and practical enactment of moral and economic self-sufficiency and political self-rule.

7. In 1989, shortly before the parliamentary elections in November, the Shankaracharya signaled his intention to reorganize Jaṉ Kalyāṇ as a political party, Bharat Jaṉ Kalyāṇ, though that aim remains unrealized. In 1996, there were a few local units of Jaṉ Kalyāṇ in Chennai that met occasionally for devotional singing and prayer.

8. *Bharat* is one of the names for India preferred among Hindu nationalists. *Karma* refers to a Hindu theological concept, referring to the moral weight of action; *jnana* refers to esoteric, theological knowledge; *dharma* refers to the Hindu moral/legal notion of action that is appropriate on the basis of caste, gender, life stage, and occupation; *bhumi* refers to the earth or land. *Dharmo Rakshati Rakshata* means "dharma protects those who protect dharma."

9. For example, to mark his fifty-third birthday, a pamphlet was released outlining prayers to accompany *pūja, Stōttira Maṇikālai* (1987).

10. This practice appeared to be modeled on one of the ritual obligations prescribed for upper-caste male householders—the prayers known as *cantiyāvantaṉam.* Its gender-neutral reworking is worth noting as a gesture of inclusiveness consistent with the other enlargements of women's ritual roles that the movement conceded. However, this appeal to women should be read in tandem with the other implicit exclusions of caste and class that the movement enacted.

11. Ja<u>n</u> Kalyāṇ's efforts to engage elite women as recruiters and volunteers was consistent with the model of elite voluntarism that has been encouraged by the Indian government since independence. Reliance on voluntarism enabled the state to reduce its own expenditures in these areas (Caplan 1985; Committee on the Status of Women in India 1974); by conferring honor and recognition on these service providers, the state also offered routes to prestige for these women and their families.

9

Tradition Revisited

In this book I have woven particular women's stories into a larger story that comprises the collective history and experience of upper-caste urban elites, with its stakes in anticolonial nationalism and the official nationalism of the Indian state. It is of some importance that Smārtas, like other elites who enjoyed limited degrees of privilege under colonial rule, sought to refashion their community identity as they made efforts to define and speak for a pan-Indic "national culture," beginning in the late nineteenth century. This project was initially enabled by the rise of nationalist movements in colonial India. Decolonization, however, did not bring an end to it. Smārta claims on Indian culture continued to be lodged in ways that have had consequences for political and cultural life in southern India. There are ongoing, unresolved conflicts at both state and national levels about caste-based affirmative action, as well as about the more basic problem of whether entitlements should be allotted and how—issues that will only become more fractious with India's economic liberalization. These claims, moreover, have had implications for the production of scholarly knowledge about South Asia. It was a Smārta-brokered South Asian culture that informed one of the major paradigms of area studies—the Great Tradition/Little Tradition dichotomy. This fact lends additional significance to my study. Exploring the context in which Smārtas have reckoned the boundaries of Indian culture and have offered themselves as its spokespersons has enabled me to consider how and why, in the academic study of South Asia, certain kinds of questions have been consistently more askable than others, and why images of South Asia as quintessentially Hindu have persisted.

Though Smārtas did not speak in one voice for or about Indian culture, a recurrent feature of their efforts lay in their patterns of gendered representation. In the anticolonial nationalisms authored initially by elite men, an idealized womanhood—modest, self-sacrificing, patient, and chaste—came to be associated, intimately and inextricably, with what was deemed authentic Indian tradition, and elite women were taken to be its embodiments. Women stood both as the corrupted products of foreign depredations and as promises of nationalist redemption. This dual image was continuous with earlier reformist discourses that depicted women as the indices of civilizational progress and sought social reform on women's behalf. Though these representations entailed persistent contradictions, they rendered women and womanhood more visible within public culture as political actors and nationalist icons. Women's everyday domestic practices became available as signifiers within nationalist discourses, and the home became one stage for defining and contesting the nation. These developments, in conjunction with the transnational emergence of feminist ideas and organizations, fostered collective action by elite women, such as the Women's Indian Association, as well as dispersed but no less important experiments in domestic life. The latter were entailed, for example, in women's commitments and resistances to Gandhian nationalism. In many households, conflict erupted among kinswomen and between women and men around women's involvement in the spinning and wearing of *khadi* and the purchase of jewels. Gandhi advocated simplicity in consumption, with goals of both economic self-sufficiency and the moral reconstitution of India's populace. Nevertheless, the silk saris and gold jewelry that he urged women to abandon were (and continue to be) semantically dense markers of feminine auspiciousness and family honor. Women could not reject them without courting disapproval from family members and risking a crisis of personal identity, for such gestures challenged normative images of Brahman femininity.

I contend that the intersecting terrains of Brahman domesticity and femininity today cannot be understood apart from each other. Neither is explicable without attention to these earlier moments. I am not suggesting that women in the 1980s and 1990s have acted out colonial scripts or that colonialism should be the sole point of departure in explaining current Indian politics and culture. Rather, I argue that current discourses on normative femininity incorporate many traces of these moments. These are present in the divergent role expectations for Brahman women, in which they reflect urban elites' modernist aspirations and their reformulations of tradition in those contexts. Women's ritual and body signs were valued as features of authenticating traditions, but at the same time women were expected to ensure the transmission of modernity by rationalized home management and by undergoing (and enacting) educational and social reform.

My take on these issues derives from a broader claim that the cultural encoding of femininity involves historically contingent practices instead of being a determinate outcome of holistic, transhistorical systems of meaning. I approach the histories and contradictions of modernity as matters of habitus, encrypted in the patterned actions of domestic life, its ritualized moments, its moral etiquette, and its aesthetic expressions. During the latter part of the twentieth century, homes in urban India have been increasingly defined through, and bounded by, consumption, with consumption itself becoming more freighted with social, semiotic, and economic significance. Ritual and the domestic practices with which it is entwined symbolically, behaviorally, and functionally have become important sites for this consumption and for the status production work that accompanies it. Yet these practices were not simply glosses for class ideology, narrowly understood. Rather, their roles in status production (and thus the local meanings of class and caste as categories) depended on generative cultural logics, which I have characterized as aesthetic to underscore the significance of sensory engagement and local judgments of beauty in these systems of action. The dress and body signs of upper-caste femininity make and mark embodied personhood, inscribed with caste and gender difference. Class, nation, and the dichotomy of modernity/tradition can be read on these surfaces.

I have attempted to show how these embodying and signifying practices engage women's desires and intentions without fully determining women's subjectivities. My attention to embodied practices has offered an entry into issues of female agency—authorship—without ignoring the equally critical questions of authorization—the contexts and constraints formed by historical sedimentations of action, desire, and possibility (Fox 1989, 68–76). Women's negotiations of womanhood, within the hegemonic discourses of gender, caste, class, and nation, revealed improvisations that some might interpret as signs of subversion or noncompliance. There were, for example, apparently deliberate transgressions authored by some women in the context of ritual practice, such as Sunithi's declaration that menstruating women could enter her household shrine area (Chapter 5). With equal conviction, other women's action might be understood as accommodation, for example, Janaki's paraphrase of the Laws of Manu on the marginality of women and Sudras (Chapter 4). What I have argued is that in their ritual actions and in their narrations about those actions, these women and the others whose stories I told were engaged in subject-making practices, in which consent and resistance were entwined. The arenas of domestic ritual practice were sites for ongoing experimentation and improvisation. Action drew on a deep and pervasive pool of religious discourses and imagery—Sanskritic texts as well as film magazines, newspapers, and novels; formalized ritual sequences as well as everyday lives of work and leisure. Instead of denoting distinct historical periods or styles of action, modernity and tradition were objectified, represented, and argued about in the socially and historically situated practices through which gender, caste, and class were made and unmade, and in the everyday realizations of national imaginaries.

Navarāttiri in a New Key

The bulk of the fieldwork on which this book is based was done in 1985 and in 1987–1988. In 1996 I returned to Chennai for four months to initiate a new project dealing with religious sites as local spaces of public memory. I was fortunate to be there during the season of Navarāttiri, the festival that I describe in the book's Prologue. Witnessing this festival in 1996, in a climate of ascending Hindu nationalism and greater penetration of globalizing capitalism, helped to catalyze the questions about gender and elite cultural politics that this book explores. As such, it will help bring its project to closure.

Navarāttiri is the nine-night festival honoring the goddesses Lakshmi, Durga, and Saraswati; women create elaborate displays comprising miniature figures, *pommai* (dolls). The figures represent deities, humans, and animals and are often arranged in tableaux that depict rituals, games, and village life. One young woman, Antal, had worked with her mother, Vijayalakshmi, for weeks preparing a special display; its theme, she told me, was "*shakti* power." One section of her display recalled those of other households, with the Dasavatara (the ten avatars of Vishnu), the Ramapaṭṭāpiṣēkam (the god Rama and his entourage), Ashtalakshmi (the eight forms of the goddess Lakshmi), a figure of the god Shiva lost in meditation, and finally—at the center—images of the goddesses Saraswati, Lakshmi, and Durga, and a *kalacam,* the decorated bronze water pot that is worshiped as the icon of the goddess during the festival. The figures were conventionally arranged as a *kolu* on a series of open, steplike shelves. That was only one part of her display, though. On an adjacent table top, "*shakti* power" was in full force. Antal had made small figures to represent important women in India—Mrs. Gandhi, Mother Theresa, and Madhuri Dixit. She had also created figures that depicted different types of women—mothers, scientists, actresses, office workers, teachers, and students. As backdrops, she had made posters lettered with verses by early Tamil nationalist Subramania Bharati in praise of India's "new woman."

The image of Antal's *kolu* captures many of the themes explored in this book in that it seems to assert the continuing imbrication of femininity and domesticity in elite culture. It also conveys something of the complexity of the domestic worlds in which public culture is produced and mediated in urban India. I visited Antal's home and about seventy others because I had been enlisted by a neighbor to serve as a judge in the *kolu* contest that a local newspaper, the *Adyar Times*, was sponsoring. I had hesitated accepting the job initially. Evaluating the quality of a local cultural performance evoked the worst, most orientalizing caricature of anthropology. My neighbor pressed me, though, because she had been having a hard time getting a local volunteer. If I didn't do it, she would have yet another task on an already overloaded schedule. She also emphasized the need to avoid bias: "The judges shouldn't be locals; they would not be fair or objective." My cojudge was as nonlocal as I was; Gowri was Marathi and originally from Mumbai. She and her husband ran a handicraft shop in the city. It turned out to be easy to follow Gowri's lead, as she had pretty clear ideas about how to evaluate the entries, perhaps reflecting the criteria that she and her husband used to select merchandise.

Simple emplotments of the contest might treat modernity as either heroic or tragic. That is, the contest could be interpreted as a perversion of (pristine) tradition by media-drunk capitalists. Or its inverse might be entertained: The contest might be viewed as a cultural survival—a residue of a past that has withstood the incursions of the aforementioned media-drunk capitalists. The contest itself belied such narratives. Listening to the entrants' descriptions of their displays and to Gowri's conversations with them allowed me to participate in an open-ended, multilayered discourse on modernity and tradition. The *kolu*'s spatial and material commentary on the boundaries and boundary crossings between public and domestic, rural and urban, tradition and modernity was also a narration of womanhood. Women's work gendered the spaces of modernity and tradition while being the catalyst for imagining possible lives, themselves mediated by consumption and by print and electronic capitalism.

The Contest

Our three-day blitz of Adyar, a middle-class commercial and residential section of Chennai, took place at the height of heavy monsoon rains, albeit in the comfort of a chauffeured Ambassador touring car. The hospitality that is an earmark of this festival made our visits pleasurable, though by the end of each day we were staggering under the weight of the gifts that we had received from the women whose homes we visited, in accordance the festival's etiquette. Moreover, Navarāttiri in southern India incorporates aspects of competitive display. Women who visited each other's homes appraised the artistry of the displays and their monetary value; they noted those with histories and compared the hospitality gifts and sweets they received; they scrutinized the cleanliness and furnishings of each other's homes, and the quality of clothing, jewelry, and cosmetics. All of this was done with an interest in the respectability, wealth, taste, and beauty of the homes and their *kolus*. Thus, like other domestic activities discussed in this book, this festival involved status production, lending cultural salience to class inequality.

In 1996, the contest was in its third year. It had begun in 1994 as a way for new community newspapers to gain readership and advertiser support. These newspapers were English-language weeklies. Consumption oriented, they were dominated by advertising but also contained news articles on municipal affairs, as well as performance, book, and restaurant reviews. They were geared to a readership comprising a multilingual urban elite (encompassing but not limited to Smārtas) whose members regularly traversed, communicated, and consumed within transnational circuits. A wave of these weeklies came on the scene in 1994, under the patronage of a wealthy publisher. The weeklies began as free circulation and have continued as such. In 1996, many of Chennai's administrative divisions had such papers. The papers were among the vehicles through which an emergent class culture, mediated via domestic consumption, was represented and negotiated.

These factors made the 1996 festival exponentially different from those I had encountered earlier. Competitiveness, more than being explicit, framed and defined the event. The displays themselves, on average, were far more elaborate than those I had seen in earlier years. They were larger—sometimes occupying two rooms of a residence. I'm sure that this reflects the wealth of the neighborhoods that were invited to participate. In those areas, white-collar professionals, many of them government employees, were highly represented. Because pictures of winning entries appeared in newspapers and stories about them spread through dispersed social networks, the images became circulating templates that moved across the city and, in many cases, transregionally and transnationally. Although the displays might have begun with ties to local specificities, their visual and oral representations were quickly absorbed into imaginaries that were mobile and proliferating. My own photographs, subsequently shared with the U.S. relatives of some of my friends, were small but instructive examples. The contest, besides being a vehicle for negotiating status, trafficked in objectifications of modernity and tradition. The content of displays can illustrate.

The large-scale production of the objects (both handcrafted and machine manufactured) has contributed to high degrees of standardization in their colors, styles, sizes, and modes of arrangement. Oral histories that I collected indicated that some elements have recurred as core features over the past thirty to forty years. Certain images were, in people's narratives, emblematic of the festival. Besides Ganesha and the goddesses to whom Navarāttiri was dedicated, the images included Dasavatara and Ashtalakshmi sets, tableaux of marching bands, cricket games, weddings, and figures of Cēṭṭiyar merchants with their wares. Another set that I saw in a majority of homes was the village, often envisioned as a pilgrimage site (see Figure 9.1). People sometimes described it as a "typical" south Indian village. For many, these sorts of sites indeed constituted rural India. Their own encounters with pilgrimage sites were part of geographies of identity—visits were sometimes associated with life cycle rituals and were facilitated by the presence of the combined tourism and pilgrimage circuits that India's government has strenuously promoted, now by soliciting private investment. Yet these spaces of local pasts were juxtaposed with spaces of modernity in many displays. Disney scenes and characters were present in more than one home. More common, though, were the scale models of urban Chennai that have become popular, along with depictions of bus and rail connections between the metropolitan area and its rural fringe. One woman's entire front room was taken up with the imagery of Indian current events (Figure 9.2). A schoolgirl's display evoked the national development models of the 1950s with its "modernized village" featuring solar- and wind-powered technology, smokeless cookers, and new schools.

While taking note of the redundancies in the collections, I was struck even more by my fellow judge's evaluation of these more or less standard displays. Before we visited any homes, I asked her how she thought we should evaluate the entries. She had already thought about that issue and gave me a concise reply that specified four dimensions. The first was its theme—the message that unified the display; second was the neatness and artistry of its decoration; third was the extent to which the religious basis of the festival was communicated; and last was originality. The originality criterion was simultaneously ambiguous and revealing. I had assumed initially that by originality she meant creativity—the degree to which the participant had made the display her own; her personal, creative flair. As we evaluated displays, I found that at times she did mean this; in fact, the prize-winning entries were such. However, there was another sense to originality that Gowri also intended—the display's invocation of the "original" form of the festival. The historical origins of this festival are disputed, and the path by which the current domestic version arose has been characterized in a variety of ways. But these issues were beside the point, for what Gowri sought was not a historical narrative. In each house, she pressed our host to tell us why they celebrated Navarāttiri: "They should know why it is done, isn't it?" For Gowri, a correct account included reference to the three goddesses that the festival honored; Gowri also looked for the degree to which the display confirmed the host's own narrative. The highest marks went to displays such as Antal's, which showed evidence of originality (understood as authenticity) but

FIGURE 9.1 A Navarāttiri *Kolu* with a Tableau of a South Indian Village, 1996. Photograph By Author.

FIGURE 9.2 A Navarāttiri *Kolu* Made to Represent Current Events in India, 1996. Photograph By Author.

also presented a theme in keeping with the festival's original message, and did so in an innovative manner.

The other winning entries paid similar attention to originality. One young woman had made a series of *kōlams* surrounding the *pommai* display and described her theme as the "revival" of culture. Another woman had worked with her unmarried son, a professional archaeologist, to create a display that spread throughout the three rooms of their home's upper story. This display was organized as a small museum dedicated to the history of India, beginning with the first documented evidence of settlement and culminating in the present, "the age of the *Adyar Times*" (Figure 9.3). Rather than the conventional figures and tableaux, this *kolu* comprised stacks of books on which objects associated with specific temporal eras were placed. The display was arranged so that viewers were required to follow a predetermined path that began with the earliest prehistoric evidence and terminated with a reflective metacommentary on the exhibit—a collection of objects associated with archaeological and historical modes of investigation. First prize went to a woman whose display, "Green Revolution" (in English), covered nearly all table and floor surfaces in her living room. She intended to celebrate what she considered the benefits of southern India's distinctive heritage. This she characterized as its fidelity to "natural" (using the English word) products and ways of life, virtues consistent with Gandhian philosophy. This heritage was expressed in several forms. It was displayed as handicrafts—via the small, beaded figures made by her mother-in-law—and as an agrarian lifeway—via the sprouted seeds[1] that formed the decorative borders for her displays. A final element of the heritage she sought to represent was its practice of disciplined consumption; this she symbolized with a wedding tableau labeled "Simple Wedding" (in English). This commonly used phrase referred to a ceremony conducted without the provision of a large dowry or elaborate gift exchanges. She emphasized the fact that everything in her display had been produced in her own home and pointed out that several large *kōlams* had been made using dry foodstuffs from her kitchen—dals, rice, powders, and seeds.

Gowri's choice of prizewinners may have been idiosyncratic, but the results of her judgment became part of the shared memory of the festival for readers of the weeklies, as well as for the friends, neighbors, and relations of the winners. The discourses and visual images that provided templates for the festival were proliferating over wider spaces, for more dispersed audiences, and in fairly compressed time spans. Though its objectifications of locally understood ideas of modernity and tradition were dramatic, the festival was merely one of the many forms of public culture that stem from and help define domesticity—practices that

FIGURE 9.3 A Navarāttiri *Kolu* Made Using Books, 1996. Photograph By Author.

derive from and impart meaning through gendered metaphors and women's agency.

Ethnographies and Feminisms

In this book I have explored the ambiguities of the muting that is sometimes attributed to Hindu women. I have suggested that muting is not simply a silencing—an absence of speech or action. Rather, it encompasses ambiguous forms of expression that are sites of ongoing force and resistance. Muting both reproduces constraints on women's agency and offers a zone of free play and contestation. Looked at in this way, the women's narratives retold here evoke Foucault's vision of the capillary qualities of power: its productiveness, prolixity, and instability, as well as the inseparability of force and resistance. I (like some cultural and feminist theorists) find these formulations appealing because they open the possibility for more nuanced and context-sensitive views of agency, enabling us to set aside the either/or trappings of societal constraint versus individual will and structure versus agency. Indeed the materials assembled here point to the limits of the two understandings of subjectivity that have dominated modern social theory until recently. Neither the autonomous, ratiocinating "agent" of liberal humanism nor the vacuous, interpellated "subject" of poststructuralism has the capacity to address the contradictions that generate women's muting in Hindu contexts. I have, however, taken poststructuralist criticism as a point of departure. The narratives presented here necessitate questioning the stability of womanhood as a cultural category and looking to the manifold grammars of femininity that exist at specific sociocultural and historical conjunctures.

My work is informed by feminist concerns that are manifested in my interest in the historical and cultural constitution of differences and inequalities among women, as well as between women and men. I have sought to convey how Smārta women experienced and explained gendered differences and inequalities in the contexts of ritual practice, though I recognize that my own positioning as a fieldworker, which was shifting and relational, is a constituent element of that which I have sought to understand. I turn to this issue warily. I do not want my work to be read as confessional anthropology but as an effort to position my project in its own conditions of possibility, thus revealing the limits and situatedness of its outcomes. Right from the start, my own experiences in the field showed the limits of universalistic notions of womanhood. I was recognizable in some contexts as a woman, though I was ambiguous and even transgressive of some images of feminine normativity in other contexts. Despite the fact that I worked most closely with other women, the dynamics of power and history militated against any comforting assumptions of our common identity. What did they make of me as a woman, and as a white woman? Sunithi created a space for connection by indicating the conjunction of Mary (a double reference to me and to the Christian Virgin Mary) and Māriyamman, and by suggesting that I was Karumāriyamman's vehicle for spreading her renown abroad. Similarly, other women's willingness to disclose sexual and medical details of their lives was contingent on my being assimilable to their images of womanhood. Even an upper-caste male's dismissal of my work (recounted in Chapter 5) recognized me in this light, for the things that limited understanding were my non-Hindu background and my femininity. Like his wife, I was constitutionally unfit to participate in religious practices.

Their recognition of my femininity, however, was no guarantee of common interests or experience. My presence in Chennai as an ethnographer depended on histories of conflict and conquest. Area studies programs and curricula were developed as part of postwar development and modernization projects initiated by the U.S. government and private foundations such as Ford and Rockefeller (Hancock 1998). My graduate education was supported, in part, with funds provided by the U.S. Department of Defense through the Foreign Language Area Scholarship program. The micropolitics of the relationships described in this book derived, indirectly, from this conflictual history. For example, the narratives of Valli (the Harijan medium discussed in Chapter 5) were, to some extent, the means by which she informed me of who I was in her world and what she expected of me. Her prior experience with an anthropologist had given her clear ideas about the information that I wanted, and she provided it with little prompting. That information had preestablished boundaries, and Valli considered it a valuable commodity. With this, she recognized and sought to redress material disparities between us—disparities that stemmed from the historical transformations that I have mentioned.

In more immediate terms, there were assumptions, idioms, and desires that often went unremarked among my friends but remained difficult for me to comprehend or accept. Ironically, though my research interests owed something to my interest in feminist theory and to my sympathy toward what I defined as feminist politics, I never ceased to feel discomfort at what I, regardless of how I tried to overcome or conceal it, viewed as their disinterest in (or hostility toward) feminism. At the same time, my everyday Indian experience of being—and not being—a woman invariably caused me to question what had been hitherto less problematic for me as a white, middle-class American woman: the ability to see my own concerns and politics as derived from a generalized feminine experience and as representative of a generalized feminist stance.

My feminine identity therefore was problematic for me and for my informants and friends. Feminine identity never stood alone; it was always intimately threaded with caste, class, age, marital and reproductive status, and ethnicity. Women distanced me because I was *not* a woman in some situations (e.g., as a dinner guest I was often treated as an honorary man) or I was a woman whose qualities could endanger their womanliness, mar their auspiciousness, and make them accountable for its loss. Regardless of my actual behavior or intentions, there were undesirable and dangerous attributes, like independence, sexual licentiousness, and boldness, that were associated with white American women. Merely being seen with me could damage a woman's reputation.

Thus I did not participate in women's devotional groups simply as a woman. Rather, it was my relationship with Minakshi, a friend who assisted me with my work, that opened these networks to me. She was married and was older than I; she had grown children (the eldest of whom was male); and she was a competent social actor in terms of the etiquette and behavioral expectations of the middle classes. By escorting me, she became a character reference of sorts. People often described her as my "guide," a commonly used English term among urban Indians that here denoted her superiority; they meant that she was my teacher. Relatedly, they designated me as a *bhakta,* a devotee. With this they softened my foreignness and my academic association, and created, provisionally, a common space of practice and emotional expression.

Minakshi herself was willing to help me because of the strength of her own devotion to the goddess. She was excited by the prospect of visiting shrines around the city and meeting other devotees and potential gurus. In effect, then, my entry was really Minakshi's entry. Very often her presence deflected attention away from me and toward her. I was marginal to the relations that were negotiated, even though I may have instigated them.

Our interactions were thus grounded in a micropolitics of knowledge. My presence, academic status, and the *bhakta* designation together marked me as a person who sought knowledge, though they also recognized me as an interrogator with whom they might or might not comply.[2] Some women attempted to mitigate my control over the situation by presenting prepackaged information, narratives already in circulation in fairly fixed forms. Another counterweight to my power (and to each other's power) was to establish clear boundaries on their authority to speak by, for example, displacing authority to the goddess or referring me to other, more authoritative, persons. One woman, watching me take notes during one of Sunithi's ritual performances, cautioned me about "testing" the goddess; I could record information but should not cross-examine her human servants.

Reflecting on the effects of Minakshi's presence on the politics of elicitation leads me to a more complicated issue. It enabled me to move to the margins and thus deflected attention from power struggles. It veiled my power as elicitor, but it complicated my relationship with Minakshi. Judith Stacey (1988) described situations like this as ethical binds (see also Abu-Lughod 1990a; Visweswaran 1994). She pointed out that an ethnographer's commitment to feminist politics does not in itself disrupt or eliminate the arrangements of knowledge and power that ethnographic practice enacts. She suggested furthermore that such arrangements may be reinforced because of the ways in which feminist research conceals those relations of power. Although I, like Stacey, cannot offer a simple way out of this ethical bind, I have tried to extend the debate by linking discourses on ethnographic reflexivity with those of ethnographic description. In re-presenting the women's narratives, I found it necessary to disclose how my position as woman ethnographer shifted as they told their stories to and around me. With this, I revealed the tensions between authority and marginality as phenomena that are embedded in ethnographic practice. The intersubjective, positional knowledge thereby created necessarily implies transformations among the subjects who author and are authorized by that knowledge (Fox 1989, 68–76).

The pursuit of questions dealing with the differential and contingent meanings of womanhood and women's experiences grounds feminist ethnography and suggests how ethnographic work might contribute methodologically and theoretically to feminist inquiry (Abu-Lughod 1990a; Stacey 1988; Behar and Gordon 1996; Moore 1994). Instead of taking femininity, or even gender, as the core issue to be explained, one might start from a consideration of the multiplicity of subject positions that women themselves negotiate in the particular circumstances of their lives (see Lamphere, Ragone, and Zevella 1997). Framing subjectivity as negotiated rather than given calls attention to its intersubjective dimensions. One's engagement with others as a feminist ethnographer furnishes a context for decentering and destabilizing one's own notions of (and expectations about) feminist practice, as well as one's identity as a feminist. The epistemological project of anthropology rests on the proposition that knowledge is created in the intensive, long-term relations of fieldwork. Although it reifies the boundaries of home and field, here and there, us and them, it is also the means of unsettling those boundaries.

I have drawn on feminist theories and feminist interventions in anthropological epistemology in order to describe and understand Hinduism in late twentieth-century India as a form of everyday practice that critically involves and is—to an important extent—about women and womanhood. What kinds of sex/gender systems are produced in the everyday worlds of Hindu practice? What are the representations that mediate these? How do these representations intersect with cultural practices of caste? of class? of deterritorialized and diasporic identities? What kinds of female communities are imaginable on these terrains? What kinds of female subjects? What kinds of emancipatory possibilities exist and how are they defined locally? Life history narratives related by or about particular individuals, even the partial stories that I have presented here, are particularly illuminating sites for exploring these questions. Further, such narratives provide opportunities to connect the often unremarked practices of daily life to collective and institutional forms of domination and hegemony such as caste and class.

To bring this home, it was the friendship between Minakshi and me—with its complex mix of love, dependence, and the cross talk of (mis)understanding—that forced me to probe the arrangements of knowledge production and to confront the heterogeneity and incommensurability of the discourses that emerged in our interactions. Those differences of desire and knowledge became more apparent as we worked together more closely and became more bound to each other emotionally. As an anthropologist, for whom knowledge was alienable, I participated in a system that designates some persons as "informants," vessels from whom information has to be extracted, and others as "participant-observers," dressed in "native" drag but toting tape recorders, notebooks, typewriters, and now computers and video cameras. I found it impossible to sustain my relationships with others in that way, though such failures were always countered by my equally forceful desire to complete my work and thus achieve a professional identity. This was the source of many of the struggles I experienced, privately and in my dealings with others. I knew that simply by recording information in my notebook I was taking it away, evaluating it according to exogenous standards, and reconstructing it. Moreover, I was committed to this, partly because of my training but also in the interests of preserving any salvageable shreds of autonomy and independence.[3]

As much as I tried to develop a sympathetic understanding of what it meant to be a *cumaṅkali,* I could not adopt that identity for myself. Married but childless, self-supporting, traveling alone, and speaking imperfect Tamil made me an oddity, to say the least. The women with whom I worked recognized this before I did and offered me an identity. For them, being *cumaṅkali*s meant tolerating my presence with affection and trying to teach me by example. They had an acute and practical understanding of the issues of "difference" about which feminist theorists write, though they also understood permeability. They lived in a world of unexpected connections between apparently unlike things, of borders and border crossings, and of always fuzzy boundaries.

My conflicting desires were partially comprehensible to Minakshi, for, like me, she earned a living by brokering information. As we became friends, I learned that although the circuits of our knowledges intersected, they did not totally converge. Minakshi was able to collaborate with me because of our mutual affection, because of her material needs, and because of the desire for knowledge that we shared. This knowledge was inseparable from the relationships in which it was created. For Minakshi, however, this knowledge was never finished nor was it alienable. It was always subject to interpretation, to repossession, and to retraction; it sustained a variety of different relationships. Borne in talk and in stories, knowledge was the stuff of connections with others, and of reputation. A book, edited, revised, and printed, enters circuits as a commodity and a credentialing instrument. As it moves, it may occasion argument, fond recollection, or embarrassment. It cannot be undone, however, or remade.

My hope is that in this book, my friends have recognized, albeit through my sensibilities, their own religious imaginations and boundary crossings, for it was their creativity that made it possible for me to imagine this book. Minakshi saw her own work with me as being guided by the goddess, as a way of honoring her; by extension, she saw this project in the same light. She told me often that my research and writing could only have been initiated and carried out because it pleased the goddess; she and I were only the instruments of the goddess. And I know, in a different way, that I could not have finished this work without her. With my writing, I hope to have given readers a way to comprehend the intelligence, generosity, and imaginativeness of Minakshi's gifts.

Notes

1. Sprouted seeds of nine grains are among the ritual objects used in some orthodox life cycle rituals.

2. This situation blurs the conventions—studying "up," "across," and "down"—with which anthropologists often categorize their interactions with informants in industrial, class-stratified nation-states (Cole 1988). I was studying "across" in that I was dealing with educated members of the urban bourgeoisie; I was studying "up" in that my status (as a non-Hindu and as a student) was inferior to that of all of my Brahman acquaintances, especially those of high academic or professional standing (see also Sheehan 1993).

3. My experience echoes, in part, the tensions among different subject positions that Dorine Kondo (1990) describes with both wit and eloquence in her book *Crafting Selves.*

Glossary

acaivam nonvegetarian diet
ācāram propriety, orthoprax conduct
acuttam uncleanliness
advaitavēdanta philosophical monism (Tamil *attuvaitamvētāntam*)
Aippaci seventh Tamil month, mid-October–mid-November
akam interior, home, self
aḻaku beauty
ampāḷ goddess
amirtam divine nectar
ammaṉ mother or mother goddess
Āṉi third Tamil month, mid-June—mid-July
Āṇṭāḷ Tamil female saint
apiṣēkam lustration
appaḷam wafer made of ground dal
āratti display of camphor before deity
arccaṉai ritual offering accompanied by prayer
āsrama life stage
Āṭi fourth Tamil month, mid-July—mid-August
akattil illai menstruation, literally "not in the house"
akattukkuttūram menstruation, literally "away from the house"
Āvaṇi fifth Tamil month, mid-August—mid-September
bhajan devotional song
bhajana group organized for purposes of devotional music
bhakti devotion to deity (*bhakta*: one who is devoted)
caivam vegetarian diet
cakkaram aniconic deity image inscribed with geometric designs having esoteric significance
cāmpār stew made of vegetables and dal
carkkaraippoṅkal sweetened rice dish
cēri slum
cītaṉam women's wealth, usually given as wedding trousseau
Cittirai first Tamil month, mid-April—mid-May
cukam health, beauty, well-being
cumaṅkali married woman with a living husband, literally "auspicious woman"
cuttam cleanliness
cūṭu catalytic heat

darshan act of seeing and being seen by a deity or an important, holy personage (Tamil *tarica<u>n</u>am*)
dharma morally appropriate action
Durga goddess in her fierce aspect (Sanskritic)
eccil saliva, contamination from contact with saliva
elumiccai viḷakku lamp made from a lime
eri burn, set aflame
Ganesha god
ghee clarified butter
hōmam sacrificial fire
iṣṭa teyvam favorite deity, deity to whom one is personally devoted
iṭli steamed cake made of fermented rice and dal
japam silent recitation of mantras
jaṭai matted hair of an ascetic
jāti category or type
kalacam water pot that is decorated and used as goddess image in *pūja*
kalāccāram cultural expressions such as literary and artistic works
kaḷai radiant appearance
kālam time, duration
Kali goddess in her fierce aspect (Sanskritic)
Kamakshi goddess in form of young girl (Sanskritic)
ka<u>n</u>am weight, bulk
ka<u>nn</u>i girl (virgin)
karma action or experience understood to be moral consequence of previous experience
karmayoga worship through service
karmayogi one who performs worship through service
ka<u>r</u>pu a woman's marital chastity
Kārttikai eighth Tamil month, mid-November—mid-December
Karumāriyamma<u>n</u> goddess in her fierce aspect (non-Sanskritic deity)
kaṭṭu to tie or bind
khadi homespun cloth, the production and use of which was championed by M. K. Gandhi
kōlam geometric design made to mark thresholds
kolu assembly (also refers to display of objects during Navarāttiri
kōpuram tower above temple entryway
kuḷi to bathe
kuṅkumam red powder connoting female auspiciousness
lakh amount of 100,000 (Tamil *lakcam*)
lakcamañcaḷ distribution of 100,000 pieces of turmeric
lakkaṇam durational period of about one hour and a half
Lakshmi goddess in her wifely aspect (Sanskritic; Tamil *laṭcumi*)
Māci eleventh Tamil month, mid-February–mid-March
ma<u>n</u>am mind, heart, intention
mañcaḷ turmeric
mañcaḷnīr water in which turmeric has been dissolved
maṅkalam auspiciousness

maṉṟam organization
maṇṭalam period of forty to forty-five days
maṇṭapam pillared hall of temple
maṇṭali association
mantra sacred utterances (Tamil *mantiram*)
Māriyammaṉ goddess in her fierce aspect (non-Sanskritic)
Mārkaḻi ninth Tamil month, mid-December–mid-January
maṭam monastery
maṭi ceremonial purity (n.); to fold (v.)
maṭimañcaḷ ritual distribution of turmeric
māviḷakku lamp made from wheat or rice flour and ghee
Minakshi goddess as young queen (Tamil *Mīṉaṭci*)
mukam face
mūrtti deity image made of stone
naivēttiyam food offering during *pūja*
nāḷ solar day
nallapeyar good reputation, literally "good name"
namaskāram respectful greeting
naṭcattiram constellation
Navarāttiri nine-night festival
nōṉpu cycle of fasting and prayer to fulfill a vow
oḷi light
oṭṭu stick, attach
pācam emotional attachment, affection
pakkam side, neighborhood, page
palakāram snack
palam strength
pañcalōkam five-metal alloy
pañcāṅkam almanac
Paṅkuṉi twelfth Tamil month, mid-March–mid-April
paṇṭikai festival
paṟa fly, soar
paricuttam ceremonial purity
pārppaṉ pejorative term for "Brahman"
paṟṟu to stick, adhere, be devoted, unite
Parvati goddess in wifely aspect
pattu food that is sticky
paṭṭu silk
pāvam sin
peṇ woman
peṇmai womanhood
pirakācam brightness
pīṭam dais, seat of power
pommai doll
poṅkal harvest festival during the month of *Tai*
poṭṭu auspicious mark on woman's forehead
prasadam transvalued leavings of food offered to deity (Tamil *piracātam*)

pūja worship (Tamil *pūcai*)
pukal̲ reputation
Puraṭṭāci sixth Tamil month, mid-September–mid-October
racam aesthetic emotion, appreciation; a thin soup
rākukālam inauspicious period of day
sadhu renouncer (Tamil *cātu*)
samskāra life cycle ceremony; refinement (Sanskritic)
sari garment worn by women, six- or nine-yard cloth tied around the waist and draped over the shoulder (Tamil *puṭavai*)
satī woman who burns herself on her husband's funeral pyre
shastra Sanskritic legal and moral treatises (Tamil *cāstiram*)
Shakti goddess, consort of Shiva; cosmic creative principle (Tamil *Cakti*)
Shiva god, "the destroyer" (Tamil *Civaṉ*)
Śrī goddess, consort of Shiva
stōttiram prayer consisting of deity praise names
swadeshi self-sufficiency (Tamil *cutēci*)
swaraj self-rule (Tamil *cuyāṭci*)
Tai tenth Tamil month, mid-January–mid-February
tāli woman's wedding pendant
tāmpūlam betel leaves and areca nuts (for chewing); also a gift that includes betel leaves and areca nuts
tēvi goddess; can be affixed to the end of a goddess's name
tēy starve, become thin or worn out
teyvam deity
tiruṣṭi malevolent or envious gaze
tiruviḷakku pūja worship of goddess in the form of an oil lamp
tīṭṭu polluting effects of menstruation or childbirth
tuvai wash clothing by beating
uḷ interior; enclosed room
upacāram hospitality; formal acts of *pūja*
uttaravu order, instruction
Vaikāci second Tamil month, mid-May–mid-June
Varalakshmi goddess in her wifely aspect, a form of Lakshmi
varṇa ranked category of castes
varṇāśramadharma moral codes according to gender and caste
Vēda sacred knowledge or the texts in which such knowledge is recorded (Tamil *Vētam*)
veḷiyē outside, exterior
Veḷḷikil̲amai Friday
vet̲t̲ilpākku betel leaves and areca nuts (for chewing)
vigraham deity image (Tamil *vikkirakam*)
viḷakku oil lamp
vipūti sacred ash
viratam cycle of fasting and prayer to fulfill a vow
Vishnu deity, "the preserver"
vīṭu house, household

References

Abu-Lughod, L. 1990a. "Can There Be a Feminist Ethnography?" *Women and Performance: A Journal of Feminist Theory* 5:7–27.

______. 1990b. "The Romance of Resistance: Tracing Transformations of Power Through Bedouin Women." *American Ethnologist* 17, 41–55.

______. 1991. "Writing Against Culture." In *Recapturing Anthropology,* edited by R. G. Fox, 137–162. Santa Fe, N.Mex.: School of American Research.

______. 1992. *Writing Women's Worlds.* Berkeley: University of California Press.

Althusser, L. 1971. "Ideology and Ideological State Apparatuses (Notes Toward an Investigation)." In *Lenin, Philosophy and Other Essays.* Translated by B. Brewster. New York: Monthly Review Press.

Ammal, S..M. 1968. *Camaittuppār.* 3 vols. Madras: S. Meenakshi Ammal Publications.

Andersen, W., and S. Damle. 1987. *Brotherhood in Saffron.* Boulder: Westview.

Anderson, B. 1991. *Imagined Communities: Reflections on the Origin and Spread of Nationalism.* Rev. ed. London: Verso.

Appadurai, A. 1981a. "Gastro-Politics in Hindu South Asia." *American Ethnologist* 8:494–511.

______. 1981b. *Worship and Conflict Under Colonial Rule: A South Indian Case.* Cambridge: Cambridge University Press.

______. 1985. "The Private and the Interior in Hindu Social Life." Paper presented at the annual meeting of the American Anthropological Association, Washington, D.C., December 4–8.

______. 1986. "Theory in Anthropology: Center and Periphery." *Comparative Studies in Society and History* 28:356–361.

______. 1988a. "How to Make a National Cuisine." *Comparative Studies in Society and History* 30:3–24.

______. 1988b. "Putting Hierarchy in Its Place." *Cultural Anthropology* 3, no. 1:37–50.

______. 1991. "Global Ethnoscapes: Notes and Queries for Transnational Anthropology." In *Recapturing Anthropology,* edited by R. G. Fox, 191–210. Santa Fe, N.Mex.: School of American Research.

______. 1996. *Modernity at Large.* Minneapolis: University of Minnesota Press.

Appadurai, A., and C. A. Breckenridge. 1976. "The South Indian Temple: Authority, Honor and Redistribution." *Contributions to Indian Sociology,* n.s., 10:187–209.

______. 1988. "Why Public Culture?" *Public Culture* 1:5–11.

Ardener, S., ed. 1977. *Perceiving Women.* London: Dent.

Asad, T. 1983. "Anthropological Conceptions of Religion." *Man,* n.s., 18:237–259.

______. 1993. *Genealogies of Religion.* Baltimore: Johns Hopkins University Press.

Austin-Broos, D. 1997. *Jamaica Genesis.* Chicago: University of Chicago Press.

Avalon, A. 1921. *The Serpent Power.* Madras: Ganesh.

______. 1927. *Shakti and Shakta: Essays and Addresses.* Madras: Ganesh.

Babb, L. 1987. *Redemptive Encounters: Three Modern Styles in the Hindu Tradition.* Berkeley: University of California Press.

Babb, L., and S. Wadley, eds. 1995. *Media and the Transformation of Religion in South Asia.* Philadelphia: University of Pennsylvania Press.

Bailey, F. G. 1957. *Caste and the Economic Frontier.* Manchester: Manchester University Press.

Baker, C. 1975. "Temples and Political Development." In *South India,* by C. Baker and D. Washbrook, 69–97. Delhi: Macmillan.

Barnett, M. 1976. *The Politics of Cultural Nationalism.* Princeton: Princeton University Press.

Barnett, S. 1977. "Identity Choice and Caste Ideology in Contemporary South India." In *The New Wind,* edited by K. David, 393–414. The Hague: Mouton.

Bastide, R. 1978. *The African Religions of Brazil.* Translated by H. Sebba. Baltimore: Johns Hopkins University Press.

Basu, S. 1998. *A City of Villages.* New York: Oxford University Press.

Basu, T., et al. 1993. *Khaki Shorts and Saffron Flags.* New Delhi: Orient Longman.

Bayly, C. 1986. "The Origins of *Swadeshi* (Home Industry): Cloth and Indian Society, 1700–1930." In *The Social Life of Things,* edited by A. Appadurai, 285–322. Cambridge: Cambridge University Press.

Bell, C. 1992. *Ritual Theory, Ritual Practice.* New York: Oxford University Press.

Behar, R. 1990. "Rage and Redemption: Reading the Life Story of a Mexican Marketing Woman." *Feminist Studies* 16:223–258.

______. 1992. *Translated Woman.* Boston: Beacon.

Behar, R., and D. Gordon, eds. 1996. *Women Writing Culture.* Berkeley: University of California Press.

Berreman, G. 1967. "Caste As a Social Process." *Southwestern Journal of Anthropology* 23:351–370.

Beteille, A. 1965. *Caste, Class and Power.* Berkeley: University of California Press.

______. 1996. "Caste in Contemporary India." In *Caste Today,* edited by C. Fuller, 150–179. Delhi: Oxford University Press.

Bharucha, R. 1994. "Somebody's 'Other': Disorientations in the Cultural Politics of Our Times." *Economic and Political Weekly* 29:105–111.

Boddy, J. 1989. *Wombs and Alien Spirits.* Madison: University of Wisconsin Press.

______. 1994. "Spirit Possession Revisited." *Annual Review of Anthropology* 23:407–434.

Bourdieu, P. 1977. *Outline of a Theory of Practice.* Cambridge: Cambridge University Press.

______. 1984. *Distinction: A Social Critique of the Judgement of Taste.* Translated by R. Nice. Cambridge: Harvard University Press.

______. 1990. *The Logic of Practice.* Stanford: Stanford University Press.

Bourguignon, E. 1976. *Possession.* San Francisco: Chandler and Sharp.

Brass, P. 1990. *The Politics of India Since Independence.* New York: Cambridge University Press.

Breckenridge, C. 1986. "The Social Use of Everyday Objects in Hindu South India." In *Dimensions of Indian Art*, edited by L. Chandra and J. Jain. Delhi: Agam Kala Prakashan.

Breckenridge, C. ed. 1995. *Consuming Modernity.* Minneapolis: University of Minnesota Press.

Brodkey, L. 1987. "Writing Critical Ethnographic Narratives." *Anthropology and Education Quarterly* 18:74–90.

Brooks, A. 1997. *Postfeminisms.* London: Routledge.

Buhler, G., ed. and trans. 1964. *The Laws of Manu.* Vol. 25, *The Sacred Books of the East.* Delhi: Motilal Banarsidass. Original edition published in 1886.

Butler, J. 1990. *Gender Trouble.* London: Routledge.

______. 1993. *Bodies That Matter.* New York: Routledge.

Caplan, L. 1975. *Administration and Politics in a Nepalese Town.* London: Oxford University Press.

______. 1987. *Class and Culture in Urban India.* Oxford: Clarendon.

Caplan, P. 1985. *Class and Gender in India.* London: Tavistock.

Cardeña, E. 1992. "Trance and Possession as Dissociative Disorders." *Transcultural Psychiatric Research Review* 29:287–300.

Casey, E. 1996. "How to Get from Space to Place in a Fairly Short Stretch of Time." In *Senses of Place,* edited by S. Feld and K. Basso, 13–52. Santa Fe, N.Mex.: School of American Research.

"Castiri." 1977. *Virata Pūja Vitānam.* Chennai: Little Flower Company.

Cattiyanatan, Amma<u>n</u>. 1985. *Śrī Turkatēvi stōttiramalai.* Chennai: Amma<u>n</u> Patippakam.

Cattiyanatan, Amma<u>n</u>, and K. M. Cami Aiyar. 1978. *Maṅkaṭu Amma<u>n</u> A<u>r</u>ucuvai.* Chennai: Amma<u>n</u> Patippakam.

Cenkner, W. 1983. *A Tradition of Teachers.* Delhi: Motilal Banarsidass.

Chaitanya, J. 1993. "*Ram Ke Nam*: Documentary as Resistance." *Economic and Political Weekly* 28:2646–2647.

Chakrabarty, D. 1992. "Postcoloniality and the Artifice of History." *Representations* 37:1–28.

______. 1994. "The Difference-Deferral of a Colonial Modernity: Public Debates on Domesticity in British India." In *Subaltern Studies 8,* edited by D. Arnold and D. Hardiman, 50–88. Delhi: Oxford University Press.

Chakravarti, U. 1986. "Pati-vrata." *Seminar* 31:17–21.

______. 1990. "Whatever Happened to the Vedic Dasi?" In *Recasting Women,* edited by K. Sangari and S. Vaid, 27–87. New Brunswick, N.J.: Rutgers University Press.

Chatterjee, P. 1986. *Nationalist Thought and the Colonial World: A Derivative Discourse.* London: Zed.

______. 1989. "Colonialism, Nationalism and Colonialized Women: The Contest in India." *American Ethnologist* 16, 622–633.

______. 1992. "A Religion of Urban Domesticity: Sri Ramakrishna and the Calcutta Middle Class." In *Subaltern Studies 7,* edited by P. Chatterjee and G. Pandey, 40–68. Delhi: Oxford University Press.

______. 1993. *The Nation and Its Fragments.* Princeton: Princeton University Press.

Chaudhuri, N., and M. Strobel, eds. 1992. *Western Women and Imperialism.* Bloomington: Indiana University Press.

Chhachhi, A. 1989. "The State, Religious Fundamentalism and Women." *Economic and Political Weekly* 24:567–578.

Clarke, C., C. Peach, and S. Vertovec, eds. 1990. *South Asians Overseas.* Cambridge: Cambridge University Press.

Clifford, J. 1986. "Introduction—Partial Truths." In *Writing Culture,* edited by J. Clifford and G. Marcus, 1–26. Berkeley: University of California Press.

______. 1988. *The Predicament of Culture.* Cambridge: Harvard University Press.

Cohn, B. 1987. *An Anthropologist Among the Historians.* Delhi: Oxford University Press.

Cohn, B., and M. Marriott. 1958. "Networks and Centres in the Integration of Indian Civilization." *Journal of Social Research* 1:1–4.

Cole, J., ed. 1988. *Anthropology for the Nineties.* New York: Free Press.

Comaroff, J. 1985. *Body of Power, Spirit of Resistance.* Chicago: University of Chicago Press.

Committee on Emotional Integration. 1962. *Report of the Committee on Emotional Integration.* New Delhi: Ministry of Education.

Committee on Religious and Moral Hygiene. 1959. *Report of the Committee on Religious and Moral Hygiene.* New Delhi: Ministry of Education.

Committee on the Status of Women in India. 1974. *Towards Equality.* New Delhi: Ministry of Education and Social Welfare.

Courtright, P. 1985. *Gaṇeśa.* New York: Oxford University Press.

______. 1995. *Satī, Sacrifice, and Marriage.* In *From the Margins of Hindu Marriage,* edited by L. Harlan and P. Courtright, 184–203. New York: Oxford University Press.

Crapanzano, V., and J. Garrison, eds. 1977. *Case Studies in Spirit Possession.* New York: Wiley

Csordas, T. 1993. *The Sacred Self.* Berkeley: University of California Press.

Data India. 1981–1990. New Delhi: Press Institute of India.

Daniel, E. V. 1984. *Fluid Signs.* Berkeley: University of California Press.

Das, V. 1977. *Structure and Cognition.* 2d ed. Delhi: Oxford University Press.

______. 1981. "The Mythological Film and Its Framework of Meaning." *India International Centre Quarterly* 8:43–56.

______. 1995. *Critical Events.* Delhi: Oxford University Press.

Davis, R. 1997. *Lives of Indian Images.* Princeton: Princeton University Press.

De Bary, W. T., ed. 1958. *Sources of Indian Tradition.* Vol. 2. New York: Columbia University Press.

De Certeau, M. 1984. *The Practice of Everyday Life.* Berkeley: University of California Press.

"Decking up the Deities." *India Today,* January 15, 1991, 74–76.

De Lauretis, T. 1987. *Technologies of Gender.* Bloomington: Indiana University Press.

Derrett, J. D. M. 1968. *Religion, Law and the State in India.* London: Faber and Faber.

Dickey, S. 1993. *Cinema and the Urban Poor in South India.* Cambridge: Cambridge University Press.

Diehl, G. 1956. *Instrument and Purpose.* Lund: Gleerup.

Di Leonardo, M. 1986. "The Female World of Cards and Holidays." *Signs* 12:440–453.
Dirks, N. 1992. "Castes of Mind." *Representations* 37:56–78.
______. 1993. *The Hollow Crown.* 2d ed. Ann Arbor: University of Michigan Press.
______. 1996. "Recasting Tamil Society." In *Caste Today*, edited by C. Fuller, 263–295. Delhi: Oxford University Press.
Driver, E. 1982. "Caste, Class, and 'Status Summation' in Urban South India." *Contributions to Indian Sociology*, n.s., 16:225–253.
Driver, E., and A. Driver. 1987. *Social Class in Urban India.* Leiden: Brill.
D'Souza, V. 1992. "Polishing the Past." *The Week*, April 5, 52–55.
Dumont, L. 1970. *Homo Hierarchicus.* Chicago: University of Chicago Press.
Eck, D. 1985. *Darśan.* 2d ed. Chambersburg: Anima.
Eisenstadt, S., N. Kahane, and D. Shulman, eds. 1984. *Orthodoxy, Heterodoxy and Dissent in India.* Berlin: Mouton.
Fabricius, P. 1972. *Tamil and English Dictionary.* Travancore: Evangelical Lutheran Mission Publishing House.
Forbes, Geraldine, ed. 1989. *Shudha Mazumdar.* Armonk, N.Y.: Sharpe.
______. 1996. *Women in Modern India.* Vol. 4.2 of *The New Cambridge History of India.* Cambridge: Cambridge University Press.
Foucault, M. 1979. *Discipline and Punish.* Translated by A. Sheridan. New York: Vintage.
______. 1980. *The History of Sexuality.* Vol. 1. Translated by R. Hurley. New York: Vintage.
______. 1991. "Governmentality." In *The Foucault Effect*, edited by G. Burchell, C. Gordon, and P. Miller. Chicago: University of Chicago Press.
Fox, R. G. 1985. *Lions of the Punjab.* Berkeley: University of California Press.
______. 1989. *Gandhian Utopia: Experiments with Culture.* Boston: Beacon.
______. 1990. "Hindu Nationalism in the Making, or the Rise of the Hindian." In *Nationalist Ideologies and the Production of National Cultures*, edited by R. Fox, 63–80. Washington, D.C.: American Anthropological Association.
______. 1991. "For a Nearly New Culture History." In *Recapturing Anthropology*, edited by R. G. Fox, 93–113. Santa Fe, N.Mex.: School of American Research.
Fraser, N. 1996. *Justice Interruptus.* New York: Routledge.
Fuller, C. J. 1992. *The Camphor Flame.* Princeton: Princeton University Press.
Gandhi, M. 1982. *Hind Swaraj.* Rev. ed. Ahmedabad: Navajivan. Original edition published in 1938.
Geetha, V., and S. V. Rajadurai. 1990. "Communal Violence in Madras: A Portent?" *Economic and Political Weekly* 25:2122–2123.
Ghose, J. C., ed. 1982. *The English Works of Rammohun Roy.* New Delhi: Cosmo.
Giddens, A. 1984. *The Constitution of Society.* Berkeley: University of California Press.
Gramsci, Antonio. 1971. *Selections from the Prison Notebooks.* Translated and edited by Q. Hoare and G. Nowell-Smith. London: Lawrence and Wishart. Original edition published in 1929–1936.
Greenough, P. 1995. "Nation, Economy, and Tradition Displayed." In *Consuming Modernity*, edited by C. Breckenridge, 216–248. Minneapolis: University of Minnesota Press.

Grewal, I. 1996. *Home and Harem.* Durham: Duke University Press.

Grosz, E. 1990. "Contemporary Theories of Power and Subjectivity." In *Feminist Knowledge: Critique and Construct,* edited by S. Gunew, 59–120. London: Routledge.

Guha, R. 1988a. "On Some Aspects of the Historiography of Colonial India." In *Selected Subaltern Studies,* edited by R. Guha and G. Spivak, 37–44. New York: Oxford University Press.

______. 1988b. "The Prose of Counter-Insurgency." In *Selected Subaltern Studies,* edited by R. Guha and G. Spivak, 45–88. New York: Oxford University Press.

______. 1989. "Dominance Without Hegemony and Its Historiography." In *Subaltern Studies 6,* ed. R. Guha, 210–309. Delhi: Oxford University Press.

Gupta, A. 1998. *Postcolonial Developments.* Durham, N.C.: Duke University Press.

Habermas, J. 1984. *The Theory of Communicative Action.* Vol. 1. Translated by T. McCarthy. Boston: Beacon.

______. 1989a. "The Public Sphere: An Encyclopedia Article." Translated by F. Lennox and S. Lennox. In *Critical Theory and Society,* edited by S. Bronner and D. Kellner, 136–142. New York: Routledge.

______. 1989b. *The Structural Transformation of the Public Sphere.* Translated by T. Burger. Cambridge: MIT Press. Original edition published in 1962.

Hancock, M. 1990. "Saintly Careers Among South India's Urban Middle Classes." *Man,* n.s., 25:505–520.

______. 1995a. "Dilemmas of Domesticity." In *From the Margins of Hindu Marriage,* edited by L. Harlan and P. Courtright, 60–91. New York: Oxford University Press.

______. 1995b. "Hindu Culture for an Indian Nation." *American Ethnologist* 22:907–926.

______. 1998. "Unmaking the 'Great Tradition.'" *Identities* 3–4:343–388.

______. Forthcoming. "Gendering the Modern." In *Unfinished Business,* edited by A. Burton. London: Routledge.

Hannerz, U. 1980. *Exploring the City.* New York: Columbia University Press.

______. 1992. *Cultural Complexity.* New York: Columbia University Press.

Hardgrave, R. 1969. *The Nadars of Tamilnad.* Berkeley: University of California Press.

Harlan, L. 1992. *Religion and Rajput Women.* Berkeley: University of California Press.

Hawley, J., ed. 1994. *Fundamentalism and Gender.* New York: Oxford University Press.

Haynes, D. 1991. *Rhetoric and Ritual in Colonial India.* Berkeley: University of California Press.

Hebdige, D. 1979. *Subculture.* London: Methuen.

Hindu Religious Endowments Commission. 1962. *Report of the Hindu Religious Endowments Commission.* New Delhi: Government of India, Ministry of Law.

Ifeka, C. 1987. "Domestic Space As Ideology in Goa, India." *Contributions to Indian Sociology,* n.s., 21:307–329.

Imperial Gazetter of India. 1907–1908. Oxford: Clarendon.

Inden, R. 1990. *Imagining India.* London: Blackwell.

Indian Law Reports. 1875–present. Madras Series. Madras: Government Press.

Irschick, E. 1969. *Politics and Social Conflict in South India.* Berkeley: University of California Press.

______. 1986. *Tamil Revivalism in the 1930s.* Madras: Cre-A.

______. 1994. *Dialogue and History.* Berkeley: University of California Press.

Jagadheesan, L. R. 1991. "Caste Politics." *Aside,* December 31, 8–11.

Jan̲ Kalyāṇ. *Member's Pledge.* 1987. Kanchipuram: Jan̲ Kalyāṇ.

Jayawardena, K. 1986. *Feminism and Nationalism in the Third World.* London: Zed.

John, M. 1996. *Discrepant Dislocations.* Delhi: Oxford University Press.

Kailasapathy, K. 1979. "The Tamil Purist Movement: A Reevaluation." *Social Scientist* 7:23–51.

Kapferer, B. 1991. *A Celebration of Demons.* 2d ed. Washington, D.C.: Smithsonian Institution Press.

Karlekar, M. 1991. *Voices from Within.* Delhi: Oxford University Press.

Kehoe, A., and D. Giletti. 1981. "Women's Preponderance in Possession Cults." *American Anthropologist* 83:549–561.

Kelly, J., and M. Kaplan. 1990. "History, Structure and Ritual." *Annual Review of Anthropology* 19:119–150.

Kelly, W. 1986. "Rationalization and Nostalgia: Cultural Dynamics of New Middle Class in Japan." *American Ethnologist* 13:603–618.

Khare, R. 1970. *The Changing Brahmans.* Chicago: University of Chicago Press.

______. 1976. *Hindu Hearth and Home.* New Delhi: Vikas.

______. 1984. *The Untouchable as Himself.* Cambridge: Cambridge University Press.

Kishwar, M. 1985. "Women in Gandhi." *Economic and Political Weekly* 20:1691–1702, 1753–1758.

Kondo, D. 1990. *Crafting Selves.* Chicago: University of Chicago Press.

Kristeva, J. 1982. *Powers of Horror.* New York: Columbia University Press.

Kriyāvin̲ Taṟkālat Tamiḻ Akarāti. 1992. Chennai: Cre-A.

Laclau, E., and C. Mouffe. 1985. *Hegemony and Socialist Strategy.* London: Verso.

Lakshmi, C. S. 1984. *The Face Behind the Mask.* New Delhi: Vikas.

______. 1990. "Mother, Mother-Community and Mother Politics in Tamil Nadu." *Economic and Political Weekly* 25:WS72–WS83.

Lambek, M. 1993. *Knowledge and Practice in Mayotte.* Toronto: University of Toronto Press.

Lamphere, L., H. Ragone, and P. Zevella, eds. 1997. *Situated Lives.* New York: Routledge.

Leach, E. 1961. *Rethinking Anthropology.* London: Athlone.

Leadbeater, C. W. 1952. *The Chakras: A Monograph.* 4th ed. Madras: Theosophical Publishing House.

LeFebvre, H. 1991. *The Production of Space.* Translated by D. Nicholson-Smith. Oxford: Blackwell.

Lelyveld, D. 1995. "Upon the Subdominant." In *Consuming Modernity,* ed. C. Breckenridge, 49–65. Minneapolis: University of Minnesota Press.

Lewandowski, S. 1977. "Changing Form and Function in the Ceremonial and the Colonial Port City in India." *Modern Asian Studies* 11:183–212.

______. 1980. *Migration and Ethnicity in Urban India.* New Delhi: Manohar.

______. 1984. "The Built Environment and Cultural Symbolism in Postcolonial Madras." In *The City in Cultural Context*, edited by J. Agnew, J. Mercer, and D. Sopher, 237–254. London: Allen and Unwin.
Lewis, G. 1986. "The Look of Magic." *Man* 21:414–437.
Lewis, I. 1989. *Ecstatic Religion*. Rev. ed. London: Routledge.
Logan, P. 1980. "Domestic Worship and the Festival Cycle in the South Indian City of Madurai." Ph.D. diss., University of Manchester.
Lopez, D. 1995. *Religions of India in Practice*. Princeton: Princeton University Press.
Madan, T. N. 1987. *Non-Renunciation*. Delhi: Oxford University Press.
Madras High Court Reports. 1863–1874. Madras: Government Press.
Mahoney, M., and B. Yngvesson. 1992. "The Construction of Subjectivity and the Paradox of Resistance." *Signs* 18:44–73.
Mani, L. 1990. "Contentious Traditions." In *Recasting Women*, edited by K.Sangari and S. Vaid, 88–126. New Brunswick, N.J.: Rutgers University Press.
Mankekar, P. 1993. "National Texts and Gendered Lives." *American Ethnologist* 20:543–563.
Manuel, P. 1993. *Cassette Culture*. Chicago: University of Chicago Press.
Marcus, G., and M. M. J. Fischer, eds. 1986. *Anthropology as Cultural Critique*. Chicago: University of Chicago Press.
Marriott, M. 1976. "Hindu Transactions: Diversity Without Dualism." In *Transaction and Meaning*, edited by B. Kapferer, 109–142. Philadelphia: Institute for the Study of Human Issues.
Marriott, M., and R. Inden. 1977. "Toward an Ethnosociology of South Asian Caste Ssystems." In *The New Wind*, edited by K. David, 227–239. The Hague: Mouton.
McGee, M. 1992. "Desired Fruits: Motive and Intention in the Votive Rites of Hindu Women." In *Roles and Rituals for Hindu Wom*en, edited by J. Leslie, 71–88. Delhi: Motilal Banarsidass.
Mencher, J. 1974. "The Caste System Upside Down or, the Not-So-Mysterious East." *Current Anthropology* 15:469–493.
Merrey, K. 1982. "The Hindu Festival Calendar." In *Religious Festivals in South India and Sri Lanka*. Edited by G. Welbon and G. Yocum. New Delhi: Manohar.
Milton Singer Papers. Department of Special Collections. Joseph Regenstein Library. University of Chicago.
Minault, G., and H. Papanek, eds. 1982. *Separate Worlds*. Delhi: Chanakya.
Mines, M. 1994. *Public Faces, Private Voices*. Berkeley: University of California Press.
Mines, M., and V. Gourishankar. 1990. "Leadership and Individuality in South Asia." *Journal of Asian Studies* 49:761–786.
Misra, A. 1993. "Benares: The Many Splendoured City." *Economic and Political Weekly* 28:2448–2453.
Mohanty, C. 1991. "Cartographies of Struggle, Third World Women and the Politics of Feminism." In *Third World Women and the Politics of Feminism*. Edited by L. Torres. Indianapolis: Indiana University Press.
Moore, H. 1994. *A Passion for Difference*. Indianapolis: Indiana University Press.
Mosse, G. 1975. *The Nationalization of the Masses*. Ithaca, N.Y.: Cornell University Press.

Mouffe, C. 1979. "Hegemony and Ideology in Gramsci." In *Gramsci and Marxist Theory.* Edited by C. Mouffe. London: Routledge and Kegan Paul.

Mudaliar, C. 1974. *The Secular State and Religious Institutions in India.* Wiesbaden: Franz Steiner.

Mukherjea, B. K. 1962. *Hindu Law of Religious and Charitable Trust.* 2d ed. Calcutta: Eastern Law House.

Munn, N. 1986. *The Fame of Gawa.* Cambridge: Cambridge University Press.

______. 1992. "The Cultural Anthropology of Time." *Annual Review of Anthropology* 21: 93–123.

Nag, D. 1991. "Fashion, Gender, and the Bengali Middle Class." *Public Culture* 3:93–112.

Nair, J. 1996. *Women and Law in Colonial India.* New Delhi: Kali for Women.

Nandy, A. 1983. *The Intimate Enemy.* Delhi: Oxford University Press.

Narayan, G. 1982. "Communal Riots Go South." *The Illustrated Weekly of India,* April 18, 20–21.

Neild-Basu, S. 1977. "Madras: The Growth of a Colonial City, 1780–1840." Ph.D. diss., University of Chicago.

Niranjana, T. 1993. "Whose Culture Is It?" *Journal of Arts and Ideas* 25–26:139–151.

Niranjana, T., P. Sudhir, and V. Dhareshwar, eds. 1993. *Interrogating Modernity.* Calcutta: Seagull.

Obeyesekere, G. 1981. *Medusa's Hair.* Chicago: University of Chicago Press.

O'Hanlon, R. 1986. *Caste, Conflict and Ideology.* Cambridge: Cambridge University Press.

______. 1992. "Issues of Widowhood, Gender and Resistance in Colonial India." In *Contesting Power,* edited by D. Haynes and G. Prakash. Berkeley: University of California Press.

O'Hanlon, R., trans. and ed. 1994. *A Comparison Between Men and Women.* Madras: Oxford University Press.

Ong, A. 1987. *Spirits of Resistance and Capitalist Discipline.* Albany: State University of New York Press.

The Organiser. 1981–1984. New Delhi.

Pandey, G. 1991. *The Construction of Communalism in Colonial North India.* Delhi: Oxford University Press.

Pandey, Raj Bali. 1969. *Hindu Saṃskāras.* Delhi: Motilal Banarsidass.

Pandian, M. S. S. 1990. "From Exclusion to Inclusion." *Economic and Political Weekly* 25:1938–1939.

Papanek, H. 1979. "Family Status Production Work." *Signs* 4:775—781.

Parry, J. 1994. *Death in Banaras.* Cambridge: Cambridge University Press.

Patel, S. 1988. "Construction and Reconstruction of Woman in Gandhi." *Economic and Political Weekly* 23:377–387.

Prakash, G. 1996. "Science Between the Lines." In *Subaltern Studies 9,* edited by S. Amin and D. Chakrabarty, 59–82. Delhi: Oxford University Press.

Pramar, V. 1987. "Sociology of the North Gujarat Urban House." *Contributions to Indian Sociology,* n.s., 21:331–345.

Presler, F. 1987. *Religion Under Bureaucracy.* Cambridge: Cambridge University Press.

Raghavan, V. 1956. "Variety and Integration in the Pattern of Indian Culture." *Far Eastern Quarterly* 15:497–505.

______. 1963. "Nationalism in Sanskrit Literature." *The Illustrated Weekly of India,* April 21, 45, 47.

______. 1964. *The Great Integrators.* New Delhi: Ministry of Information and Broadcasting.

______. 1979. *Festivals, Sports, and Pastimes in India.* Ahmedabad: B.J. Institute of Learning and Research.

Raheja, G., and A. Gold. 1994. *Listen to the Heron's Words.* Berkeley: University of California Press.

Ramacantira Castirikal, Ji. E., and Em. En. Raja. 1978. *Śrī Cantōṣimātā Pūjaiyum Kataiyum.* Chennai: Giri Traders.

Ramanathan, M. 1989. *Sister R. S. Subbalakshmi.* Bombay: Lok Vangmaya Griha.

Ramanujan, A. K. 1978. Afterword to *Samskara,* by U. R. Anantha Murthy, 139–147. Translated by A. K. Ramanujan. Delhi: Oxford University Press.

______. 1985. Afterword to *Poems of Love and War,* 231–297. Translated and edited by A. K. Ramanujan.. Delhi: Oxford University Press.

______. 1986. "On Woman Saints." In *The Divine Consort,* edited by J. Hawley and D. Wulff, 316–324. Boston: Beacon.

Ramanujan, A. K., ed. and trans. 1973. *Speaking of Śiva.* Harmondsworth, U.K.: Penguin.

Ramaswamy, S. 1993. "En/gendering Language." *Comparative Studies in Society and History* 35:683–725.

______. 1997. *Passions of the Tongue.* Berkeley: University of California Press.

Reynolds, H. 1982. "The Auspicious Married Woman." In *The Powers of Tamil Women,* edited by S. Wadley, 35–60. Syracuse, N.Y.: Maxwell School of Public Citizenship and Public Affairs.

Riley, D. 1988. *Am I That Name?* Minneapolis: University of Minnesota Press.

Robert Redfield–Ford Foundation Cultural Studies Papers. Department of Special Collections. Joseph Regenstein Library. University of Chicago.

Rudner, D. 1994. *Caste and Capitalism in Colonial India.* Berkeley: University of California Press.

Rudolph, L., and S. Rudolph. 1967. *The Modernity of Tradition.* Chicago: University of Chicago Press.

Ryerson, C. 1987. *Regionalism and Religion.* Madras: Christian Literature Society.

Sabini, J., and M. Silver. 1982. *Moralities of Everyday Life.* New York: Oxford University Press.

Sadasivan, D. 1974. *The Growth of Public Opinion in the Madras Presidency.* Madras: University of Madras.

Said, E. 1989. "Representing the Colonized: Anthropology's Interlocutors." *Critical Inquiry* 15:205–225.

Sandoval, C. 1991. "U.S. Third World Feminism." *Genders* 10:1–24

Sangari, K. 1991. "Mirabai and the Spiritual Economy of Bhakti," pts. 1–2. *Economic and Political Weekly* 25:1464–1475, 1537–1552.

______. 1993. "Consent, Agency and Rhetorics of Incitement." *Economic and Political Weekly* 28:867–882.

Sanjek, R. 1990. "Urban Anthropology in the 1980s." *Annual Review of Anthropology* 19: 151–186.

______. 1993. "Anthropology's Hidden Colonialism." *Anthropology Today* 9:13–18.

Sarkar, T. 1991. "The Woman As Communal Subject." *Economic and Political Weekly* 26:2057–2062.

Sarkar, T., and U. Butalia, eds. 1995. *Women and Right Wing Movements in India.* London: Zed.

Savarkar, V. 1969. *Hindutva: Who Is a Hindu?* Bombay: Veer Savarkar Prakashan. Original edition published in 1923.

Schieffelin, E. 1985. "Performance and the Cultural Construction of Reality: Spirit Seances Among New Guinea People." *American Ethnologist* 12:707–724.

Scott, D. 1994. *Formations of Ritual.* Minneapolis: University of Minnesota Press.

Scott, James. 1985. *Weapons of the Weak.* New Haven: Yale University Press.

______. 1990. *Domination and the Arts of Resistance.* New Haven: Yale University Press.

Scott, Joan. 1988. *Gender and the Politics of History.* New York: Columbia University Press.

______. 1991. "The Evidence of Experience." *Critical Inquiry* 17:773–797.

Secondary Education Commission. 1952–1953. *Report of the Secondary Education Commission.* New Delhi: Ministry of Education.

Seshadri, H. V. n.d. *Hindu Renaissance Under Way.* Bangalore: Jagarana Prakashana.

Sharma, U. 1986. *Women's Work, Class and the Urban Household.* London: Tavistock.

Sheehan, E. 1993. "The Academic As Informant." *Human Organization* 52:252–259.

Singer, M. 1955. "A Sacred Center in a Polluted World." Robert Redfield—Ford Foundation Cultural Studies Papers, box 17, folder 2, page 21. Department of Special Collections, Joseph Regenstein Library, University of Chicago.

______. 1972. *When a Great Tradition Modernizes.* Chicago: University of Chicago Press.

Singer, M., ed. 1959. *Traditional India.* Austin: University of Texas Press.

Singh, A. 1976. *Neighborhood and Networks in Urban India.* Delhi: Marwah.

Smith, F. 1992. "Indra's Curse, Varuna's Noose, and the Suppression of the Woman in the Vedic Srauta Ritual." In *Roles and Rituals for Hindu Women,* edited by J. Leslie, 17–43. Delhi: Motilal Banarsidass.

Sperber, D. 1974. *Rethinking Symbolism.* Cambridge: Cambridge University Press.

Spivak, G. 1987. *In Other Worlds.* New York: Routledge.

______. 1988. "Subaltern Studies: Deconstructing Historiography." In *Selected Subaltern Studies,* edited by R. Guha and G. Spivak, 3–32. New York: Oxford University Press.

Srinivas, M. N. 1956. "A Note on Sanskritization and Westernization." *Far Eastern Quarterly* 15:481–496.

Srinivasan, A. 1985. "Reform and Revival." *Economic and Political Weekly* 20:1869–1876.

Stacey, J. 1988. "Can There Be a Feminist Ethnography?" *Women's Studies International Forum* 11:21–27.

Stein, B. 1980. *Peasant, State, and Society in Medieval South India.* Delhi: Oxford University Press.

Stōttira Maṇimālai. 1987. Chennai: Sri Jeyentira Pakta Samajam.

Stoller, P. 1989. *Fusion of the Worlds.* Chicago: University of Chicago Press.

Stree Shakti Sanghatana. 1989. *"We Were Making History."* London: Zed.

Subramanian, V. 1988. "Karmayoga and the Rise of the Indian Middle Class." *Journal of Arts and Ideas* 14–15:133–142.

Sunder Rajan, R. 1993. *Real and Imagined Women.* New York: Routledge.

Sunil, K. 1987. "The Curious Case of the Missing Monk." *The Illustrated Weekly of India,* September 13, 9–17.

Swallow, D. 1982. "Ashes and Powers." *Modern Asian Studies* 16:123–158.

Tamil Lexicon. 1982. 6 vols. Madras: University of Madras.

Tarlo, E. 1996. *Clothing Matters.* New Delhi: Viking.

Thapar, R. 1966. *A History of India I.* Harmondsworth, U.K.: Penguin.

Tharu, S., and K. Lalita, eds. 1993. *Women Writing in India.* Vol. 2, *The Twentieth Century.* New York: Feminist.

Tharu, S., and T. Niranjana. 1996. "Problems for a Contemporary Theory of Gender." In *Subaltern Studies 9,* edited by S. Amin and D. Chakrabarty, 232–260. Delhi: Oxford University Press.

The Hindu. 1981–1993. Chennai.

Thiruchendran, S. 1997. *Ideology, Caste, Class, and Gender.* New Delhi: Vikas.

Thompson, E. P. 1963. *The Making of the English Working Class.* New York: Vintage.

Tiruppaḷniyeḻucci, Tiruvempāvai, Tiruppāvai. 1987. 3d ed. Chennai: Giri Traders.

Trawick Egnor, M. 1982a. "The Changed Mother, or What the Smallpox Goddess Did When There Was No More Smallpox." *Contributions to Asian Studies* 18:24–45.

______. 1982b. "On the Meaning of *Sakti* to Tamil Women." In *The Powers of Tamil Women,* edited by S. Wadley, 1–33. Syracuse: Maxwell School of Citizenship and Public Affairs.

Trawick, M. 1990. *Notes on Love in a Tamil Family.* Berkeley: University of California Press.

Tucker, R. 1978. *The Marx-Engels Reader.* New York: Norton.

Turner, V. 1967. *The Forest of Symbols.* Ithaca, N.Y.: Cornell University Press.

______. 1969. *The Ritual Process.* Ithaca, N.Y.: Cornell University Press.

Van der Veer, P. 1994. *Religious Nationalism.* Berkeley: University of California Press.

Van der Veer, P., ed. 1995. *Nation and Migration.* Philadelphia: University of Pennsylvania Press.

Vasudevan, R. 1989. "The Melodramatic Mode and the Commercial Hindi Cinema." *Screen* 30:29–50.

Vatuk, S. 1972. *Kinship and Urbanization.* Berkeley: University of California Press.

Visweswaran, K. 1990. "Family Subjects." Ph.D. diss., Stanford University.

______. 1994. *Fictions of Feminist Ethnography.* Minneapolis: University of Minnesota Press.

______. 1996. "Small Speeches, Subaltern Gender." In *Subaltern Studies 9,* edited by S. Amin and D. Chakrabarty, 83–125. Delhi: Oxford University Press.

Wadley, S. 1975. *Shakti: Power in the Conceptual Structure of Karimpur Religion.* Chicago: University of Chicago, Department of Anthropology.

______. 1983. "Vrats: Transformers of Destiny." In *Karma: An Anthropological Inquiry,* edited by C. Keyes and E. V. Daniel, 147–162. Berkeley: University of California Press.

Wadley, S., ed. 1982. *The Powers of Tamil Women.* Syracuse: Maxwell School of Citizenship and Public Policy.

Ward, C. 1989. "Possession and Exorcism." In *Altered States of Consciousness and Mental Health,* edited by C. Ward, 125–144. Newbury Park, N.J.: Sage.

Washbrook, D. 1975. "The Development of Caste Organization in South India, 1880–1925." In *South India,* by C. Baker and D. Washbrook, 150–203. Delhi: Macmillan.

______. 1976. *The Emergence of Provincial Politics.* Cambridge: Cambridge University Press.

______. 1989. "Caste, Class and Dominance in Modern Tamil Nadu." In *Dominance and State Power in Modern India,* edited by F. Frankel and M. S. A. Rao, 1:204–264. Delhi: Oxford University Press.

Weinstein, J. 1974. *Madras.* Beverly Hills: Sage.

Wiebe, P. 1975. *Social Life in an Indian Slum.* Delhi: Vikas.

White, D. 1996. *The Alchemical Body.* Chicago: University of Chicago Press.

Williams, R. 1973. *The Country and the City.* London: Chatto and Windus.

______. 1977. *Marxism and Literature.* London: Oxford University Press.

Winslow, M. 1983. *A Comprehensive Tamil and English Dictionary.* New Delhi: Asian Educational Services. Original edition published in 1862.

Wolff, K., trans. and ed. 1964. *The Sociology of Georg Simmel.* New York: Free Press.

Women's India Association. 1934. "WIA Home for Women." In *Women's India Association Annual Report, 1933–1934.* Madras: Women's India Association.

Woodruffe, J., and M. P. Pandit. 1965. *Kularnava Tantra.* Madras: Ganesh.

Zwicker, T. 1984. "Morality and Etiquette in the Reproduction of Hierarchical Caste Relations in South Asia." Master's thesis, University of Pennsylvania.

Index